A HISTORY
OF
CYNICISM

Current and forthcoming titles in the Bristol Classical Paperback series:

A HISTORY
OF
CYNICISM

From Diogenes to the 6th Century AD

Donald R. Dudley

Second Edition
Foreword and Bibliography by Miriam Griffin

PAPERBACKS

This impression 2003
This edition published in 1998 by
Bristol Classical Press
an imprint of
Gerald Duckworth & Co. Ltd.
61 Frith Street, London W1D 3JL
Tel: 020 7434 4242
Fax: 020 7434 4420
inquiries@duckworth-publishers.co.uk
www.ducknet.co.uk

First published in 1937 by Methuen & Co. Ltd.

A catalogue record for this book is available
from the British Library

ISBN 1 85399 548 7

Printed in Great Britain by
Antony Rowe Ltd, Eastbourne

FOREWORD

'Not until D.R. Dudley's *A History of Cynicism from Diogenes to the Sixth Century AD* (London 1937) did the literary and philosophical significance of the Cynics begin to be acknowledged by modern scholars.'

So write the editors of the latest volume on the Cynic movement. Dudley's work is not, however, a museum piece, important only in the history of scholarship. It remains still, as the same editors go on to say, 'the best general introduction in English'.[1]

Written when Dudley was a research fellow at St. John's College, Cambridge, the book has all the energy and ambition of youth. It covers the whole history of the Cynic movement in antiquity, which lasted nearly a millennium; it explores the phenomenon from all angles: as an ascetic way of life, as a philosophical critique of conventional moral values, and as a source of literary techniques suitable to its debunking mission. Dudley subjected the evidence, much of it anecdotal, to detailed critical examination. But his aim was the general one of exploring what he saw as 'a tendency deeply rooted in human nature, and asserting itself whenever the rights of the individual need upholding against the political, moral or economic constraints of society'.[2] Writing in the thirties when Germany, Italy and Russia were becoming increasingly totalitarian, Dudley predicted a reaction towards individualism. He would have been pleased to see these centralised systems disintegrate but disappointed to see the materialistic form the new individualism would take, so unlike the austerity and spirituality of the Cynics.

For nearly forty years after its publication, Cynicism still remained a neglected subject, though Dudley's book maintained its place as a standard work. But recently, growing interest in Hellenistic history and literature, and particularly in Hellenistic philosophy, has led to the Cynic movement being taken more seriously. From the mid-seventies, editions of the fragmentary texts and studies of leading Cynic figures started to appear and, in 1991, an international conference was held on 'Ancient Cynicism and Its Influence'.

Despite this flurry of activity, the picture drawn by Dudley has not been superseded but rather refined. Indeed some of the scholarly views he adopted at the time, and which have been questioned by scholars in other areas, have been simply accepted uncritically into the literature on Cynicism on his authority. It may help the reader to note two key examples: the existence of a genre called Diatribe[3] and the notion that the Cynics and Stoics of the so-called 'Philosophical Opposition' under Nero and the Flavian Emperors were advocating the replacement of hereditary succession by a principle of adoption.[4]

Given the renewed interest in the subject and the lack of a more recent general history to take its place, the reprinting *A History of Cynicism* needs no apology.

NOTES

1. Branham, R. Bracht and M.-O. Goulet-Cazé, *The Cynics: The Cynic Movement in Antiquity and Its Legacy* (California, 1996), 1; 422.
2. p. 209.
3. The works referred to by ancient writers as διατριβαί were not thereby assigned by them to a distinct literary genre: 'Cynic-Stoic Diatribe' was an invention of German scholars (G. Schmit, 3.24, *Der Kleine Pauly* 2 (1967), Nachträge, 1577-8). Used in antiquity to mean a way of spending time, or a philosophical discussion or school, or one of many types of philosophical discourse, the term Diatribe is now rejected altogether by some scholars (e.g. H. Jocelyn, Liverpool Classical Monthly 7 [1982] 3-7; 8 [1983] 89-91) but retained by others as a convenient modern term to denote the ancient tradition of popular philosophical discourse characterised by a pointed style, vivid imagery, colloqualism and informal structure.
4. That there was no 'principle of adoption' and no evidence for the Cynics or Stoics embracing such an idea was already shown by J. Béranger, 'L'hérédité du Principat', *REL* 17 (1939) 172ff., and has been generally accepted by Roman historians. The Emperors who practised adoption all lacked sons and were using the traditional remedy of the Roman aristocracy. In many cases, they adopted near relatives. Even Pliny, making a virtue of necessity by praising the adoption of Trajan by Nerva as 'the selection of the best man',

ends his *Panegyric* by praying that Jupiter gives Trajan a son. Marcus Aurelius, who was a Stoic, did not hestitate about the succession of his son Commodus. The Stoic philosopher Seneca accepts hereditary succession (*Cons. Marc.* 15.2; *Cons. Polyb.* 12.5) and defends it (*Ben.* 4.30-2).

BIBLIOGRAPHY

A chronological discussion of the most important work on the Cynics before and after Dudley's book is given in M. Billerbeck (ed.), *Die Kyniker in der modernen Forschung* (Amsterdam, 1991) 1-28; now supplemented by L.E. Novia, *The Philosophy of Cynicism: An Annotated Bibliography* (London, 1995). A selective bibliography of the more recent works, organised by category and giving special attention to works in English, is available in R. Bracht Branham and M.-O. Goulet-Cazé (eds.), *The Cynics, The Cynic Movement in Antiquity and Its Legacy* (California, 1996) 421-3. The evidence for the early Cynics has now been collected and annoted by G. Giannantoni, *Socratis et Socraticorum Reliquiae*, 4 vols. (Naples, 1990). An English translation of the major sources is promised in the *Routledge Encyclopedia of Philosophy*, s.v. Cynics.

The whole of the Cynic tradition, ancient and modern, is treated by H. Niehues-Pröbsting, *Der Kynismus des Diogenes und der Begriff des Kynismus* (Munich, 1979). *Aufstieg und Niedergang der Römischen Welt*, W. Haase and H. Temporini, (eds.), vol. 36, contains a number of important chapters on Cynicism, including M.-O. Goulet-Cazé on Book VI of Diogenes Laertius (36.4 [1992] 3880-4048) and on Cynicism in the imperial period (36.4 [1990] 2720-2833). The proceedings of the international conference of 1991, mentioned above, are published in M.-O. Goulet-Cazé and R. Goulet (eds.), *Le Cynisme ancien et ses prolongements: Actes du Colloque international du C.N.R.S.* (Paris, 1993). Various important papers (some in English) are collected in M. Billerbeck (ed.), op. cit., 1991. The most recent work in English is the collection of papers in R. Bracht Branham and M.-O. Goulet-Cazé (eds.), op.cit., 1996. The Introduction to the latter volume (1-27) provides a succinct and readable account of Cynicism, based on the latest scholarly work.

M.T. Griffin

January 1998   Somerville College, Oxford

PREFACE

THE research of which this book is the outcome was mainly carried out at St. John's College, Cambridge, Yale University, and Edinburgh University. In the help so generously given to my work I have been no less fortunate than in the scenes in which it was pursued. I am much indebted for criticism and advice to Professor M. Rostovtseff and Professor E. R. Goodonough of Yale, to Professor A. E. Taylor of Edinburgh, to Professor F. M. Cornford of Cambridge, to Professor J. L. Stocks of Liverpool, and to Dr. W. H. Semple of Reading. I should also like to thank the electors of the Henry Fund for enabling me to visit the United States, and the College Council of St. John's for electing me to a Research Fellowship. Finally, to the unfailing interest, advice and encouragement of Mr. M. P. Charlesworth of St. John's I owe an especial debt which I can hardly hope to repay.

These acknowledgements do not exhaust the list of my obligations ; but I hope that other kindnesses have been acknowledged either in the text or privately.

D. R. D.

CAMBRIDGE
March, 1937

ix

CONTENTS

INTRODUCTION

THE Emperor Julian, speaking of the Cynic philosophy, says that ' it has been practised in all ages . . . it does not need any special study, one need only hearken to the god of Delphi when he enjoins the precepts " know thyself " and " alter the currency " '. In claiming the Delphic god as the founder of Cynicism Julian is guilty of an obvious anachronism ; for Cynicism cannot be shown to antedate Diogenes of Sinope. But from the fourth century B.C. Cynicism endured to the last days of the ancient world ; Cynics were common in the days of Augustine ; they may have been known in the Empire of Byzantium. Long life is not of itself a criterion of worth ; and it cannot be denied that Cynicism survived when much of immeasurably greater intellectual value perished. To the student of ancient philosophy there is in Cynicism scarcely more than a rudimentary and debased version of the ethics of Socrates, which exaggerates his austerity to a fanatic asceticism, hardens his irony to sardonic laughter at the follies of mankind, and affords no parallel to his genuine love of knowledge. Well might Plato have said of the first and greatest Cynic, ' That man is Socrates gone mad.'

But to the student of social history, and of ancient thought as distinct from philosophy, there is much of interest in Cynicism. The Cynics are the most characteristically Greek expression of that view of the World as Vanity Fair, and the consequent rejection of all current values, and the desire to revert to a life based on the minimum of demands. It is a phenomenon to be found at several stages of Western civilization ; at different periods the moving causes have been political or economic injustice, religious enthusiasm, or reaction from an over-developed urban civilization. ' Vanity of Vanities, saith the preacher, all is Vanity '—the author of Ecclesiastes was, like the Cynics, a product of the Hellenistic age, a time when old standards had been discarded, and the individual was left to the mercy of capricious but irresistible forces. The Cynics were missionaries, and their message was that life could be lived on any terms the age could impose. It is particularly easy for the modern observer to see only the grotesque aspect of Cynicism, and to miss its real significance. This is partly due to the fact that Cynicism is usually presented to us in histories of Greek philosophy, where it forms an interlude of semi-comic relief between Socrates and Plato, or between Plato and the Stoics. But a most important reason is that the Cynics represented a standard with which we are unfamiliar—that of the minimum. Through long exposure to statistics, we can readily grasp any conception that involves a norm—the cost of living, the real wage of the working man, and so on—but in the modern world no one voluntarily lives, as did the Cynics, at subsistence level. Our civilization admittedly has the disadvantage that it may be completely shattered by war : but in other respects we have far greater security than was known to the Hellenistic world. Slavery, in particular, is so remote from us that it is hard to comprehend how real a terror it was to the Greeks of that period. Yet one has only to consider how powerful were the pirates in the Mediterranean until their suppression by Pompeius, to see that any traveller by ship was running a real risk of being captured and sold into slavery. Exile has only recently been the lot of thousands of citizens of European States ; in the Hellenistic world it existed not only as a common form of punishment, but also as one of the normal risks attendant on a high position in politics. Again, during this period several cities were completely destroyed, as Thebes by Alexander, Lebedos and Kolophon by Lysimachus, and most notable of all such catastrophes in the Greek world, Corinth by the Romans.

Conditions in the Roman Empire bore a sufficiently close resemblance to those of the Hellenistic age that the Cynic mission was again in demand. Exile, slavery, loss of home and possessions, are the frequent burthen of the Cynic diatribe ; if their thought on these subjects seems commonplace, it should not be forgotten that they were dealing with what their audience felt as very real terrors, and that they were performing a valuable service in showing that even these could be surmounted.

The present account tells the history of Cynicism from

the time of Diogenes to the last years of the Roman Empire in the West. No continuous account is available of later date than that of Zeller, since when a good deal of new material has accumulated, both from the discovery of papyri and in the normal course of research. I have tried to embody the lessons of this new material in my narrative ; which, however, claims to be rather more than a cento of the conclusions of other scholars. Its central theme is that the traditional view of Cynicism as a minor Socratic school, founded by Antisthenes, must be abandoned. Antisthenes had no direct contact with the Cynics, who never formed a school of philosophy at all, being intolerant of organization and impatient of theory. I have argued that the traditional view has been established by two interested parties—Alexandrian writers of *Successions of Philosophers* and the Stoics. The former wished to trace all philosophical genealogies back to Socrates wherever possible ; the latter, desirous of showing themselves as the true heirs of Socrates, made great play with the connexion of their founder Zeno with the Cynic Crates, and turned Diogenes into a Stoic saint. The sympathy for Cynicism which always marked the more austere wing of the Stoics was based on genuine affinities, and indeed Cynicism did preserve a recognizable version of the Socratic ethics in action. But the ' succession ' Socrates-Diogenes-Crates-Zeno is a fabrication.

Another current view of Cynicism which may be misleading is that which describes it as ' the philosophy of the proletariat '. To the modern reader such a phrase suggests an attempt to replace the existing social order by a new system. But with the exception of Cercidas and the reform party at Megalopolis, and possibly the Cynics of Alexandria in the second century A.D., we shall not find Cynicism involving any kind of political action on behalf of social reform. The Cynic ' anarchy ' never became so practical as to organize the murder of tyrants, and their invective against wealth was as much for the spiritual benefit of the rich as for the material betterment of the poor. Indeed, by preaching that poverty and slavery are no bar to happiness, the Cynics implied that a social revolution would be superfluous.

The conclusion of this study is that Cynicism was really a phenomenon which presented itself in three not inseparable aspects—a vagrant ascetic life, an assault on all established values, and a body of literary genres particularly well adapted to satire and popular philosophical propaganda. The third aspect is the one to which scholars have hitherto devoted most attention ; and the researches of Gerhard, Geffcken, Wendland, and others have shown how important and fertile was its influence on Hellenistic and Roman literature. It is here touched on only in passing, for my object has been rather to give an account of individual Cynics, and to show them at work in that rôle which they variously symbolized as the Scout of God, the Schoolmaster, the Doctor of Mankind.

CHAPTER I

ANTISTHENES. NO DIRECT CONNEXION WITH CYNICS. HIS ETHICS

THE orthodox account of Cynicism regards Antisthenes as the founder of the sect. This is due to the influence of Diogenes Laertius, who says that Antisthenes 'learned his hardihood from Socrates, and inaugurated the Cynic way of life '.[1] His pupil was Diogenes of Sinope, Crates was a pupil of Diogenes. Zeno, the founder of Stoicism, was a pupil of Crates. There is thus an apostolic succession from Socrates to the Stoics. But the validity of the tradition which makes Antisthenes the founder of Cynicism has been questioned in both ancient and modern times.[2] This is hardly surprising, for a comparison between Antisthenes and the generally accepted picture of his 'pupil and successor' Diogenes shows more points of divergence than of similarity. Both were ascetics : both stressed the opposition of πόνος and ἡδονή : both used Heracles as an example of πόνος. But the resemblance hardly goes further. We know from the unquestionable authority of Aristotle [3] that Antisthenes and his pupils were deeply interested in the problems of neo-Eleatic logic ; Diogenes designated the Megarians, the inheritors of that logic, as 'bilious '.[4] Antisthenes had a liking for Homeric interpretations ; Diogenes remarked that ' it was surprising that grammarians should investigate the ills of Odysseus, yet be completely ignorant of their own '.[5] Antisthenes wrote treatises on rhetorical subjects ; Diogenes ' despised rhetoricians who made a great fuss about justice in their speeches, but never practised it '.[6] Poor and ascetic Antisthenes certainly was ; but it was in the manner of a companion of Socrates. He possessed a house and small piece of property,[7] used a bed

[1] vi. 2.   [2] See Chap. 2, App. A.
[3] Top., 104, B. 21 ; Met., 1024b, 32, and 1043b, 24.
[4] D.L., vi. 24.   [5] id., ib. 27.   [6] id., ib. 28.   [7] Xen., *Symp.* 38.

and furniture, would accompany Socrates to the banquets of the wealthiest men in Athens. Diogenes lived in the open air, or in his tub ; the staples of his diet were dried figs and water. Antisthenes frequented the lectures of the Sophists, and derived his living from teaching ; Diogenes ' poured scorn on all his contemporaries ',[1] and lived the life of a beggar. Again, Alcibiades was reproved by Antisthenes for the crime of incest ; the ἀναιδέια of Diogenes abolished all such barriers. These are striking differences and are recognized as such by ancient upholders of the ' Cynic succession ' from Antisthenes to Diogenes. To minimize them, they adduce stories which try to show that Diogenes reproved Antisthenes for not practising what he preached ; thus he is made to ' liken Antisthenes to a brazen trumpet, which gave forth a great noise but was unable to hear itself '.[2] So in modern times Gomperz, though accepting the ' succession ', regards Diogenes as ' the founder of a practical Cynicism '. But a priori the traditional view seems unlikely, and one is not disposed to accept it unless well supported by early evidence.

Such evidence, however, is significantly lacking. Aristotle refers to the pupils of Antisthenes as Ἀντισθένειοι, not as κυνικοί, and he further implies that they were mainly interested in logical studies. The only fragments which we possess of Cynic writers contemporary with Diogenes are those of Crates and Onesicratus of Astypalaea. None of these mentions Antisthenes. Crates claimed Διογένους εἶναι πολίτης.[3] Onesicratus, asked by the Indian Gymnosophist whether any of the Greeks had led an ascetic life, replied, ' Yes, Pythagoras and Socrates and Diogenes, and I was a pupil of his.'[4] Middle Comedy has no reference to Antisthenes ; for examples of notorious poverty and asceticism it makes use of a sect of Pythagoreans. In point of fact it is most unlikely that Diogenes and Antisthenes can have been contemporaries at Athens. The researches of Seltman [5] on the coinage of Sinope suggest that Diogenes in all probability

---

[1] D.L., vi. 24.
[2] Dio Chrys., viii, p. 275 ; Stobaeus, Flor., xiii. 19.
[3] D.L., vi. 93.   [4] Apud Strabo., xvi. 83-4.
[5] A fuller account of Mr. Seltman's researches is given below in connexion with the chronology of Diogenes.

came to Athens later than 340 B.C., Antisthenes died soon after 366.[1] A story which probably derives from Theophrastus,[2] and hence may represent a contemporary account, shows Diogenes himself claiming to have been converted to philosophy, not by the teachings of Antisthenes, but by the practical example of a mouse ; and which further suggests that when he arrived at Athens he was already a devotee of the ascetic life. It is only in the later writers, Epictetus, Dio Chrysostom, Aelian, Stobaeus, Diogenes Laertius, and Suidas, that we hear of a connexion between Antisthenes and Diogenes ; and it is significant that they do not name any other pupils of Antisthenes apart from Diogenes, and that their stories about the relations between the two emphasize Antisthenes' surliness to pupils and Diogenes' dissatisfaction with his practical example. The tradition of a connexion seems to have arisen some time between Onesicratus and Epictetus ; the problem is to suggest among whom, and when, it may have made its appearance. Ancient literary fabrications are usually most readily discovered by the formula *cui bono?* ; so here, who would stand to gain if Diogenes were portrayed as the pupil of Antisthenes ?

The answer is partly suggested by an anecdote which appears in Diogenes Laertius' life of Zeno.[3] Coming to Athens after his shipwreck, says this account, Zeno one day sat down in a bookseller's shop. Now the bookseller was reading aloud the second book of Xenophon's *Memorabilia*, which so delighted Zeno that he asked where such men as Socrates might be found. Very opportunely, Crates passed by, and the bookseller said, ' Follow that man.' From that day on, Zeno became Crates' pupil. . . . The Stoics recognized the merits of Cynicism, ' the wise man will play the Cynic, for Cynicism is a short cut to virtue, as Apollodorus says in his Ethics '.[4] They

---

[1] The birth of Antisthenes is usually placed *c.* 443, to fit the tradition that he fought at ' Tanagra ' (? Delium, 423). Xenophon's *Symposium*, the dramatic date of which is 421, shows him as a youngish man, but already an intimate companion of Socrates. But there is guarantee of Xenophon's chronological good faith on the point. Diodorus Siculus (xv. 76) speaks of Antisthenes as being alive in 366, and Plutarch (Lyc., 30) quotes a remark of his on the battle of Leuctra. We know that Diogenes was well known in Athens, *c.* 330.

[2] D.L., vi. 22.   [3] id., vii. 2.   [4] id., ib. 121.

probably regarded Cynicism as representing in its purest form
the ethical tradition of Socrates, and would be particularly
anxious to show that they themselves were the direct inheritors
of that tradition. Hence was constructed the 'succession'
Socrates—Antisthenes—Diogenes—Crates—Zeno : and hence
Epictetus can use Socrates, Antisthenes, and Diogenes as
good divinity for Stoic moral beliefs.[1] The Stoics would be
aided and abetted by another body of interested persons, the
Alexandrian writers of *Successions of the Philosophers*.[2] Their
schemata treated Socrates as of great importance, indeed as
the virtual turning point of Greek philosophy. Any sect
that professed φιλοσοφία must trace back its pedigree to
Socrates ; how pedigrees came to be invented is clearly seen
when we consider how Hedonists of the third century were
linked up to Socrates via Aristippus. From the diagram in
Appendix C we see how in the 'successions' adopted by
Diogenes Laertius he is the nodal point of the 'Ionian'
philosophy. The succession from Socrates via the Cynics
to the Stoics seems to have been established by Sotion of
Alexandria (*c.* 200–170 B.C.), the most voluminous and influential of these writers. He was probably followed in this
by Heracleides of Lembos, and Antisthenes and Sosicrates
of Rhodes. This succession had become orthodoxy by the
end of the Alexandrian period, and was apparently followed by
such first-century and later authors as Diocles, Pamphila, and
Favorinus. True there were dissenters (e.g. Hippobotus did
not regard the Cynics as one of the 'ten ethical schools ') ;
but in Diogenes Laertius we have preserved the Schemata of
the Alexandrian writers of διαδοχάι (Successions). He prefers,
he says, to regard Cynicism as a school of philosophy. It is a
αἵρεσις, on a par with Stoicism, with which it has κοινωνία.[3]
Antisthenes learnt καρτερία (endurance) from Socrates, and
' was the first founder of Cynicism '.[4] He it was who gave
the impulse to the indifference of Diogenes, the continence
of Crates, and the hardihood of Zeno, himself laying the
foundations of their code '.[5] Both Cynics and Stoics are
thus ἀπ' Ἀντισθένους, though this is elsewhere amended to
' the more manly sect of Stoics ' (ἡ ἀνδρωδέστατη Στωϊκή).[6]

---

[1] So Epict., i. xvii. 12, also iii. xxiv. 51.
[2] Cf. Hicks, *Diog. Laert.* (Loeb series), Introd., p. xxiv.
[3] D.L., vi. 104.　　[4] id., ib. 2.　　[5] id., ib. 15.　　[6] id., ib. 14.

' Some persons think that the Cynic school derives its name from the Cynosarges, and Antisthenes was himself called ʿΑπλοκύων ʼ[1] (or ʾΑυτοκύων). But Diogenes Laertius fails to give any anecdote or apophthegm in which Antisthenes figures as a κύων ; and we recall that Aristotle refers to his pupils as ʾΑυτισθενέιοι. The supposed ' hostile ' references in Plato and Isocrates make no use of the opportunity such a nickname would afford. The original κύων was undoubtedly Diogenes himself. He is so called by Aristotle [2] : Cercidas of Megalopolis addresses him as ' ἀλαθάως | Διογένης Ζανὸς γόνος οὐράνιος τε κύων ʼ.[3] The origin of the nickname is clear when we consider the use of the term in Homer. As is well known, it denotes shamelessness or audacity ; Helen applies it to herself in a fit of remorse ; [4] the enraged Hera calls Artemis κύον ἀδδέες (' shameless bitch ') ; Liddell and Scott use this passage as evidence that κύων was not so strong a term of abuse as with us ; but the Homeric goddesses were not given to mincing their words : the serving-maids of Penelope are called ' bitches ' by Odysseus.[5] The name was undoubtedly first applied to Diogenes in a hostile sense, owing to his ἀυάιδεια, or habit of ' doing everything in public ', and was retained by him and the later Cynics for its potentialities for allegory. The original and the later allegorizing explanations of the name are preserved by a scholium on Aristotle.[6]

There are four reasons why the ' Cynics ' are so named. First because of the ' indifference ' of their way of life (διὰ τὸ ἀδιάφορον τῆς ζωῆς), for they make a cult of ἀδιαφορία and, like dogs, eat and make love in public, go barefoot, and sleep in tubs and at crossroads. . . . The second reason is that the dog is a shameless animal, and they make a cult of shamelessness, not as being beneath modesty (ʾΑιδώς), but as superior to it. . . . The third reason is that the dog is a good guard, and they guard the tenets of their philosophy. . . . The fourth reason is that the dog is a discriminating animal which can distinguish between its friends and enemies. . . . So do they recognize as friends those who are suited to philosophy, and receive them kindly, while those unfitted they drive away, like dogs, by barking at them.

---

[1] id., ib. 13.
[3] *Apud* D.L., vi. 77.
[5] Od., xviii. 338.

[2] Rhet., iii. 10. 7.
[4] Il., vi. 344 and 356.
[6] Ed. Brandis, p. 23.

The first certain application of the term κυνικός to any of Diogenes' followers is a fragment of Menander's *Didumi*.[1]

συμπεριπατήσεις γὰρ τρίβων᾽ ἔχουσ᾽ ἐμοὶ
ὥσπερ Κράτητι τῷ κυνικῷ ποθ᾽ ἡ γυνή

Now there is no evidence that either Crates or Diogenes made use of the Cynosarges ; hence one may infer that the etymology deriving Cynic from the Cynosarges was an invention of the writers of διαδοχάι, very probably by analogy with the Stoa and the Academy.

Etymologically, then, the attempt to connect Antisthenes with the κυνικόι breaks down.   But Diogenes Laertius further says that Antisthenes adopted what afterwards came to be recognized as the insignia of the Cynic, the τρίβων, the wallet, and the staff.   The sources he gives for this statement enable us to perceive its unreliability.

He was the first, Diocles tells us, to double his cloak, and be content with that one garment and to take up a staff and wallet.   Neanthes too asserts that he was the first to double his mantle.   Sosicrates, however, in the third book of his *Successions of Philosophers* says this was first done by Diodorus of Aspendus, who also let his beard grow and used a staff and wallet.[2]

The significance of Diodorus of Aspendus we shall see shortly. Meanwhile, one remarks that Neanthes, writing probably in the third century, only suggests that Antisthenes doubled his cloak ; we have seen that, like Socrates, he probably wore the simplest clothing.   It is only in Diocles, writing in the first century A.D., that the staff and the wallet are thrown in.   In the *Life of Diogenes*,[3] it is stated that

some say Diogenes was the first to fold his cloak because he was obliged to sleep in it as well, and he carried a wallet to hold his victuals . . .   He did not lean upon a staff till he grew infirm : but afterwards he would carry it everywhere, not indeed in the city, but when walking along the road with it and with his wallet ; so say Olympiodorus, once a magistrate of Athens, Polyeuctes the orator, and Lysanias the son of Aeschrio.[4]

The three persons named were contemporaries of Theo-

[1] In. D.L., vi. 93.   [2] id., ib. 13.
[3] id., ib. 22, 23.   [4] id., ib. 23.

phrastus, and von Fritz [1] contends with great probability that the reference to Diogenes comes from a dialogue of Theophrastus in which they figured. This gives us a good early tradition ; and implies that the staff and the wallet formed the equipment of the vagabond beggar. Odysseus entered the palace at Ithaca ' in the likeness of an aged and woeful beggar, leaning on a staff, and wretched was the raiment he wore on his body ' ; and Irus wore ' a miserable wallet, full of holes, and slung by a twisted cord (Od., xvii. 335 ; xviii. 108). Aristophanes in the *Acharnians* [2] says that amongst the ' Properties ' kept by Euripides for that unhappily conceived character, Telephus, were a ragged cloak (ῥακίον), a basket (σπυριδίον), and a beggar's staff. For Antisthenes, who was no beggar, such a get-up would be pointless. It was, however, used in his day by the ascetic Pythagoreans, whom we know of through the Telauges of Aeschines, and to which sect Diodorus of Aspendus belonged. Aeschines [3] mentions the θύλακος, the pouch or wallet, carried by Telauges ; the Middle Comedy [4] has references to a κώρυκος, a leather wallet, as the distinguishing mark of these philosophers. Clearly this served the same purpose as the σπυριδίον of Telephus or the πήρα of Diogenes.

Diogenes Laertius, though himself regarding Cynicism as one of the minor Socratic schools, lets it be known that others held a different view. We have seen how Hippobotus [5] refused to regard the Cynics as one of the ten ethical schools ; elsewhere it is remarked that ' certain persons regard Cynicism as a mode of life [6] not as a sect of philosophy '. This view is fortunately preserved by the Emperor Julian. He quotes with approval the dictum of Oenomaus of Gadara, himself a Cynic, that ' Cynicism is neither Antisthenism nor Diogenism ' . . .

For [says Julian] in all ages men have practised this philosophy. . . . It does not need any special study, one should merely hearken

---

[1] *Quellen-Untersuchungen zu Leben und Phil. des D. von Sinope*, 1926.
[2] Acharn., 11, 435, 448, 453.
[3] Cf. Dittmar, Aeschines von Sphettos, 417.
[4] Antiph., fr. 11. 76 ; fr. 11. 67.   [5] D.L., 1. 19.
[6] id., vi. 103.

to the Delphic god when he enjoins these two maxims—γνῶθι σεάντον and παράχαραξον τὸ νόμισμα. Hence obviously the founder of this philosophy is he who is responsible for all the goods the Greeks possess, the god at Delphi.[1]

Though he grants that Cynicism is a ' type of philosophy ',[2] and one that ' rivals the noblest ', he insists that it is ' universal and most natural '.[3]   Noteworthy is his express statement that in his time no serious Cynic treatises were preserved; [4] either the voluminous writings of Antisthenes, known at least in part to Diogenes Laertius, had in the interim perished, or else Julian did not connect them with Cynicism.   When he does mention Antisthenes together with Diogenes and Crates, it is as a writer of myths ; [5] Hesiod, Xenophon, and Plato are also named in this connexion.   Throughout, Julian emphasizes that Cynicism is a way of life : he will describe its true nature for the benefit of those ' about to enter upon this way '.   He insists that one should distinguish the outward manifestations from the rationale, the true feature, of the Cynic life.[6]   *Cucullus non facit monachum*, nor staff and wallet the Cynic.

We have seen, then, that it is extremely unlikely that there was any personal contact between Antisthenes and Diogenes. But it cannot be denied that the resemblance between the ethics of Antisthenes and those of the Cynics was sufficiently close to make the tradition of such connexion a plausible fiction.   The earliest and best authority for Antisthenes' ethics is the *Symposium* of Xenophon.   It will be remembered that each of the chief guests at the banquet was required to state what he was most proud of, and afterwards to deliver a speech justifying his choice.   Antisthenes professed to be proud of his wealth, a statement which immediately provoked attention, for at the time he ' did not possess an obol '.[7]   When his turn came to elaborate his choice, he explained that he had spoken figuratively, " I think, gentlemen, that men's poverty and wealth is to be sought for, not in their estates, but in their souls '—an essentially Socratic view (cf. Apology 29D–30B). Material wealth is a malignant disease

for some despots destroy whole families, kill men wholesale, and

---

[1] Julian, 188C–D.   [2] id., 182C.   [3] id., 187C.
[4] id., 186B.   [5] id., 209A.   [6] id., 201A.
[7] See Note 1, Chap. I.

often enslave entire cities, for the sake of money . . . for my own part my possessions are so great that I myself can hardly discover them all ; yet I have enough so that I can eat until I am no longer hungry and drink to the point of not being thirsty, and I clothe myself so that I do not feel the cold more than my opulent friend here, Callias. When I get into my house I regard the walls as exceedingly warm tunics, and the roof as an exceptionally thick blanket ; and I have sufficient bedding to make it a hard task to get me awake of a morning. When my body needs sexual satisfaction, whatever lies to hand is good enough for me. So the women I associate with are exceeding grateful to me, for no one else will approach them. In fact, all these possessions seem to me so enjoyable that I could not wish for greater pleasure from them, but indeed for less ; for some of them do seem to me more pleasurable than is advisable. The most valuable possession I derive from my wealth is this, that even though someone were to deprive me of all I possess, I see no occupation so humble that I could not derive adequate livelihood from it . . . and one should note that wealth of this sort makes men generous. For Socrates, from whom I acquired my wealth, did not dole it out to me by measure and weight, but gave me all that I was capable of bearing. Similarly, I myself am not miserly to anyone, but I openly show my abundance to all my friends, and I share out to anyone who desires it the wealth that is in my soul [cf. Apology 31B, 33B]. But you will observe that the most luxurious of all my possessions is that I always have leisure to go to see whatever is worth seeing, or hear whatever is worth hearing, and, (what I prize above all) can pass the whole day at leisure in the company of Socrates (cf. Theaet. 172D).

The doctrine, expounded in Socratic phraseology, is the familiar one in later Greek philosophy, of asceticism as the surest way of attaining εὐδαιμονία (happiness). Now the evidence of Aristophanes and Ameipsias shows us that asceticism of some kind was practised in the ' Socratic circle '. The *Clouds* describes the inhabitants of the ' Thinking-Shop ' as ' those pale-faced, barefooted wretches, like Chaerephon and Socrates ' ; and suggests that the prospect confronting the initiate is τύπτειν, πεινῆν, διψῆν | ἀνκμεῖν, ῥιγοῦν, ἀσκὸν δείρειν, while there are references to Socrates' need of a cloak and sandals, and the generally unwashed and unshaven character of his companions.[1] Clearly some sort of asceticism must have characterized them if the burlesque was

[1] ll. 103-4, 441-2 (Oxford Text).

to be plausible : the evidence of Plato, without containing any direct reference as to its origin, certainly suggests that Socrates followed an ascetic mode of life.   Thus in the *Phaedrus* (229A) he is represented as being ' always barefooted ', in the *Symposium* (174A) an occasion when he, for once, wore a new cloak and sandals is explained away as being a gesture in honour of the Banquet to which he was going ; and, more explicitly, we have the testimony of Alcibiades (*Symp.* 219B) of Socrates' remarkable endurance of hunger, cold, fatigue. This side of Socrates' character is given in greater detail in the *Memorabilia*,[1] but as it is uncertain whether or to what degree Xenophon is there influenced by Antisthenes' own portrayal of Socrates, perhaps his evidence should not be unduly pressed.[2] But clearly this brand of asceticism is a very Socratic thing. Socrates neglected the pursuit of sensual pleasures, just as he neglected his own financial interests, to concentrate on the chief object of his ' mission ' the ' care of his soul ' and the exhortation to his fellow-citizens to care for theirs.[3]   It should be distinguished from two other ways of life with which it has sometimes been confused : the αὐτάρκεια of a man like Hippias ; and the rigid asceticism, which becomes an end-in-itself, of Diogenes and his associates.[4]   The latter practised, as we shall see, absolute simplicity of living, absolute renunciation of comforts.   But Socrates, as is known from the *Symposium* of Plato, could enjoy good living when it came his way : and so

---

[1] Especially in 1. 2. 1, 1. 3. 3, and 1. 6. 2.

[2] Joel (*Der echte und der Xenophontische Sokrates*) regards Xenophon as throughout dependent upon Antisthenes, and uses the *Memorabilia* to reconstruct Antisthenes' ethical system.   More recently H. Gomperz (*Die Sokratische Frage als geschichtliches Problems : Historische Zeitschrift*, 1924), while admitting Joel's premisses that the Socrates of the *Memorabilia* is the Socrates of Antisthenes, attacks his conclusions that this is therefore not the Socrates of history.   Antisthenes, according to him, was the most faithful disciple of Socrates : his picture of the Master is likely to be the most authentic.   Other scholars regard the *Memorabilia* as, in the main, an independent attempt to give a portrait of Socrates, though it may borrow details from Plato and Antisthenes.   The controversy is clearly one which falls outside the scope of this essay ; but in discussing the probable influence of Socrates upon Antisthenes, I have thought it wiser to draw parallels from the early Platonic dialogues, and to use the *Memorabilia* only as supplementary to inferences based on other evidence.

[3] Cf. *Apology* 29D, 30d.   [4] See Note 2 to Chap. I.

in the *Symposium* of Xenophon, Antisthenes drinks his Thasian wine, though he does not omit to add that he enjoys it less than he would simpler fare if he were really thirsty. Antisthenes also used a house, a bed, and other comforts with which Diogenes dispensed.

Even the scanty doxographical section [1] of Diogenes Laertius' biography shows the influence of Socrates as paramount in Antisthenes' ethics. The familiar Socratic doctrine that ἀρετή may be taught appears, and ἀρετή seems to have been defined in a Socratic way. It is self-sufficient as regards happiness, needing nothing else but the strength of a Socrates, it is ' a weapon that cannot be taken away ' ; again, as wisdom it is ' the safest kind of wall ' which must be constructed ' in our own impregnable reasoning '. This last implies the Socratic view of virtue as knowledge ; and the unity of the virtues appears in an Antisthenean doctrine preserved in a commentary on Homer. ' Antisthenes says that if the wise man does anything, he does it in accordance with virtue as a whole.' (Schol. Lips. on Il., xv. 123). Further, the titles of some of his works are those of ' virtues ' which we know to have been investigated by Socrates. There are for instance writings on Courage (cf. *Laches*), on Injustice and Impiety (cf. *Euthyphro*), on Justice and Courage (cf. *Protagoras*). It is probable that in these works the same method was pursued as that which appears in the early Platonic dialogues, i.e. ' popular ' instances of the virtue under discussion were taken and shown to be inadequate by the true standard. This is suggested by a quotation from Antisthenes preserved by Athenaeus (xii. 534c) via Satyrus Ἀντισθένης ὁ Σωκρατικὸς ὡς δὴ αὐτόπτης γεγονὼς τοῦ Ἀλκιβιάδου ' ἰσχυρὸν αὐτὸν καὶ ἀνδρώδη καὶ ἀπαίδευτον καὶ τολμηρὸν καὶ ὡραῖον ἐφ' ἡλικίας πάσης γενέσθαι φησιν.

The point lies in ἀπαίδευτος ; ἰσχύς and ἀνδρεία are virtues when they are of the right brand, the Σωκρατικὴ ἰσχύς ; this was what Alcibiades lacked, owing to his want of παιδέια.[2]

---

[1] D.L., vi. 12, 13.
[2] Cf. Dittmar, *Aeschines von Sphettos*, p. 86, n. 68. He regards the quotation as from the *Cyrus* of Antisthenes. Müller prints it under the fragments of the *Alcibiades*. The point probably cannot be definitely settled.

In intimate connexion with this view of ἀρετή (Virtue) are
the tenets of Antisthenes about the σοφός which occur in the
same passage of Diogenes Laertius. ' The σοφός will rule his
life, not in accordance with the established Laws, but according
to those of Virtue. ' The σοφός is self-sufficient.' ' The
σοφός will love, for he alone knows how to love.' The Virtue
of the wise man, which is ' self-sufficient as regards happiness ',
is precisely that which Socrates insisted could be taught.[1]
This is brought out most clearly in the *Phaedo* (82A ff.) where
Socrates implies two levels of ἀρετή ; the first, a δημοτικὴ καὶ
πολιτικὴ ἀρετή . . . ἐξ ἔθους τε καὶ μελέτης γεγονυῖα ἄνευ
φιλοσοφίας τε καὶ νοῦ, the practisers of which will be rein-
carnated as bees, ants, wasps or other ' social animals ', or as
worthy men (μετρίοι ἄνδρες) : the other, that of οἱ ὀρθῶς
φιλοσοφοῦντες and παντελῶς καθαροί and also of οἱ φιλομαθεῖς
who shall ' enter the communion of the gods '. Since it
occurs in the *Phaedo*, this distinction is in all probability that
of Socrates ; and it is one of great importance for subsequent
Greek thought. From the time of Socrates onwards, the
gulf between the σοφός and the ordinary human being and
his standards tends to widen, not only in Antisthenes but also
in such Platonic passages as *Theaetetus* 175A ff. (where the
philosopher is totally indifferent to birth, wealth, fame,
or rank), till eventually it becomes unbridgeable when we
arrive at that paragon of inhuman virtue, the σοφός of the
Stoics.

This view of the σοφός was Antisthenes' reason for stressing the doctrines of ἡδονή and πόνος : doctrines which the
Alexandrian writers of *Successions* relied upon to prove his
spiritual affinity with Zeno and the Stoics. Again, the
influence of Socrates may be traced. In the great speech in
the *Phaedo*, describing the life of the philosopher, it is stated
that such a man will above all seek to emancipate himself from
the flesh and its desires, its pleasures, and its pains, for every
instance in which ἡδονή or λύπη is felt, is a nail which nails
the soul more firmly to the body.[2] ἡδονή and λύπη, pleasure
and pain, are thus the chief enemies of the man who is trying
to ' tend his soul '. εὐτελεία and σωφροσύνη are prophylactic
against ἡδονή, but what antidotes can be found for λύπη
which generally comes from circumstances outside our con-

[1] Cf. Burnet, *Thales to Plato*, p. 174.   [2] *Phaedo*, 83B ff.

trol ?[1] The remedy of Antisthenes was πόνος (toil), a word which he was perhaps the first to use in a technical sense. Socrates never uses πόνος in this way in any Platonic writing,[2] and the fact that he does so use it in Xenophon's *Memorabilia* may be due to the influence of Antisthenes.

'That toil is a good thing', says Diogenes Laertius, 'he established by the example of Heracles the Great and Cyrus, choosing one from the Greeks, the other from the barbarians.' This sentence has been used as evidence for attributing cosmopolitanism to Antisthenes, but it will not really bear that interpretation. In fact, what Antisthenes did was merely to choose two examples from that gallery of great figures, some historic, some legendary, familiar to every educated person of his day. Admittedly few figures in that gallery were 'barbarians', and of those few were cast in the rôle of hero, but such was undoubtedly the case with Cyrus. The great king, who appears in a favourable light even in the Old Testament, appears to have exercised a fascination over the Greeks throughout the fifth century. For Antisthenes, he appears not only as an example of the value of πόνος, but, as also for Xenophon, as the ideal of βασιλεία.

The choice of Heracles to exemplify πόνος is of course an obvious one. 'Who of all the sons of Zeus', asks Unjust Logic in the *Clouds*, 'endured the most hardships and greatest toil ?' 'Why, Heracles,' is the answer, and from the practice of that hero the moral is drawn that hot baths do not really have an enervating effect. But a favourable portrayal of Heracles, though it was certainly not originated by Antisthenes, appears to have been a recent tradition in his time. Cyrus also figured later in Cynic allegory, but did not play so prominent a part therein as Heracles, who became a veritable patron saint to the Cynic movement.

The ethics of Antisthenes, then—probably largely through his portrayal of Socrates—had a considerable influence on the Cynics. But the narrow concentration on ethics to the exclusion of all other aspects of philosophy, the chief characteristic of Diogenes and the Cynics, is not found in the case of

---

[1] Cf. the case of the unfortunate Dionysius, 'the Renegade', also suffered such agonies from ophthalmia that he could not bring himself to admit that Pain was αδιάφορον (D.L., vii. 166).

[2] In the *Phaedo* he says οἱ φιλοσοφοῦντες . . . καρτεροῦσι.

Antisthenes. The titles of his works cover ethics, logic, politics, and what were later called metaphysics, and we know that he was interested in rhetoric and in the 'interpretation' of Homer. His philosophy presumably formed a coherent whole, though there is not sufficient evidence to reconstruct it. But the impression left by an examination of what are known to have been his doctrines in various departments of knowledge is that there is little here that is original. His logical position was that of the 'neo-Eleatics': the influence of Socrates is paramount in his ethics: his political views are a synthesis compounded of the Socratic ideal of the σοφός, the 'Sophistic' opposition between νόμος and φύσις and the reactions of a 'Socratic man' to the events of contemporary history. In his interest in 'names' one may suspect the influence of Prodicus: that of Gorgias is undoubted on his style and his rhetorical studies: in Homeric 'interpretation' he followed the already popular method of allegory. The conclusion is that here is a typical minor figure of that time of intellectual ferment, the age of Socrates and the Sophists; probably Cicero's judgement of him is fair enough 'homo acutus magis quam eruditus'. But Antisthenes' philosophy was a structure which rested on flimsy foundations. Its basis was the 'neo-Eleatic' logic: and before long the difficulties with which that system was confronted and the solutions it propounded were alike swept away by the *Sophistes* of Plato. This probably accounts for the contemptuous tone of Aristotle's references to Antisthenes,[1] and suggests that Antisthenes' logical treatises were quickly obsolete. But there is ample warrant of his popularity in ancient times. He was accepted as one of the canons of pure Attic style: Dionysius of Halicarnassus groups him with Andocides, Antiphon, Lysias, Critias, and Xenophon: Phrynichus ranks him with Plato, Demosthenes, and Critias. This popularity he must have attained as a writer of Σωκρατικοὶ λόγοι.[2] The Socrates of his dialogues was undoubtedly the ascetic, the 'man with a mission', an aspect of the Master which tended to be obscured in the later Platonic dialogues, where Socrates becomes increasingly the mouthpiece for Plato's own thought. The *Memorabilia* of Xenophon are to some extent a reaction

---

[1] Cf. Met. 1024*b*, 27 ff., 1043*b*, 18.
[2] See note 3 to Chap. I.

against Plato's portrayal of the Master : Antisthenes, together with other disciples, may well have felt that some such corrective was needed.

To the Stoics and to the Alexandrian writers of *Successions*, Antisthenes would be most familiar as the author of Socratic discourses, in which the tradition of Socrates the ascetic was predominant. Antisthenes himself was known to have been master of a philosophic ' school ' ; his ethics bore a marked resemblance to those of the Cynics and Stoics : he was therefore the obvious choice as the first link in the ' apostolic succession ' in which the Stoics wished to link themselves up to Socrates. Antisthenes thus became the ' founder of Cynicism ', and achieved a position in the history of philosophy to which his achievements as a thinker scarcely entitled him. We may agree with Vallette that he was the ' precursor of Cynicism ', but for the founder of the sect we must turn to Diogenes of Sinope.

NOTES TO CHAPTER I

1. Antisthenes must have possessed money at some time to be able to attend the lectures of Gorgias. In Xenophon's *Symposium* he appears to possess a small piece of land. Perhaps, as Burnet thinks was the case with Socrates, his poverty was of rather recent date in 421 or thereabouts (*Symp.*, iii. 8).

2. It has been suggested that the αὐτάρκεια of Hippias, who once appeared at an Olympian festival wearing a cloak, girdles, ring, sandals, &c., all made by himself (Plato, *Hipp.* 368b), had an influence on Antisthenes' view of self-sufficiency. This is to confuse two fundamentally different methods of approach to the problem. For the individual αὐτάρκεια may be obtained either by (*a*) an extension of one's accomplishments and aptitudes till they can fulfil all the ' desires ' (this is πολυτροπία : the versatility of a man like Hippias), or (*b*) an elimination of the ' desires ' till they reach a point at which their demands are light and readily satisfied (this is εὐτελεία, the method of Antisthenes and Socrates. This same point may be illustrated if we consider αὐτάρκεια in the meaning frequently used in Thucydides—' independent ' in the political sense, of a city which is sufficient to itself in both military and economic resources. If a state has relatively low ' demands ' (i.e. a ' low standing of living '), the occupations of its citizens will be few and simple. If its desires become more complex (i.e. it is attaining a ' high standard of living '), then its citizens must engage in all manner of industries for it to be

self-sufficient. The two states of society are contrasted in Rep. 370 and 373.

3. Panaetius accepted his Socratic dialogues as genuine : he is grouped with Xenophon and Plato not only by Diogenes Laertius (ii. 47), but also by Epictetus (ii. 17. 35), Fronto (de. eloc. 98), Lucian (ad. doct. 27) and Julian (215C).

CHAPTER II

DIOGENES AND HIS ASSOCIATES

(a) ' EVEN bronze groweth old with Time, but thy fame, Diogenes, not all Eternity shall take away. For thou alone didst point out to mortals the lesson of self-sufficingness, and the easiest path of life.' [1] The prophecy has in a way been fulfilled; for Diogenes is one of the more familiar figures of antiquity. Yet with him, as with other historical personages, the very merits of a good story have obscured rather than illuminated its moral, αὐτάρκεια is forgotten but the tub survives, nor does one bother to inquire closely precisely why Alexander was asked to stand out of the sun. In classical times, too, the reputation of Diogenes was subjected to a similar process; for it rested largely on that Greek delight in personality for its own sake, quite apart from its didactic value. A people who can enjoy a good story can always invent one; hence Diogenes soon after his death became a literary stock figure, and as such, like Sir John Falstaff, achieved a reality almost independent of his historical existence. Small wonder, then, that it is hard to establish about him anything that by the severer standards of historical criticism can be admitted as fact. It is a task which must be attempted, but with caution; the case of Diogenes is one in which irrefutability can be purchased at too high a price. If judgement is to be entirely suspended because so few of the stories about him can be verified, then the baby is emptied away with the bath water. All Aberdeen stories may be invented, yet the inference remains that the Aberdonians are a thrifty race. So, in analysing the anecdotes about Diogenes, one should expect the illumination rather of character than of fact. If from such an analysis a coherent individual portrait emerges, it may be possible to account for Diogenes' influence on later literature and thought.

[1] *Anth. Pal.*, xvi. 334; said by D.L. to have been inscribed on a memorial at Sinope.

A scrutiny of the available sources shows the difficulty of arriving at a satisfactory estimate of Diogenes.[1] Though these sources vary in value, they have, apart from Philodemus, a common feature in their lateness. They are the outcome of a considerable literature which grew up round Diogenes for at least two centuries after his death, and which is only known to us from references in later authors. It is necessary to form some idea of this literature before attempting any estimate of the ' historical ' Diogenes.

The literature under consideration falls into two classes. In the first may be put the Cynic and Stoic works, in which Diogenes appears as the ideal σοφός, demonstrating in divers situations, the virtues of αὐτάρκεια, and exemplifying the quality of παρρησία in contact with the great historical figures of the day. In the second class is the general literature of the writers of *Successions* (διαδοχάι), and the collectors of anecdotes, for whom the individuality and humour of Diogenes would have particular attraction. Of the Cynic authors the first to be considered is Crates. Crates wrote shortly after the death of Diogenes, and his works contain genuine reflections of his master's teachings ; though in the surviving fragments there are few direct references to Diogenes, they are our best authority for contemporary Cynic practices. Metrocles of Maroneia,[2] the associate of Crates, compiled a book of χρεῖαι ; perhaps here originated the ' literary ' Diogenes whose apophthegms were used and probably added to by Bion of Borysthenes. Invention was soon busy with the life as well as the sayings of Diogenes. von Fritz [3] adduces good reasons for thinking that the story of the ' Sale of Diogenes ' was the invention of Menippus ; a subject also handled by a certain Eubulus,[4] of whom nothing else is known. At any rate the legend seems to have established itself, for it was used by Cleomenes [5] in his book *On Pedagogues* ; like Eubulus, Cleomenes would seem to have taken particular interest in showing Diogenes as the ideal παιδαγωγός and οἰκονόμος. The Stoics [6] made use of Diogenes for the purpose of moralizing, but they seem to have found a certain amount of bowdlerizing necessary, as will appear when we consider

---

[1] See Note 1 to Chapter II.
[3] op. cit., pp. 22–5.
[5] id., ib. 75.

[2] D.L., vi. 33.
[4] D.L., vi. 30.
[6] id., ib. 32, 37, 43.

the authenticity of the writings attributed to Diogenes himself.

The general literature may be said to start with Theophrastus, who referred to Diogenes in the *Megarian dialogue*,[1] and who wrote a book entitled τῶν Διογένους συναγωγή [2]— ' a compendium of the works (or apophthegms ?) of Diogenes ' —a title which suggests that already inventions and falsifications were current. Whether the ' Eubulides ' who wrote περὶ Διογένους [3] is the contemporary and opponent of Aristotle, or a confusion with the Eubulus mentioned above, cannot be decided. Sotion,[4] the best known of the writers of διαδοχάι, appears to have treated of Diogenes in his fourth and seventh books ; von Fritz [5] argues that he approved a Stoic redaction of Diogenes' works ; Stoic criticism seems also to have influenced Sosicrates and Satyrus.[6] Diocles of Magnesia [7] was apparently particularly interested in the Cynics, he was a close friend of the Cynic Meleager of Gadara. Antisthenes of Rhodes,[8] another writer of διαδοχάι, is quoted by Laertius for details of the death of Diogenes.

Such are the available references for the Diogenes-literature of the fourth and third centuries B.C. ; in all probability they only represent a portion of it. For the Cynics and Stoics Diogenes became a second Heracles, the ideal σοφός who could be used to emphasize any worthy moral or exemplify any desirable characteristic. These stories would be reflected in the general literature, and augmented by anecdotes which grew up around him as the embodiment of independent common sense and ready repartee. Almost all of this literature is lost ; but such traces as we have been able to follow show how the story of Diogenes, like a snowball rolled downhill, gathered additions to itself as it went along.

I return to the later sources which form the only available evidence for Diogenes. Unsatisfactory though they are, the researches of von Fritz have shown how to make the best use of them. Since all are based on the lost Diogenes-literature whose traces we have endeavoured to follow, their value will clearly depend on the facilities they offer for deciding the trustworthiness of their sources. On this criterion von

---

[1] id., ib. 22. [2] id., v. 43. [3] id., vi. 20.
[4] id., ib. 26, 80. [5] op. cit., pp. 55–8. [6] D.L., vi. 80.
[7] id., ib. 20, 56. [8] id., ib. 77, 87.

Fritz shows that little profit is to be had from the accounts
of Diogenes in Epictetus, Dio Chrysostom, or Julian.   Their
writings form an individual and coherent whole, in which
borrowings from earlier sources have been assimilated and
may not readily be resolved again.   Partial exceptions to this
are the tenth oration of Dio, which contains a passage ultimately derived from the *Oedipus* of Diogenes, and the sixth
oration of Julian, which is, however, of more value for Crates
than Diogenes.   It is otherwise with Diogenes Laertius, whose
literary demerits are to our advantage.   His *Life of Diogenes*
is a cento whose component parts may be dissected out ; and
in many cases he himself names his sources.[1]

Diogenes was born at Sinope [2] in Pontus, a city of commercial importance but on the outer rim of the Greek world.
His father was apparently a man of position, but for some
reason Diogenes was exiled, and finally came to Athens.   These
events were narrated in widely different accounts, some of
which are retailed by Diogenes Laertius.[3]

Diocles relates that he went into exile because his father was
entrusted with the money of the State and adulterated the coinage.
But Eubulides in his book on Diogenes says that Diogenes himself
did this and was forced to leave home along with his father.   Moreover, Diogenes himself actually confesses in his *Pordalus* that he
adulterated the coinage.   Some say that having been appointed to
superintend the workmen they urged him to do this, and that he
went to Delphi, or to the Delian oracle in his own city, and inquired
of Apollo whether he should do what he was urged to.   When
the god gave him permission to alter the political currency, not
understanding what this meant, he adulterated the State coinage,
and when he was detected, according to some he was banished,
while according to others he voluntarily quitted the city for fear
of banishment.   One version is that his father entrusted him with
the money and that he debased it, in consequence of which the
father was imprisoned and died, while the son fled, came to Delphi,
and inquired not whether he should falsify the currency, but what
he should do to gain the greatest reputation ; and that then it was
he received the oracle.

The path of rationalizing criticism is clear, and Schwartz [4]
and von Fritz follow it confidently.   According to the latter,[5]

---

[1] See Note 2 to Chapter II.   [2] D.L., vi. 20.   [3] id., ib. 21.
[4] *Charakter-kopfe*, ii. (1911), 23.   [5] op. cit., p. 20.

the case is palpably one of invention ; its basis is that Diogenes himself used the paradox παραχάραττειν τὸ νόμισμα 'Alter the currency,' and thus gave rise to the stories. As for the banker father, he becomes explicable in the light of Diogenes' mission (παραχάραττειν τὸ νόμισμα) ; for did not Socrates have for mother a μαῖα (midwife) and pride himself on his μαιευτικὴ τέχνη ? He follows Schwartz in regarding the oracle as an invention imitating the famous reply to Socrates. In the absence of material evidence, such criticism is of course the best method of handling the problem. But according to tradition one of the lessons taught by Diogenes was that a great deal of theory may be upset by a small amount of brute fact. The impossibility of motion having been proved by argument, he got up and walked. A similar comment on the arguments of Schwartz and von Fritz is supplied by Mr. Seltman in a paper read to the Cambridge Philological Society.[1] This paper establishes that there was a Sinopean monetary magistrate called Hicesias at a time when the coinage of Sinope was subject to παραχάραξις to a degree unparalleled in any other Greek city at any period. It further suggests for Diogenes' arrival in Athens a much later date than the traditional one, thus strengthening the contention that his association with Antisthenes is an invention. On the other hand, Mr. Seltman's research not only confirms the traditional account of Diogenes' parentage and exile, but also throws a good deal of light on the reasons for his subsequent assault on established values. His father had been an important State official, he had himself occupied a position of trust ; the father, through pursuing a patriotic policy, had been unjustly thrown into prison, and had perhaps died there ;[2] the son, already well on in years, had been forced to leave his country. He had ample justification for feeling a grudge against society, and for such contemptuous bitterness as appears in the remark, 'Most men are so nearly mad that a finger's breadth would make the difference.'[3]

The story of the oracle Mr. Seltman accepts as founded on fact. The embittered Diogenes, smarting under the loss of

[1] I am greatly indebted to Mr. Seltman for his kindness in allowing me to read the MS. of this paper, which has not appeared in print. For a summary of his arguments cf. Note 3 to Chap. II.
[2] D.L., vi. 21.   [3] id., ib. 35.

his position, asks, ' What shall I do to become famous ? '
' Alter the currency,' is the response. It is a hypothesis, as
any explanation of the story must necessarily be. But there
is much force in Schwartz's contention that the story is an
imitation of the famous response given to Socrates. ' Is there
any one wiser than Socrates ? ' had been the question of
Chaerephon ; to which that of Diogenes bears resemblance.
Schwartz does not adduce, as he might have done, the very
similar story of the oracle given to Zeno.[1]

It is stated by Hecato and Apollonius of Tyre in his first book on
Zeno that he consulted the oracle to know what he should do to
attain the best life, and that the god's response was that he should
take on the colour of the dead. Whereupon, perceiving what this
meant, he studied ancient authors.

Now it is perhaps significant that stories which look like
imitations of the response to Socrates should be told about
the Stoic ' saints ', Diogenes and Zeno. The Stoics, at least
down to Panaetius, believed in oracles—

they say that divination in all its forms is a real and substantial
fact, if there is really Providence. And they prove it to be actually
a science on the evidence of certain results : so Zeno, Chrysippus
in the second book of the de Divinatione, and Athenodorus, and
Posidonius . . .[2]

It is quite possible that the Stoics, concerned to link themselves up with Socrates, should have circulated these stories
of how divine advice had also been given to two other sages
of the *Succession*. But whether the story of the oracle be
an invention or no, there is little doubt that Diogenes himself made effective use of the phrase παραχάραττειν τὸ νόμισμα.
Diogenes Laertius says ' he himself admits in the *Pordalus*
ὡς παραχάραξαι τὸ νόμισμα '.[3] One can readily imagine the
allegorical value to be extracted. ' I was exiled for literally
" altering the currency " ; my philosophy teaches men to
" alter the currency " in another sense. Let us strike out of
circulation false standards and values of all kinds.' Perhaps
further, ' Socrates said that his work was done at the
command of the Delphic god : I make the same claim for
mine.'

[1] D.L., vii. 2.   [2] id., ib. 149.   [3] id., vi. 20.

However this may be, we can safely regard as authentic the story of Diogenes' exile. Even in the fourth century, when political life was less intense, exile was to the Greek a great calamity. To be cut off from his friends, from his familiar life, above all, to be deprived of his civic status, was for the individual affected a searching test of character. ' Diogenes [1] would himself say that all the evils of tragedy had alighted on his head, for he was without city or home, cut off from his native land, a beggar and a wanderer, with food for but a day.' Yet by this means was he led to philosophy.[2] There is a curious and delightful story of the method of his conversion which, as it derives from Theophrastus, may well preserve a contemporary account. It says that Diogenes was converted (πόρον ἐξεῦρε τῆς περιστασέως) by watching a mouse running about, not looking for a place to lie down in, not afraid of the dark, not seeking any of the things that are considered dainties.[3] The precise date of his arrival at Athens is uncertain : on the evidence adduced by Mr. Seltman it cannot have been much earlier than 340 B.C.[4] If this date is correct, it at once discountenances several features of the traditional account of Diogenes. He cannot have been a ' pupil ' of Antisthenes, who died not much after 366, he can hardly have come into frequent contact with Plato. But it in no way conflicts with our only reliable evidence : that of Aristotle's Rhetoric,[5] that he was familiar in Athens as ὁ κύων in about 330 : and the notice in Diogenes Laertius [6] (presumably from the Chronica of Apollodorus) that ' he was an old man in the 113th Olympiad ', i.e. 328–325. A passage of Diogenes Laertius,[7] again probably derived from Theophrastus, suggests that he arrived in Athens already a devotee of an ascetic mode of life. ' For he wrote to a certain person to buy him a cottage, and when there was a delay about it, he took up his abode in a tub in the Metroon.' This episode probably took place at the beginning of his stay in Athens : later he seems to have slept in the porticoes of temples. The view that Diogenes was already an ascetic at the time of his arrival at Athens is also plausible in the light of his career. For while at Athens he directed on the ideas and conventions

---

[1] id., ib. 38.   [2] id., ib. 49.   [3] id., ib. 22.
[4] See Note 4 to Chap. II.   [5] Rhet., iii. x. 7.
[6] D.L., vi. 81.   [7] id., ib. 22.

of the Greek πόλις the most uncompromising criticism it had ever known. The stringency of this attitude becomes more understandable if it came from a penniless exile, already devoted to an extreme form of asceticism, and originating from the far ends of the Greek world.

Very few details of his life in Greece can be settled with confidence. Eubulus'[1] story of his capture by pirates, and his subsequent purchase by the Corinthian Xeniades, is convincingly exposed by von Fritz[2] as an invention, perhaps originating with the Διογένους πρᾶσις[3] of Menippus. Tradition connects his name with other cities besides Athens. Perhaps he visited Sparta; he was at any rate an admirer of Spartan institutions.[4] Numerous stories connect him with Corinth; Dio Chrysostom[5] says that he alternated between Athens and Sparta as did the Persian king between Sousa and Ecbatana; other accounts[6] make Corinth the scene of his old age and death. Schwartz[7] is perhaps too drastic in regarding all the Corinthian stories as false, and based on the Διογένους πρᾶσις. Our earliest source, the passage derived from the Theophrastus[8] quoted above, shows that Diogenes was accustomed to wear the garb of the wandering beggar, and that he made journeys even in his old age. Diogenes was a man with a mission; as such, he would be most likely to visit the great games, with their crowds of spectators from all parts of the Greek world. There are anecdotes in existence which connect him with these festivals;[9] he may well have visited Corinth in order to be present at the Isthmian games. The date of his death is not certain. The tradition (for which Demetrius[10] is quoted) that he died on the same day as Alexander the Great, is pretty clearly an invention. More trust may be placed in the statement that he was an old man in the 113th[11] Olympiad (i.e. 328–325). Presumably he died some time after 320. Of the manner of his death we hear most varied accounts,[12] some of them obvious fabrications; there is further divergence as to whether it took place at Athens or Corinth.[13] A circumstantial account is given on the authority of Antisthenes of

---

[1] D.L., vi. 30. [2] op. cit., pp. 22–6. [3] D.L., vi. 29.
[4] Ar., *Rhet.*, iii. x. 7. [5] D.L., vi. 197. [6] D.L., vi. 77.
[7] op. cit., p. 4. [8] D.L., vi. 22. [9] id., ib. 60; Julian, vii.
[10] D.L., vi. 80. [11] id., ib. prob. from Apollodorus.
[12] id., ib. 77–80. [13] id., ib. 77.

Rhodes [1] that it was in the gymnasium of the Craneion at Corinth, and that Diogenes committed suicide by holding his breath. Suicide of this kind is also alluded to in a fragment of Cercidas of Megalopolis, [2] and is thus clearly an early Cynic tradition. There is nothing inherently improbable in the story that he died at Corinth ; the Corinthians [3] are said to have carved a dog on his tomb, which was seen by Pausanias. [4] But whatever the place of his death, there is no doubt that Athens is the most important scene for his life. The great majority of stories about him introduce Athenian personages, customs, and localities ; the inference clearly is that most of his time was spent in Athens, the ' mother-city of philosophy ' in his day as for many years after.

Divergent traditions are also preserved about the writings of Diogenes. Diogenes Laertius [5] first gives a list of 21 works (14 dialogues and 7 tragedies), without quoting an authority. He then says that ' Sosicrates in the first book of his *Successions*, and Satyrus in the fourth book of his *Lives*, allege that Diogenes left nothing in writing, and that the sorry tragedies (τὰ τραγωδάρια) are by his friend Philiscus of Aegina '. Finally we have a list on the authority of Sotion, which excludes the tragedies, and gives the title of only five dialogues which occur in the first catalogue. Diogenes Laertius [6] was particularly interested in bibliography ; he gives bibliographies for 32 philosophers in all, including all the leading Stoics mentioned. This last fact, together with the evidence of Philodemus, [7] περὶ τῶν Στωϊκῶν, gives a clue to the list of Sotion. From Philodemus we see how the desire of the Stoics to link themselves up with Socrates, and the ' Succession ', Socrates–Antisthenes–Diogenes–Crates–Zeno, involved the canonization of all these persons as Stoic Saints. This left later Stoic moralists with some very awkward matters to gloss over, particularly in connexion with the *Republic* of Zeno, and the *Republic* and tragedies of Diogenes. These works had been acceptable to the early Stoics : Cleanthes [8] praised the *Republic* of Diogenes : Chrysippus [9]

---

[1] id., ib. [2] id., ib. 76. [3] id., ib. 78.
[4] See Note 5 to Chap. II. [5] D.L., vi. 80.
[6] Cf. Hope, op. cit., pp. 122–6.
[7] Herc. Pap., 155a, 33a : see Cronert, *Kolotes und Menedemos*, 54–67.
[8] Philo. d., col. xiii. [9] id., D.L., vii. 34.

attested its genuineness and that of the *Republic* of Zeno.
But both works contained ' praises ' of cannibalism and incest,
and were highly unpalatable to the later Stoa. Naturally they
were a ready mark for the School's opponents ; [1] we see in
Philodemus how these assaults were parried. ' Zeno was a
young man at the time, we must pardon youth [2]—besides he
was not always Zeno,[3] he was once a mere nobody.' [4] As for
Diogenes, ' it [the *Republic*] was not his at all, but was written
by some evil-minded persons '. Now the same views of
cannibalism and incest were apparently to be found in the
tragedies, particularly the *Oedipus* and the *Thyestes* ;[5] they
were accordingly declared not to be his at all, but by Philiscus
of Aegina, or according to Favorinus, Pasiphon.[6] The
tradition is reflected in Julian.[7]

As for the tragedies of Diogenes, which are and are admitted to
be the composition of some Cynic—the only point of dispute being
whether they are by the master Diogenes or his pupil Philiscus—
what reader would not abhor them, and find in them an excess of
infamy surpassing that of harlots ? . . . We must judge of the
attitude of Diogenes to gods and men, not . . . from the tragedies
of Philiscus—who by ascribing their authorship to Diogenes grossly
slanders that sacred person—but from his deeds.

As the *Republic* and the tragedies are absent from the catalogue of Sotion, we may with confidence agree with von
Fritz [8] that this represents a Stoic redaction. The general
bowdlerizing which went on in the Alexandrian period in the
interest of morals is familiar from the ' athetized ' lines of
Homer ; there is an interesting passage of Diogenes Laertius [9]
in which he apparently censures the bibliographers for not
doing their duty by an indecent passage of Chrysippus. The
view of Sosicrates and Satyrus represents a bolder type of
criticism which, not content with ' athetizing ' objectionable
works or placing them on an Index Expurgatorius, roundly
declare that no authentic works of the philosopher exist.

In conclusion, the inference is that the *Republic* and the
Tragedies were genuine works of Diogenes, as in all probability

---

[1] von Arnim, *Stoic vet. fr.*, 1, 249–56.
[2] Philod., col. xv. 5.   [3] id., 1. 15.   [4] id., col. xvi.
[5] id., col. vii.   [6] D.L., vi. 73.   [7] vii. 211E–212.
[8] op. cit., pp. 55–7.   [9] D.L., vii. 188.

were the dialogues mentioned in both catalogues, i.e. the *Cephalion, Pordalus, Aristarchus,* and *Eroticus.* We are in no position to pronounce about the authenticity of the remaining works.[1]

No materials are available for tracing any development in Diogenes' theory or practice. He is presented to us as a constant factor in the society of his day, criticizing conventional values, exposing shams, unimpressed by reputation of any kind. The stories of his highly disconcerting appearances [2] in the lecture-rooms of the philosophers are probably apocryphal ; yet it is likely enough that few of them escaped his criticism. The traditions that show him as a ' pupil ' of Antisthenes have been shown to be late ; but they contain a reflection of truth. For the conception of the ideal σοφός, as Socrates was portrayed by Antisthenes, contained potentialities which as yet had not been realized. We have seen that the chronological evidence makes it highly improbable that Diogenes can ever have come into personal contact with Antisthenes ; and the evidence of Aristotle shows that the school in the Cynosarges was chiefly devoted to logical studies. It is probable, then, that Diogenes was merely influenced by a reading of Antisthenes' books, much as hearing Xenophon's *Memorabilia* is said to have ' converted ' Zeno to philosophy. He seems at any rate to have been impressed by Antisthenes' theory of the ideal σοφός, though denying that the author had done much to put his theories into practice.[3] There is a story, found in Aelian [4] as well as Diogenes Laertius, to the effect that Plato used to say of Diogenes, ' That man is Socrates—gone mad.' The story is at least ben trovato ; Diogenes represents the Socratic σοφός with its chief features pushed to extremes. Frugality in him becomes strict asceticism : εἰρωνεία is represented by παρρησία : σωφροσυνή by ἀπαθεία. The Socratic disregard of the opinions of the mob [5] becomes the Cynic ἀναίδεια. Like Socrates, Diogenes [6] contrasted the skill of the craftsman with the haphazard conduct of other human affairs ; like Socrates, again, his mission was to exhort people not to care for money and moneymaking

---

[1] See Note 6 to Chap. II. [2] D.L., vi. 40, 53, 39.
[3] Dio Chrys., viii. 275 ; Stob., *Flor.*, xiii. 19.
[4] D.L., vi. 54. Ael., xiv. 33. [5] Cf. *Crito.*
[6] D.L., vii. 70.

but for their own souls. But there was this difference—
Diogenes was less hampered than Socrates by the ties of
family or civic life or the influence of national tradition.
Thanks to his exile he was wholly independent, Pythagoras'
spectator looking at the πανήγυρις of life. It was, he pronounced, a world of fools : the standard of values was
completely distorted. ' He would often vociferate that the
gods had given men the means of living easily, but this had
been lost sight of because we require honeyed cakes, unguents,
and the like.' [1] Again, ' Things of value are bartered for what
is worthless, and vice versa. At all events, a statue fetches
3,000 drachmae, while a quart of barley-flour is sold for a
couple of copper coins.' [2] Or to revert to the metaphor of
παραχάραξις, the conventional coin then in circulation was
bad, for it was falsely struck, without reference to a true
scale of value—what was needed was that it should be defaced
and put out of circulation. The mission of Diogenes thus
became a thoroughgoing onslaught on convention, custom, and
tradition in all aspects. He endeavoured to convert men to a
truer way of life, not, like Socrates, by dialectic, nor by allegory,
as did Antisthenes, but by the practical example of his daily
life. There is a story that his pupil Hegesias once asked for
the loan of one of the master's books. ' You are a simpleton,
Hegesias,' was the reply ; ' you don't choose painted figs,
but real ones ; yet you would pass over the true training
(τὴν ἀληθινὴν ἄσκησιν) and apply yourself to written rules.'
In different accents, it is the cry of St. Francis of Assisi, ' I
am your breviary, I am breviary.' In such a policy there was
no room for compromise ; it demanded absolute freedom in
speech, absolute fearlessness in deed. Hence παρρησία and
ἀναίδεια, twin qualities which later made Cynicism famous,
or at least notorious. ' παρρησία is the finest thing in the
world,' Diogenes [3] is reported to have said. Its value to the
σοφός is clear ; it enabled him to resist the coercion of tyrants
and to expose the pretensions of ' intellectuals ' and politicians.
Tradition is unanimous that Diogenes himself was remarkable
for his powers of ridicule and repartee. Anecdotes show him
in conflict with Antisthenes, Eucleides, Plato, and Aristotle
amongst the philosophers, with Demosthenes, Philip, Alexander, Perdiccas, and Craterus among statesmen and ' tyrants '.

[1] D.L., vi. 44.   [2] id., ib. 36.   [3] id., ib. 35.

Few or none of these stories are likely to be authentic. Some are obvious inventions for setting in opposition the Cynic σοφός and the evil tyrant : or the man of common sense and the ' sophist ' ; others involve chronological impossibilities. The only certain example of his apophthegms is that quoted by Aristotle—' Taverns are the mess-tables of Attica.' [1] There is little point in retailing any of the stories from Diogenes Laertius ; they belong rather to an anthology of Greek humour than a discussion of philosophy.[2]

The counterpart of παρρησία in speech is ἀναίδεια in action. Again, one cannot verify any of the numerous anecdotes which illustrate this characteristic. Some merely offend against Greek views of good manners, others against more universal views of decency. We have no right to accept one set and reject another. This quality of ἀναίδεια has been shown to be the most likely origin of the nickname κύων, shamelessness being the peculiar characteristic of the dog, according to the Greek view ; there is also the evidence of the early Stoics, who seem to have approved or even practised the quality, to the embarrassment of their successors. Again we see the uncompromising nature of Diogenes. For him, whatever is ' according to nature ' is proper at all times and in all places.

It was his habit to do everything in public, the works of Demeter and of Aphrodite alike. He used to produce such arguments as this. ' If taking breakfast is nothing out of place (μηδὲν ἄτοπον), neither is it out of place in the market-place. But taking breakfast is nothing out of place, therefore it is nothing out of place to take breakfast in the market-place.' [3]

A typical bit of eristic reasoning ; we shall see again that Diogenes employed such sophisms if they suited his turn.

---

[1] Ar., *Rhet.*, iii. x. 7.
[2] Perhaps I may here be permitted to record the personal impression that the stories about Diogenes are decidedly *funnier* than those Diogenes Laertius tells about other philosophers. This may be due to a variety of reasons. Perhaps some of the apophthegms, however they have later been ' contaminated ' in detail, did originate with Diogenes ; no doubt his reputation served as a magnet which would attract to itself a good story ; lastly, the source of several such stories may be Bion of Borysthenes, who himself possessed a pretty wit.
[3] D.L., vi. 69.

It is clear that his writings attacked custom, convention, and tabu of every kind. Incest was defended as natural in the *Oedipus* and *Republic* ; the doxographical portion of the *Life* in Diogenes Laertius says that ' he saw nothing improper in stealing from the temples, nor from eating the flesh of any animal ; nor indeed in cannibalism, for one could find examples of it amongst the customs of foreign nations '. Of course, these statements cannot be taken at their face value to imply that Diogenes recommended incest and cannibalism. We have most of them on the authority of sources hostile to the Cynics, and we do not know in what context they occurred in Diogenes.[1] The argument from foreign customs is familiar enough from the fifth century ; we need only cite one of the antinomies of the Δισσοὶ λόγοι,[2] which develop the theme νόμος πάντων βασιλεύς, to show that καλόν and αἰσχρόν are the same. ' If you brought together all the αἰσχρά and put them in a big heap . . . and assembled representatives of all people and told them to take away only what is καλόν, you would have nothing left.' Interesting is the argument with which Diogenes is supposed to have justified cannibalism in the Thyestes.[3]

According to right reason, as he puts it, all elements are contained in all things, and pervade everything ; since meat is not only a constituent of bread, but bread of vegetables ; and all other bodies also, by means of certain invisible passages and particles, find their way in and unite with all substances in the form of vapour. This he says in the *Thyestes* . . .

This is clearly a bit of popularized Anaxagorean physics, and it is strange to find it in Diogenes, who was so opposed to the natural sciences. One's first reaction to the mention of ' vapour ' is to suppose that Diogenes may have been confused with his namesake, Diogenes of Apollonia. But reference to the *Thyestes* is quite explicit ; and when we consider the ' sophism ' by which Diogenes justified his habit of breakfasting in public it seems likely enough that he would similarly seize on a bit of popular science and exploit it for his own ends. The point is important because it will reappear in a discussion of Diogenes' educational theories.

The ἀναίδεια of Diogenes was therefore didactic ; under-

----

[1] See Note 7 to Chap. II.
[2] In Diels, *Frag. der. Vors*'. 83, 18.   [3] D.L., vi. 73.

taken to expose the artificiality of convention. The same
explanation may be adduced for his notorious eccentricities—
how he went about in broad daylight with a lighted lantern,[1]
looking for an honest man : how he would enter a theatre
when every one else was leaving it.[2] There is a good deal of
the showman about such actions ; they were done for propaganda. Diogenes is said to have compared himself with the
trainers of choruses ' who pitch the note too high that the
rest may get the right one '[3]—incidentally a sidelight on Greek
music. παραχάραξις as such is negative in its immediate
results—it invalidates a currency hitherto legal tender. But
this is subordinate to a positive purpose, to restore the true
currency which, according to the laws of economics, bad
money has driven out of circulation. Was Diogenes sufficiently faithful to the metaphor of παραχάραξις in all its
implications that he had a constructive, as well as a destructive,
side to his teachings ? The currency he sought to deface was
that which bore in any form the superscription of νόμος ; we
can see whose superscription would have symbolized for
Diogenes the restored currency of φύσις. 'He claimed that
he lived the same type of life as did Heracles, preferring liberty
to everything.'[4] The phrase τὸν αὐτὸν χαρακτῆρα τοῦ βίου
suggests that we may be dealing with the actual words of
Diogenes ; χαρακτήρ used thus is a numismatical metaphor.
The probability is increased by the fact that the sentence
occurs in the doxographical section of the biography, which
seems to depend on the writings of Diogenes. This opposition of νόμος and φύσις, paramount in the thought of Diogenes,
had of course been one of the major issues of Greek philosophy
for more than a century. The two conceptions were so familiar,
the issue between them so clear-cut, that neither the Cynics
nor the Stoics apparently found it necessary to define exactly
what κατὰ φύσιν implied. Yet it is clear that φύσις has
greatly altered from its meaning in the idealogy of Ionian
science. Kaerst has said that φύσις for the Cynics was a
' universal, invariable rational norm ',[5] but perhaps ' minimum '
is a term less liable to misunderstanding than norm. Strip
away all the accretions of convention, tradition, and social
existence, and what is left is κατὰ φύσιν. To take a modern

---

[1] id., ib. 41.   [2] id., ib. 35.   [3] id., ib. 63.
[4] id., ib. 71.   [5] *Gesch. des. Hell.*, ii. 103.

analogy, a Commission of eminent doctors have recently determined the minimum income on which a single man can support life; if their findings, $X/-$ per week, can be regarded as irreducible, then such a standard of living is in the Cynic sense κατὰ φύσιν. It is the οὗ οὐκ ἄνευ applied to human affairs. Hence Diogenes' constant endeavour to reduce his wants to the ' natural ' standards ; hence appeals to the habits of primitive man and of animals, who may be supposed to have preserved that standard in its least corrupted form. We have already seen how Diogenes considered the ways of the mouse and was wise ; the sixth oration of Dio Chrysostom puts into his mouth several such appeals to the example of animals. They are at least in his spirit, though they cannot be proved to be derived from any of his writings, and a sample may be quoted :

Thanks to their delicacy men live a more wretched life than animals. For animals drink water, and eat plants, and mostly go naked the year through ; they never enter a house nor use fire ; yet unless they meet a violent end they live the span of life allotted by nature to their species. . . . There are those who say that man cannot live as do the other animals because his body is so delicate, and he is hairless, unlike many beasts, and unprotected by fur or feathers, and without a thick skin. Diogenes would retort that men are so frail by reason of their mode of life, for they shun heat and cold so far as they can. Hairlessness is not of itself a disadvantage, he would instance frogs and other animals, whose bodies are much softer than that of man . . . yet who in many instances live throughout the winter in the coldest water.[1]

That ' life in accordance with nature ' brought happiness was his inevitable contention ; reinforced by the usual ascetic argument that the ' very contemning of pleasure is in itself the greatest of pleasures '. Confronted with the pleasure of the life according to Diogenes, the reaction of *l'homme moyen sensual* must have been like that of the Victorian country squire who, hearing of the somewhat insipid pleasures to be provided for his entertainment in the next world, remarked that he hoped he would be given grace to enjoy this sort of thing when he got there. But Diogenes had a recipe for the acquisition of grace—it lay in ἄσκησις, ' training ', in the

---

[1] Dio Chrys., *Or.*, vi.

stricter sense of the word. ' Nothing in life ', he maintained,
' can be brought to a successful issue without training, but
that alone is capable of overcoming everything.' [1] Hence he
used to roll in hot sand in summer and in snow in winter,
using every means of inuring himself to hardship (πανταχοθεν
ἑαυτὸν συνασκῶν).[2] The theory of ἄσκησις is expounded
in more detail in the doxographical section of the Laertian
biography.

He would affirm that training is of two kinds, mental and physical ;
the latter being that whereby, with constant exercise, perceptions
are formed such as secure freedom of movement for virtuous deeds ;
and one half of this training is incomplete without the other, good
health and strength being equally included among the essential
things for the soul as for the body.[3]

The whole passage is technical to a degree one does not associate
with Diogenes ; von Fritz thinks that it comes from one of
the Stoic compilations fostered on to him. But it can be
shown that the theory of sensation and the dependent theory
of education were known in the fourth century : that the
interdependence of mental and gymnastic training was a
doctrine current in the circle of Diogenes : that Diogenes and
the contemporary Cynics would borrow scientific terms when
convenient. The inference is that, though the theories in the
passage cannot have been the inventions of Diogenes, they
may well have been expounded in his writings.[4]

Stobaeus [5] shows how Diogenes allegorized the story of
Medea (presumably in the ' tragedy ' of that name) to exemplify
the virtues of πόνος .

Diogenes said the Medea was a σοφή, and not a sorceress. For she
took over flabby men, whose physique had been ruined by luxury,
and by making them toil at gymnastic exercises and by sweat-baths,
she made them strong and healthy again. Hence arose the legend
that she boiled their flesh and made them into young men.

This insistence on ἄσκησις and πόνος in education was of
course no new thing in Greece. For three hundred years the
young Spartans had been brought up on an ἐπιπόνος ἄσκησις
which revolted the taste of Athens—' we live at our ease, yet

[1] D.L., vi. 71.   [2] id., ib. 23.   [3] Hicks' translation.
[4] See Appendix II.   [5] Flor., xxix. 92.

we are ready to face the same dangers that they do.'[1]   Hence
it is not surprising to find stories which show Diogenes as
an admirer of Sparta. ' Where have you seen good men,
Diogenes ? ' he was asked.   ' Good men nowhere,' was the
answer, ' but I have seen good boys at Sparta.' [2]   So too
asked, on his way from Sparta to Athens, whence and whither
he was going, he replied, ' From the men's apartments to the
women's.' [3]   It was an admiration sometimes shared by Plato,
though elsewhere, particularly in the Laws, he criticizes the
Spartans for organizing their state for war as the be-all and
end-all, and Spartan education for only teaching one aspect
of virtue, namely courage, and only the less difficult parts of
that.   But it is in Aristotle [4] that we find philo-Laconism
most explicitly condemned as obsolete.

The Spartans brutalize their children by their laborious exercises,
and do not attain their object, which is to make them virtuous.
When they alone were assiduous in their drill, they were superior
to others, but now they are beaten both in war and in the gymnasium. . . . We should judge the Spartans, not from what they
were, but from what they are ; for now they have rivals who
compete with them : formerly they had none.

But Diogenes' approval was presumably only of the method
of Spartan education.   At Sparta more than any other city of
the Greek world, the State dominated the individual.   Even
the Athens of the fourth century, which all the efforts of
Demosthenes failed to galvanize into its old political zest,
seemed too narrow to the devotee of αὐτάρκεια ; assuredly
there was no place for the citizen of the world at Sparta.   For
the cosmopolitanism of Diogenes does seem to have been a
new phenomenon.   It is of course a truism to say that the
fourth century was an age when men felt the city-state
cramping : there had been amalgamations, federations, a
growing sense, as in Lysias and Isocrates, of the unity of the
Hellenic race : there had also been such sympathetic observers
of the ' barbarian ' as Xenophon.   But the cosmopolitanism
of Diogenes was not the well-travelled man's interest in alien
cultures, like that of Herodotus, but rather a reaction against
every kind of coercion imposed by the community on the

---

[1] Thuc., ii. 39. 1.   [2] D.L., vi. 27.   [3] id., ib. 59.
[4] *Politics*, 1338B, 20.

individual. 'The only true commonwealth', he maintained, 'is that which is as wide as the universe.' [1] Again, asked whence he came, he replied with the famous word κοσμοπολίτης, 'I am a citizen of the world.' [2] It is essential not to read too much into this profession. For us 'cosmopolitanism' as a conception carries an emotional colour which is the legacy of Alexander, transmitted through the Roman Empire and the Catholic Church. But as Tarn [3] says, the phrase as used by Diogenes was one of negation, meaning, 'I am not a citizen of any of your Greek cities.' Because he happened to enunciate it at a period when Alexander was in fact trying to set up the first 'international state', a great deal of speculation has grown up about the possibility of Cynic influence on the great conqueror. Such speculation generally makes much of the fact that on Alexander's staff were two men who 'heard' Diogenes, Onesicratus and Anaximenes. Of itself this does not seem convincing; Alexander was not a man who took the advice of others, either on military or political points; and if he had neglected the political ideas of the great Aristotle he was not likely to attach much weight to those of two admirers of a notorious eccentric of the Athenian streets. And in fact we find no trace in Diogenes of those two great ideas which are the pivots of Alexander's system—the Brotherhood of Man and the King as Living Law. Tarn shows that the conception of the Brotherhood of Man in all probability originated with Alexander, and is in direct contrast with the 'cosmopolitanism' of the Cynics and early Stoics. When, a few years after the death of Alexander, Alexarchus set up on Mt. Athos his little 'world-state' of Ouranopolis, with its coinage on which the King and his consort were symbolized by the sun and moon, the citizens by the stars; when Demetrius Poliorcetes wore a robe on which were figured the hosts of heaven: they were reflecting the conception that the universe is a common city of gods and men. For Zeno, as Tarn says, it was a common city of gods and wise men; that this was true of Diogenes seems likely from his contention that 'all things are the property of the wise: for all things belong to the gods, the gods are friends to the wise: friends share all property in common:

[1] D.L., vi. 72. [2] id., ib. 63.
[3] 'Alexander the Great and the Brotherhood of Man', *Proceedings of the British Academy*, xix, 1932.

therefore all things are the property of the wise.'[1]   Between the
σοφός and the rest of the world a deep gulf is fixed ; and only
the σοφός is a member of the ὀρθὴ πολιτεία ἐν κόσμῳ.   We
have no early evidence that Diogenes was interested in kingship; the σοφός being sufficient unto himself would need no
overseer.   It is only the literary Diogenes who appears, as in
Dio Chrysostom, as the monitor of Alexander.   The historical
Diogenes is better reflected in the story of how, on hearing
that the Athenians had given Alexander the title of Dionysus,
he remarked, ' Well, you'd better make me Serapis.'[2]
All the best evidence for Diogenes emphasizes his insistence
on the αὐτάρκεια (self-sufficiency) of the individual.   Philodemus, who attacks Cynic doctrines which mostly seem to
derive from the *Politeia* of Diogenes, says that ' they [the
Cynics] attach no validity to any of the cities we know, nor to
any law '.[3]   Crönert[4] mistakenly contrasts this with a passage
from the doxographical portion of Diogenes Laertius.

As to law : he would say that it is impossible for a society to exist
without law.   For without a city no benefit can be derived from
that which is civilized : the city is civilized (ἀστεῖον) : there is no
benefit in law without a city : therefore the law is something
civilized.[3]

But as von Fritz[6] shows, there is no conflict between the
views if we remember that for Diogenes τὸ πολιτεύεσθαι and
τὸ ἀστεῖον were not desiderata, since they were not κατὰ
φύσιν. ' The privilege of the gods is to want nothing, and
of those like the gods to want but little.'[7]
We can only get a disjointed idea of the other doctrines
developed in the *Republic*.   Philodemus says that Diogenes
there discussed the uselessness of weapons, and agrees with
Athenaeus[8] that he advocated a bone currency.   It seems
almost certain that the *Republic* of Diogenes, like that of Plato,
dealt with the position of women.   They were to wear the
same dress as men, and to exercise nude in public, as at
Sparta ;[9] they were to be held in common.   ' The only marriage he recognized was the union of the man who per-

[1] D.L., vi. 72.   [2] id., ib. 63.   [3] Herc. Pap., 339.
[4] op. cit., p. 65, n. 318.   [5] D.L., vi. 72.
[6] op. cit., p. 59 seq.   [7] D.L., vi. 104.   [8] iv. 159C.
[9] Herc. Pap., No. 339, Col. ix.

suades with the woman who lets herself be persuaded. And for this reason he thought that children should be held in common.'[1] If Philodemus is throughout drawing on the writings of Diogenes, we gather that intercourse was to be permitted without restriction of place, person, or sex.[2] It goes without saying that all distinctions of rank and birth were to be abolished. Such appears to have been the ' ideal state ' of Diogenes. That it might be realized he carried on a violent opposition, not merely to the customs and conventions, but to the ordinary business of existing communities.

He would praise those who were about to marry and refrained, those who intended to go on a voyage and never set sail, those who thinking to engage in politics do no such thing, those also who purporting to raise a family do not do so, and those who make ready to associate with tyrants and yet never approach them after all.[3]

It is the extreme of individualism. To call it a political system at all is doubtless a contradiction, unless we are prepared to admit with Blake the possibility of a benevolent anarchy.

It would be an exaggeration to speak of any Cynic ' school ' in the regular sense of organized teaching and a common body of doctrine. But Diogenes must have been a familiar figure to every Athenian of his time : and no doubt many persons listened to his discourses, if only out of curiosity. ' He was heard by Phocion the Honest and Stilpo of Megara and many other political personages,' says Diogenes Laertius ; with them may be counted Onesicratus of Astypalaea, who was to play a not undistinguished part in the expedition of Alexander. But in addition Diogenes does seem to have gathered round himself a circle of disciples, who practised the way of life he proclaimed. The circle was probably not large ; as Diogenes said, ' He was a dog whom all admired, yet few dared go hunting with him.'[4] Diogenes Laertius[5] gives the names of some half-dozen persons who presumably belonged to this little group ; two of them seem to have had nicknames, from which one gathers that they were well-known eccentrics. By far the most famous was Crates of Thebes ; there were also Hegesias, from Diogenes' own city

[1] D.L., vi. 72.   [2] Herc. Pap., No. 339, Col. ix.
[3] D.L., vi. 29.   [4] id., ib. 33.   [5] id., ib. 84.

of Sinope and perhaps a close attendant of Diogenes, for he was called ' The Dog-collar ' (ὁ Κλοιός), Philiscus of Aegina, Menander ' a great admirer of Homer ', called, we are not told why, Δρυμός (oakwood), Monimus of Syracuse, satirized by Menander as carrying not one wallet but three, and perhaps also Pasiphon and Androsthenes.   What form Diogenes' ' teaching ' took is fairly clear.   Music, astronomy, geometry, dialectic, he had abandoned all ; [1] the discourses which he delivered with such great persuasiveness [2] were no doubt informal lectures on ethical subjects, enlivened by analogies from the crafts and from the habits of animals, and illustrated by quotations from Homer and the allegorical interpretation of myths.   Such discourses were the spoken precursors of diatribe ; but that form of composition, later the best-known Cynic literary genre, does not seem to have been employed by Diogenes.   The catalogues of his works given by Laertius comprise only ' dialogues ' and ' tragedies '—the latter being probably burlesque parodies, like the sixty ' tragedies ' [3] attributed to Timon of Phlius, and bearing more resemblance to the mime than to the drama proper.   Parody and allegory were of course familiar enough before Diogenes, and he does not seem to have played any part in the development of those genres which we shall find typical of later Cynic literature.

The influence of Diogenes during his own lifetime was probably not great.   Though Theophrastus thought it worth while to write a book about him, the general attitude towards him was most likely one of amused tolerance.   But he was to be of much greater significance in the succeeding century than in his own.   The reason for this is symbolized, probably not intentionally, in one of the many stories about his death. The romance of Eubulus told how he was asked in what manner he wished to be buried.   ' On my face,' he replied, and explained that in a short time down was going to be changed to up—the reference is explained as being to the newly gained supremacy of Macedon.[4] τὰ κάτω ἄνω στρεφέσθαι serves well as a description of the effects of the period of the Diadochi, when the old city-state, and the ideals for which it stood, long moribund, were finally buried.   The civilization fostered by the πόλις had had many of the char-

---

[1] D.L., vi. 104.   [2] id., ib. 76.   [3] id., vii. 110.
[4] id., vi. 31.

acteristics of a hot-house plant; but now the greenhouse
was broken and the inmates exposed to the cold. Everywhere the individual found himself confronting an unfriendly
world, with no other refuge than his own resources could
provide. Bevan attributes the sketchiness of Stoic physics
to the sheer urgency of erecting some kind of defence to serve
men in their bitter need—one does not dig foundations in a
hurricane.[1] Antisthenes had said that wisdom was the safest
wall, and that a fortress must be constructed in our own impregnable reason. The metaphor of the fortress is frequently
echoed in Hellenistic philosophy. Crates found the island
of Pera, the Cynic Paradise, a safe refuge from a sea of
troubles; the city of Diogenes, he said, was impregnable
before the attacks of Fortune. Fortune, Tyche, ruling deity
of the Hellenistic world, was the hostile power against whom
Philosophy now erected her castles. Designed by different
builders, her fortresses varied in complexity; the earliest and
simplest of them all was that designed by Diogenes, and by
him most stoutly garrisoned.

(b) Diogenes' pupils : Onesicratus.

' One of Diogenes' distinguished pupils,' according to Diogenes Laertius, was Onesicratus of Astypalaea.[2] His career
was one of considerable interest. A great admirer of Diogenes,
he later joined the expedition of Alexander, in which he
played a not unimportant part, being the pilot of the King's
ship, and chief navigating officer under Nearchus in the famous
voyage through the Persian Gulf. On his return to Greece
he wrote a work about Alexander, which Diogenes Laertius
implies was modelled on the Cyropaedia of Xenophon. His
book, we gather, was popular, and was seen by Aulus Gellius
on the book-stalls of Brundisium, together with those of
other romancers. Romance, indeed, appears to have been its
chief ingredient—' all Alexander's companions ', says Strabo
austerely, ' appear to have greater affection for fable than for
fact, but the stories of Onesicratus cap them all.' Nevertheless, Strabo cites him on the habits of the elephant, on
the banyan tree, on the great whales of the Southern Ocean,

[1] *Stoics and Sceptics*, p. 32.
[2] Fragments and references in Jacoby, *Frag. d. Griech. Hist.*, 134
(1929).

and on the far lands of Taprobane and Cathay. It is interesting to see how he represented a sect of Indian fakirs as so many Cynics, living the life of πόνος, and holding beliefs about a vanished Golden Age. Cynic, too, is the way in which he writes of the simple virtues of savage races;

of the country of Mousicanus he writes at some length, praising it . . . saying that its inhabitants are known for their longevity (they attain an age of a hundred and thirty years), and for their simple and healthful life, despite the fact that their country offers abundance of every commodity. They have public organizations for meals, as do the Spartans. . . . They use neither gold nor silver, although mines exist in their country. Instead of slaves they use the young men in their prime, as do the Cretans with the Aphamiotae, and the Spartans with the Helots. They cultivate no science except that of medicine—indeed, some Indian tribes consider highly developed skill in the art of war and kindred subjects as positively wicked. They have no laws except for the punishment of murder and insolence. . . .

Onesicratus is not an important figure in the development of Cynicism. He himself did not lead the κυνικὸς βίος; yet more than any Cynic he was ' a wanderer over the face of the earth '; and in discovering Diogenes' doctrines on the banks of the Indus he shows how, in the minds of its admirers, Cynicism is already not a school of philosophy, but a way of life.

(c) Monimus.

In contrast with Onesicratus, Monimus of Syracuse appears to have been one of the small coterie who lived after the example of Diogenes. What little Diogenes Laertius says about him apparently derives from Sosicrates; and as it makes use of the story of ' the Sale of Diogenes ' is presumably untrustworthy as to detail. But it may be true that Monimus was the slave of a Corinthian banker, who after being driven out by his master took to the Cynic life. He is said to have been a follower of Crates as well as Diogenes, and was mentioned by Menander in the *Groom*. (a) ' There was once a certain Monimus, Philo, a wise man, but something too paradoxical.[1] (Ph.) You mean the man who carried

---

[1] Allison thus renders ἀδοξότερος. Hicks translates ' not so very famous '.

the Wallet ? (a) The wallet ? Rather three Wallets ! [1] Yet
he never spake a word to match the saying " know thyself ",
nor such familiar watchwords. No, the squalid mendicant surpassed them all, for he declared all human supposition to be illusion (τὸ γὰρ ὑποληφθὲν τύφον εἶναι πᾶν
ἔφη). From this illusory world Monimus turned to seek the
truth (ἐμβριθέστατος ἐγένετο. ὥστε δόξης καταφρονεῖν, πρὸς
δ' ἀλήθειαν παρορμᾶν).' Perhaps an indication of where he
found truth is to be derived from the statement that he
wrote two books περὶ ὁρμῶν ; which taken in connexion with
the phrase πρὸς ἀλήθειαν παρορμᾶν suggests that truth was to
be found from the ' impulses ', or what we should call the
' instincts '. That νόμος has no validity because it violates
the natural instincts is one of the arguments used by Antiphon,[2]
' The law has laid down for the eyes what they should see
and what they should not, for the feet whither they should go
and whither not. . . .' A transgression of the Law of Nature
brings punishment, οὐ διὰ δόξαν ἀλλὰ δὶ ἀλήθειαν. That
truth should be found through the instincts would obviously
accord well with Diogenes' insistence on the life according to
Nature ; but probably the very scanty evidence will not admit
our being too definite in attributing this doctrine to Monimus.
The other writings assigned to him by Diogenes Laertius
are an *Exhortation to Philosophy* and some ' humorous writings,
blended with covert seriousness ' (παίγνια σπουδῇ λεληθυίᾳ
μεμιγμένα). This last term can cover a wide range of com-
positions, as is clear from the works of Crates, which contained parodies of Homer, of elegiac verse, of hymns, and of
tragedy. τὸ σπουδαιογέλοιον [3] was of course the distinguishing mark of Cynic literature ; Demetrius [4] says, ' The moralists
often employ humorous forms of composition on suitable
occasions, as at festivals or banquets, and in attacks on luxury.
. . . Such is the manner of Cynic literature.' An example
of these γνῶμαι is quoted by Stobaeus : [5] ' Monimus said
that it was better to lack sight than education. For under one
affliction you fall to the ground, in the other deep under-
ground (τὸν μὲν γὰρ εἰς τὸν βάθρον, τὸν δ' εἰς τὸ βάραθρον

---

[1] Whence Allison deduces that he was a hunchback and also had
a paunch ! More likely the point is that he was greedy.
[2] Ox. Pap., 1364, Vol. xi.
[3] Strabo, xvi. 759.   [4] Dem., de el. 170.   [5] ii. 13. 88.

ἐμπίπτειν).' The diatribe was probably not to be found among the παίγνια of Monimus ; but in the absence of references little can be said about his works. They do not seem to have had a great reputation, and it is significant that there are no allusions to him in the remains of Teles.

(d) Crates.

A figure of far greater importance in the story of Cynicism is that of Crates of Thebes. By later writers he was classed with Antisthenes and Diogenes as the Cynics *par excellence* ; in his own day he was referred to in the comedies of Menander and Philemon, and apparently introduced as a character by Antiphanes ; Zeno collected and published his apophthegms in a work which is probably the source of most later anecdotes ; he is referred to several times in the extant fragments of Teles. Plutarch, always interested in any famous Boeotian, wrote his biography, which apparently served as a source for the references in the sixth oration of Julian. There are allusions in Seneca, Epictetus, Athenaeus, Marcus Aurelius, Demetrius, Gregory Nazianzen, and Origen. Finally there is the biography by Diogenes Laertius, which quotes Zeno, Menander, Eratosthenes, Diocles, Demetrius of Magnesia Antisthenes of Rhodes, Hippobotus and Favorinus. Crates played a greater part than Diogenes in the development of Cynic literary genres, and the fragments [1] of his work which survive are extensive enough to give the impression of a high order of talent, particularly in the use of parody.

The evidence for the chronology and the events of his life is scanty. He appears to have been a whole generation younger than Diogenes, for his ' floruit ' is given as the 113th Olympiad (328–325),[2] in which Diogenes was an old man. Tradition agrees that he was originally a man of wealth, but renounced his possessions to take up the life of a Cynic. Details of this renunciation vary ; the Cynic tradition is perhaps that preserved by Diocles,[3] who says that on the advice of Diogenes he gave up his farms to sheep-pastures, and threw his money into the sea. If any trust may be placed in the stories which show him already a Cynic at the time of the destruction of Thebes by Alexander in 335,[4] we could

---

[1] Collected by Diels in *Frag. Poet. Phil. Grace*, Vol. 1 (1901).
[2] D.L., vi. 87.   [3] id., ib. 87.   [4] id., ib. 93.

infer that he came under the influence of Diogenes between 340–335. The rest of his life seems to have been spent mainly in Athens. The account of his association with Zeno, and with Demetrius of Phalerum after his fall in 307,[1] suggests that he lived through the last decade of the fourth century ; and since he appears to have died in old age his death can hardly have taken place much before 290. It is said that he was buried in Boeotia.

If Diogenes is regarded as the embodiment of αὐτάρκεια Crates may stand for that of φιλανθρωπία, variously symbolized in the conceptions of the Cynic as the Watchdog, as Doctor, or as Scout, working in the interests of humanity. ‘ He would go into any house ’, says Plutarch,[2] ‘ and they would receive him gladly and with honour, and hence he was nicknamed the Door-Opener (Θυρεπανοίκτης),’ ‘ It was he ’, according to Julian,[3] ‘ who was the originator of the noble doctrines of Zeno.’ And they say that on his account the Greeks would write over their doorways ‘ Entry for Crates, the Good Genius ’.[4] Apuleius is more explicit.

Crates, the follower of Diogenes, whom the Athenians of his time revered as a household deity (*lar familiaris*). No house was ever barred against him ; however private the rooms of the head of the family, Crates would enter it, and that most opportunely, for he was the umpire and arbiter of all family disputes and quarrels. Poets speak of the hero Heracles, and how by his valour he overthrew wild animals, monsters, and giants, and rid the earth of them ; our philosopher was in truth a very Heracles in contending against Anger, Envy, Greed, Lust, and other plagues and evils of the human soul. Of such pests would he free men's minds. . . .

It is the familiar comparison, so dear to the Cynics themselves, and which Lucian uses of Diogenes. ‘ Like Heracles, I march and fight against lusts. . . . I am the deliverer of mankind and the healer of their woes.’ But the methods of Diogenes were harsh : ‘ Other dogs ’, he would say, ‘ bite their enemies, I bite my friends, for their salvation.’ The nature of Crates was much more genial ; possibly because he had not suffered injustice as had been the lot of Diogenes.

‘ He passed his whole life jesting and laughing, as though

---

[1] Plut., de. adul. et amic.   [2] id., qu. con., ii. i. 6.
[3] Or., vi. 200B.   [4] ἀγαθῷ δαίμονι, obelized in Teubner text.

on perpetual holiday,'[1] says Plutarch—his very reproofs were delivered not with bitterness, but with kindliness—a kindliness which on one occasion pleasantly surprised Demetrius of Phalerum.

We are less dependent on secondary sources for an estimate of Crates than was the case with either Antisthenes or Diogenes ; his teaching can be deduced from the extant fragments of his own writings. Its lesson was that of a simple, practical asceticism. ' Prefer not the oyster to the lentil, to bring us to confusion,' runs fragment 6 ; the moral is, as Plutarch explains, ' that luxury and extravagance are not the least of the causes which produce revolution and tyranny in cities '. Simplicity and Good Judgement must replace Luxury and Extravagance—' Hail, Lady Mistress, the delight of the wise, Simplicity, offspring of famed Prudence, those who pursue the path of Justice honour thy virtue.'[2] But asceticism, and even philosophy, are not ends in themselves. They are means to the supreme end, which is of course εὐδαιμονία, or what was synonymous to the Cynic, ἀπάθεια. Philosophy should be pursued till we realize the worthlessness of δόξα and τιμή, which are both τῦφος (illusion). Through asceticism and ' philosophy ' we may come to ' the island of Pera ', the Cynic paradise described in perhaps the best-known fragment of Crates.

Fr. 4. 5. 6. (Diels)
There is a city, Pera, in the midst of the wine-coloured sea of τῦφος,[a] fair and fruitful it is, and exceeding squalid,[β] owning—naught. Thither sails no fool nor parasite, no lecher whose delight is in harlots, but it beareth thyme [γ] and garlic, figs and loaves. For such men fight not against each other, nor yet do they take up arms for petty gain, nor for glory. . . . [fr. 5]. Free they are [i.e. the inhabitants of Pera] from Lust the enslaver of men, they are unbent by it : rather do they delight in Freedom, and immortal Basileia [δ] . . . [fr. 6]. She ruleth their hearts and rejoiceth in her own possessions, no slave is she to gold nor to the wasting desires of Love, nor to aught that has to do with Wantonness.[3]

Such were the amenities of the island of Pera ; less lyrical is fragment 12, ' thou knowest not what power the wallet brings, and a quart of lupins, and caring for naught '. The philoso-

---

[1] de. an. tranq., 4. 226E.   [2] Fr. 12D.
[3] See Note 8 to Chap. II.

phers of the schools were lost in τῦφος. ' τῦφος ', says Marcus
Aurelius,[1] ' is a great deceiver ; it especially bewitches you
just when you think you are making headway on worthy
matters. For consider what Crates says about Xenocrates
himself '—presumably an allusion to the τῦφος of the master
of the Academy, though the remark is not quoted. On the
authority of Zeno,[2] we are told how

Crates was once sitting in a cobbler's shop reading aloud the
Protrepticus of Aristotle, which was written for Themison, the king
of Cyprus. Aristotle there says that no one possessed better
qualifications for philosophy than Themison, for he had ample
wealth to expend on it, and a great reputation as well. While
Crates was reading the cobbler listened attentively and at the same
time continued stitching, and Crates remarked to him, ' Philiscus,
I think I must write an " Exhortation to philosophy " for you, for
I see you are better qualified than the man to whom Aristotle
dedicated his book.'

Fragments 1 and 2 are an attack on the Megarians.

(1) Yes, and Stilpo too I saw, suffering bitter woes, in Megara,ᵃ
where they say is the bed of Typhon. Endlessly did he dispute,
and many a comrade was round him. They wasted time in the
verbal pursuit of Virtue.ᵝ . . . (2) and I saw Asclepiades the
Pheliasian and the bull of Eretria (Menedemus).[3]

A passage of Teles [4] attributes to Crates an attack on Hedonist
doctrines which is interesting both in its content and as a good
example of the lively style of Cynic moralizing :

If we must judge the happy life [says Crates] by a favourable
balance of pleasures, then no man will be truly happy. For if you
choose to consider the several stages of a man's life, you will readily
see that there is an overwhelming preponderance of pain. First
of all, half of our entire life, the portion spent in sleep, is indifferent.
Then the first stage, that of infancy, is exceedingly trying. The
child is hungry, and the nurse tries to rock it to sleep ; it is thirsty,
and she washes it : it would like to go to sleep, but she makes a
row with the rattle. Should it escape the nurse, it gets into the
hands of the tutor, the trainer, the schoolmaster, the music master,
the painter. Advance a stage, and up comes the teacher of mathe-

---

[1] vi. 13.
[2] *Apud* Strabo, 95, 21.
[3] See Note 9 to Chap. II.
[4] Hense, p. 38, 3.

matics, the geometrician, the riding-master ; the boy has to be up with the dawn, never a moment's spare time. And now he is an ephebos : now he goes in fear of the prefect, the trainer, the drill-sergeant, the master of the gymnasium, by all of whom he is beaten, bullied and hustled about. If there are watches to be kept the ephebi must keep them : if there are guard-duties they perform them : if there are transport operations, they must embark on them. Now the youth has come to man's estate, he is in his prime. He goes on military expeditions and embassies on behalf of the State : engages in political life, is strategus, choregus, agonothetus. He lauds the days when he was a boy. Time goes on, he comes to be an old man. Once more the attendant lies in wait for him : he longs for his youth: quotes Euripides, ' Youth is ever sweet to me, Old Age lieth heavier than Etna.' So I can't see how any one can live a happy life, if one is to judge from the criterion of a favourable balance of pleasures.[1]

The diatribe of Teles which uses this passage is entitled $περὶ$ $τοῦ$ $μὴ$ $εἶναι$ $τέλος$ $ἡδονήν$. A work of Chrysippus on the same subject is thought to have been an attack on Epicurus ; but from the nature of the hedonist doctrines here assailed it seems likely that we have to deal with the views attributed in Diogenes Laertius to Aristippus. As has been said, the ' end ' for the Cynics was $εὐδαιμονία$, which is equated with $αὐτάρκεια$. Aristippus [2] substituted for this that $ἡδονή$ against which Diogenes had marched ' like another Heracles '. De-throned from the position of $τὸ$ $τέλος$, $εὐδαιμονία$ was defined by Aristippus in a way which was most repugnant to the Cynics. The end being the ' individual ' pleasure ($ἡ$ $κατὰ$ $μέρος$ $ἡδονή$) $εὐδαιμονία$ is the sum-total of all ' individual ' pleasures, in which are included pleasures both of the past and of the future. Further, $εὐδαιμονία$ is desirable not for its own sake, but for the sake of the particular pleasures. This doctrine was attacked on similar grounds by Hegesias. His followers

denied the possibility of happiness [i.e. as defined by Aristippus], for the body is afflicted with much suffering, in which the soul shares and is thereby disturbed. Moreover, expectations are frequently upset by Fortune. From all of which it follows that happiness cannot be attained.[3]

---

[1] See Note 10 to Chap. II. [2] D.L., ii. 87, 88.
[3] id., ib. 93, 94.

Cicero[1] says that in a book of Hegesias entitled Ἀποκαρτερῶν the story is narrated of a man who was committing suicide by fasting, and who, when his friends tried to dissuade him, replied by enumerating the evils of life (*vitae humanae enumerat incommoda*). The controversy is reflected in two epigrams of the *Anthology*,[2] in which the ' evils of life ' are set out by Posidippus, and the good things of life by Metrodorus.

The standards of the ordinary man were of course no less afflicted with τῦφος than those of the dogmatists. ' He used to say that it is impossible to find anybody wholly free from flaws ; but, as in a pomegranate, one of the seeds is always going bad.'[3] Popular standards of values were satirized in the ' famous day-book ' (ἡ ἐφημερὶς ἡ θρυλουμένη) :[4] apparently an ironic picture of a wealthy man's account-book.

' Set aside ten minas for a chef, a drachma for the doctor. Five talents for a flatterer, for council—smoke. A talent for a whore, three obols for a philosopher.'

In strong contrast to these distorted standards were the ' natural ' values of the κυνικὸς βίος. The simplicity and frugality of Crates' own life are attested by the fragments of his work as well as the evidence of his follower Metrocles. ' Gather lentils and beans, my friend ; if you do this you will readily set up a trophy of victory over Want and Poverty.'[5] Elsewhere Poverty appears as the friend rather than the enemy. ' I am a citizen of the lands of Obscurity and Poverty, impregnable to Fortune, a fellow-citizen of Diogenes.'[6] Satisfied with his quart of lupins, he could care for naught. Though deformed and a hunchback, he appears to have practised the ἄσκησις of gymnastics which Diogenes so emphasized.[7] In a passage of Teles Metrocles contrasts the expensive life of a student at the Academy or under Theophrastus with the simplicity of a disciple of Crates.

Metrocles says, that when he studied under Theophrastus and Xenocrates, though he had a liberal allowance from home, he was actually afraid of starvation, and was constantly in a state of want and penury. But when he transferred to Crates, he could have

---

[1] Tusc., i. 83.   [2] ix. 359, 360.   [3] D.L., vi. 89.
[4] id., ib. 85.   [5] Fr. 7.   [6] D.L., vi. 93.
[7] id., ib. 92.

maintained a second person besides himself without any allowance. For formerly it was essential to have sandals . . . a cloak, a retinue of servants, a well-furnished household, to contribute to the common table fine wheaten bread, dainties above the common level, sweet wine, and to furnish the entertainments which came his way. Such a mode of life was there considered liberal. But when he changed over to become a follower of Crates there was none of that. Living on a much simpler scale he was satisfied with a rough coat and barley-bread and common herbs, and felt neither regret for his former mode of life nor dissatisfaction with that of the present. . . . If he wished to anoint himself, he would go into the baths and use oil-lees ; sometimes too he would go to the furnaces of the smithies, roast a sprat, mix a little oil, and sit down and make his breakfast. In summer he would sleep in the temples, in winter in the baths. Yet there was none of his previous want or penury, he had sufficient for his circumstances, and felt no desire for attendants.

Yet there are not wanting indications that with Crates the austerity of Diogenes was to some extent relaxed. It is note-worthy that no anecdotes portray him as a beggar : possibly he had not renounced all his wealth. One account, quoted from Demetrius of Magnesia, says that he deposited his money with bankers to be paid to his sons if they were ordinary men (ἰδιῶται), but to be distributed among the people if they became philosophers, for then they would want nothing. Now we have the authority of Eratosthenes for the statement that his son, Pasicles, went through the ephebate, and as he is not mentioned as a disciple of Crates, it is possible that as an ' ordinary man ' he claimed his legacy. No doubt the genial nature of Crates himself is mainly responsible for the relaxing of the rigid standards of Diogenes which appears in fragment 10, the parody of the prayer of Solon.

Muses of Pieria, fair children of Olympian Zeus and of Memory, hearken to my prayer. Give me food day by day for my stomach, but give it without slavery, which makes life poor indeed. . . . May I be rather useful than agreeable to my friends. Little desire have I for famous riches : no craving do I feel for the wealth of the Beetle, nor the substance of the Ant. But I wish to attain a portion in Justice, and to amass such wealth as may easily be borne, is easily acquired, and precious for Virtue. If I may attain to this, I will worship Hermes and the holy Muses, not with costly offerings, but with pious deeds.

A passage of Teles [1] seems to suggest that Crates did not insist on complete renunciation of wealth from his followers.

Crates replied as follows to the question, ' What shall it profit me to become a philosopher ? ' ' You will be able to open your purse readily and to dip your hand therein, not as now, fumbling and hesitating and trembling, like a paralytic. With equanimity you will see it full, and without regret empty, you will be equipped to employ money readily when prosperous ; but if penniless, you will not be harassed by longings for it. Your life will be one adapted to meet the situation, with no cravings for what you do not possess, and undisturbed by the vicissitudes of chance.'

Probably such lessons were meant for the wider circle of the hearers of Cynic discourse rather than for the devotees of the Cynic life. Nevertheless, the attitude suggests, rather than the austerity which Diogenes undeviatingly maintained to the end of his life, the remark of Aristippus on his association with Lais.[2] ' I have Lais, not she me : it is not abstinence from Pleasure which is best, but to master it without being worsted.'

Through his association with Metrocles Crates was drawn into a relationship which caused great amazement in antiquity—his *κυνογαμία* [3] with Hipparchia. The marriage seems to have been a historical fact ; it is mentioned by Diogenes Laertius, Suidas, and Apuleius in almost identical terms, which suggests that their accounts are based on a common source. This would not in itself be valuable evidence, but there is also a quotation from the *Didumi* of Menander, an epigram on Hipparchia by Antipater of Sidon, and a very striking passage of Epictetus. Exactly how the marriage came about we do not know. Probably Metrocles sent word to his family in Maroneia of how much happier he was as the follower of Crates than as a student at the great schools, perhaps he warmly eulogized his new master. But at any rate his sister Hipparchia, whose name suggests that she was of good family, fell violently in love with Crates, refused to consider her younger and more eligible suitors, and threatened to commit suicide unless she were allowed to marry him. To judge from the evidence of literature, young women were seldom so strong-minded in Greece. The idea that ' Virtue is the same

[1] Hense, p. 28, 5.   [2] D.L., ii. 75.   [3] See Appendix III.

for women as for men ' admittedly goes back to Socrates, it was adopted by Antisthenes, and developed by Plato in the Republic. As we have seen, Diogenes proclaimed that there should be no distinction of dress between the sexes, and that women should conduct their athletic exercises in public just as men did. But the theory had never been put in practice so literally as was now proposed by Hipparchia. The girl's parents appealed to Crates to dissuade her ; ' he did all he could, and finally failing to convince her, got up, took off his clothes in front of her, and said : " This is the bridegroom, here are his possessions ; now make your choice. You will never be a helpmeet of mine, unless you share my pursuits." ' This final argument failed, and Hipparchia had her way. A precise date for this marriage cannot be determined. Since Metrocles studied at the Lyceum under Theophrastus before he became a Cynic, it must have been some time later than 323, when Theophrastus became head of the Peripatetic School. The only other evidence is that of Menander : a fragment of the *Didumi* speaks of Crates having a daughter of marriageable age. Menander died *c.* 291 ; of the date of the *Didumi* nothing is known. But from the nature of the reference the marriage of Crates and Hipparchia must have taken place some fifteen years or more before the production of the play, i.e. probably earlier than 310. The evidence thus points to some time in the decade following 320 as the date for the κυνικὸς γάμος.

Hipparchia became a famous figure, ' she was nicknamed " the female philosopher "',' says Diogenes Laertius, ' and countless stories were told about her.' She was not the first woman who had adopted philosophy : one thinks immediately of Aspasia and her famous ' Salon ' : we also hear of two women, Lastheneia of Mantinea and Axiotheia of Phlious, as being pupils at the Academy. Aristippus, too, is said to have instructed his daughter in the hedonist doctrines. The fame of Hipparchia is to be explained partly by the constancy with which she adhered to the Cynic asceticism, ' she went everywhere with Crates, wearing the Cynic garb ', partly by the opportunities Cynic sexual morality gave to the inventors of scabrous stories. It is worth noting that lurid stories of the nuptials of Crates and Hipparchia appear only in Apuleius : they are absent from the earlier accounts. They may therefore be dismissed with great probability as inventions, Hipparchia being chosen as a stock figure on which to fasten examples of ἀναίδεια. A more curious and interesting comment on the marriage is that made by Epictetus.[1] In the essay ' On the Calling of the Cynic ' it is maintained that in the present order of things the Cynic will not marry or rear children, for that will interfere with his duties as the messenger, the scout, the herald of the gods that he is. If he marries

he must get a kettle to heat water for the baby . . . wool for his wife . . . oil, a cot, a cup, and many other pieces of crockery. . . . What then will become of the King, whose duty it is to be overseer over the rest of mankind—who have married ; who have had children : who is treating his wife well, who ill : who quarrels : which house stands firm, which does not ; making his round like a physician feeling pulses. See to what straits we are reducing our Cynic, how we are taking his kingdom away from him.

' Yes,' comes the objection, ' but Crates married '—Crates the *lar familiaris*, the public consultant, the best example of this kind of labour in the interests of humanity. The answer is very odd.

You are mentioning an instance of passionate love : besides, you are assuming another Crates in the person of the woman. Our inquiry is concerned with ordinary marriage, apart from special circumstances : which from our standpoint do not at present seem to concern the philosopher.

Similar language is used by Diogenes Laertius.

She fell passionately in love with Crates' discourses and ways of life (ἦρα Κράτητος καὶ τῶν λόγων καὶ τοῦ βίου) . . . she threatened to commit suicide unless she were given in marriage to him. To her Crates was everything . . . he tried to dissuade her, but her sincerity overcame him.[2]

It is another instance of Greek feeling of helplessness in the face of passionate love ; ῎Ερως ἀνίκατε μάχαν, unconquerable even by the Cynics, who can only offer as palliatives Hunger and Time; if these fail, the only course is to use the Rope. Physical intercourse would have been perfectly in accord with Cynic sexual morality ; if Diogenes had permitted τὸν πείσαντα

[1] iii. 22, 76.　　　　　[2] D.L., vi. 96.

τῇ πεισθείσῃ συνεῖναι, why should not the rôles of the sexes equally well have been reversed ? It was the element of passion in the marriage, and its permanence that astounded the Greeks. ' She even went out to dinner with Crates '— a thing only done, to use the Victorian phrase, by women of a certain class. παραχάραττειν τὸ νόμισμα, the slogan of Diogenes, was followed by Crates and Hipparchia not only in their marriage, but also in the education of their children. According to Menander, Crates himself claimed that ' he gave his daughter in marriage for a month on trial '; and on the authority of Eratosthenes we learn that he took his son Pasicles into a brothel and said, ' That is how your father married.' The marriage of Hipparchia and Crates affords one of the strangest and most interesting examples of Greek sexual morality.

Of Crates' influence on philosophy through his association with Zeno, and on literature through the part he played in the development of Cynic genres, we shall have occasion to speak later. But in one direction it is hard to evaluate his influence ; I mean his services as a ' public consultant ' to the Athenian people. In the latter half of the fifth century the ordinary man at Athens was to a remarkable degree thrown on his own resources in the conduct of his affairs. The laws of the State, of course, laid down certain limits which could not be transgressed without punishment ; but in that very important section of human affairs which does not come within the province of the law, but on which happiness so largely depends, the average man had no guide. Religion could satisfy his craving for ritual in the State ceremonies, or provide emotional stimulus in the Mystery Cults, but it gave no advice on the conduct of his everyday affairs. The two great schools of Philosophy, the Academy and the Peripatetics, were scholarly and scientific in spirit, dominated by the Platonic conception ἀδύνατον πλῆθος φιλόσοφον εἶναι; Theophrastus warned his pupils that the mastery of his doctrines would demand a world of labour. For his recurrent problems, so trivial in the general scheme of things, so important to him, the ordinary man could derive about as much help from them as could his modern equivalent from the Cavendish Laboratory. For help he had to have recourse to oracles or the interpretation of dreams, or to the advice of his friends (it is interesting to see how ancient discussions of friendship always insist that to give helpful advice is the most important function of a friend). But oracles were sometimes expensive and generally ambiguous : while probably your friends often knew little more than you did yourself. The value of advice from a man like Crates, himself detached from the ordinary business of life, would be that it was impartial, clear, and related to a known standard of values. We may picture him doing much what Socrates is made to do in the *Memorabilia*, preaching the virtues of agreement between brothers, pointing out the advantages of self-control to those who seemed much in need of it. Philosophy brought to the masses inevitably differed from the Philosophy of Plato and Aristotle ; from the noble quest to satisfy the curiosity of the intellect it has descended to become Daily Strength for Daily Needs. To us Crates, the cheerful hunchback, who renounced his wealth, made one of the few successful love-matches known in Greek literature, and had a talent for literary parody, is a pleasant and interesting figure ; for the life of the average Athenian of his day he was perhaps more important than Theophrastus or the learned professors of the Academy.

NOTES TO CHAPTER II

1. The most important is necessarily the biography by Diogenes Laertius—an extraordinary piece of uncritical exuberance. One of the longest Laertian biographies, it contains anecdote heaped upon anecdote, frequent repetitions, two or more accounts of the same event, all strung together in an inconceivable disorder of which von Fritz rightly complains. The *Florilegium* of Stobaeus contains numerous apophthegms under the name of Diogenes ; similar dicta are attributed to him by Epictetus, Maximus of Tyre, and Julian, and, less frequently, by Athenaeus, Aelian, and Plutarch. As a literary figure, he appears in the works of Dio Chrysostom and Lucian. Nine anecdotes, only one of which is retailed by Diogenes Laertius, appear in a papyrus of the first century B.C.,[1] and five apophthegms in what seems to be an Egyptian school copybook of the third or fourth centuries A.D. [2] Much more important are the fragments of Philodemus,[3] *On the Stoics*, which give evidence for the contents of Diogenes' *Politeia*.

---

[1] The so-called ' Wiener Diogenes-papyrus ', vide Cronert, *Kolotes und Menedemos*, p. 49.

[2] Papyrus Bouriant, n. 1 : Cronert, op. cit., p. 157.

[3] Hercul. Pap., Nos. 155 and 339 : ib., pp. 53–67.

2. Von Fritz divides the *Life* as follows : cap. 1–24 form a biography, probably based by D.L. on a single original ; cap. 25 opens with the sentence δεινὸς τ' ἦν κατασοβαρεύσασθαι τῶν ἄλλων, and cap. 25–69 are filled with a series of anecdotes, most of which illustrate this characteristic ; cap. 70–3 contain χρέιαι, in all probability from the same source as the biography above, c. 74 begins εὐστο-χώτατος δ' ἐγένετο ἐν ταῖς ἀπαντήσεσι τῶν λόγων, ὡς δῆλον ἐξ ὧ προειρήκαμον. and thus may link on to cap. 25–69 ; the cap. 74–fin. contain additions inserted by Diogenes Laertius himself—an epigram of his own composition, the date of Diogenes' death, a discussion of the writings attributed to him, and a list of namesakes. There are then two main portions, the Biography and the Collection of Anecdotes. The second of these depends largely on Cynic and Stoic sources, while the first derive from general literature as well. Thus analysed, the *Life* by Laertius is our chief source for Diogenes.

3. Mr. Seltman's evidence is here briefly reproduced. Sinope, as the most important city of the Euxine, issued an uninterrupted succession of good coinage throughout the fourth century. This falls into three issues—the first[1] covering the years prior to 370 (obverse a nymph's head, reverse eagle on a dolphin, the letters ΣΙΝΩ and two or more letters of a magistrate's name), the second[2] 37–362 when Sinope was under the control of the Satrap Datames of Dascylium (same as above, except that ΣΙΝΩ is replaced by ΔΑΤΑΜΑ), the third[3] 362 to at least 310 (same as first issue, except that there is often an aplustre in front of the nymph's head). Nine coins[4] are listed in the Reçueil Général des Monnaies Grecques d'Asie Mineure which bear as the name of the magistrate the letters ΙΚΕΣΙΟ, and which belong to the third series. Some time after 362, then, a magistrate of the same name as that given for the father of Diogenes was actually in charge of the Mint at Sinope. What of παραχάραξις ? Besides the three issues of good Greek coins, we find a large number of alien imitations of the currency of Sinope. Mr. Seltman cites 37 coins with Sinopean types but the Aramaic legend Ariawrath, and 18 with the Aramaic letters ABDSSN, or 55 coins in all. ARIAWRATH must be Ariarathes, satrap of Cappadocia between 351 and 333. Besides the coins bearing Aramaic legends[5] which Mr. Seltman shows cannot have been minted at Sinope, we have 40 specimens of a barbarous imitation[6] of a Sinopean type, with blundered Greek letters. The inference is clear.

During the decade after 350 the credit of Sinope was being seriously undermined by the circulation of imitations of her currency, emanating notably from the satrap of Cappadocia. What action was taken to meet the situation is readily seen. Of the 55 coins with Aramaic legends 31 (or about 60 per cent.), of the 40 barbarian coins 8 (or 20 per cent.), have been defaced by a large chisel-stamp. This was

---

[1] R.G., No. 20.   [2] id., No. 216.   [3] id., Nos. 21, 21, 22, 23.
[4] id., p. 193.   [5] id., Nos. 33–36*a*.   [6] id., No. 24.

done to put them out of circulation ; and is, Mr. Seltman argues, παραχάραξις in the true fourth-century sense. (The word was a rare one, it cannot mean the issue of false coinage, the word for which was παρακόπτειν, and besides no Sinopean coins of base metal are known.) The work must have been that of a high official at the Mint, it exactly coincides with what we are told about Diogenes' father Hicesias. Hicesias, then, was a ' sound money man ', he acted in the best interests of the State ; why did he suffer imprisonment ? Mr. Seltman has two suggestions. After the control of Datames at Sinope from 370 to 362 there was probably a pro-Persian party in the city, which could easily say that the παραχάραξις of the coins of the Cappadocian satrap was an insult which would probably lead to trouble. Furthermore, the παραχάραξις was not confined to the imitation currency : of the good Sinopean coins, 2 out of 43 listed of the first issue, 10 out of 130 of the third issue have been so defaced. This was probably due to carelessness on the part of under officials, but it could easily be turned into a serious accusation against the Master of the Mint. So for one or both of these reasons Hicesias was imprisoned, and his son Diogenes, who was an assistant at the Mint, was driven into exile.

4. Ariarathes did not become satrap of Cappadocia till 351 ; as 40 per cent. of his issues have not been ' paracharacted ', the inference is that this measure was not taken till the issue had been going on for some years.

5. The whole tradition is rejected by von Fritz,[1] who says that it is ' incredible ' that the Corinthians should not have written an epitaph for the tomb, or that Diogenes Laertius should not have retailed it if they had. Again, the scepticism seems too dogmatic ; we have no means of settling the point : the only epigram in the Anthology [2] which refers to the dog on the tomb is anonymous and undated.

6. Von Fritz' [3] attempts to show that the περὶ ἀρετῆς, περὶ ἀγαθοῦ, and Philiscus are Stoic compilations are not convincing ; the first two could well be alternative titles for dialogues in the early catalogue ; either for instance would fit the τέχνη ἠθική. Von Fritz objects to the Philiscus because, ' There is no analogy in antiquity for a philosopher to name a dialogue after one of his pupils.' But Theaetetus was a member of the Academy, though perhaps rather a fellow-student than a pupil of Plato. (Aristotle wrote a Eudemus named after a fellow-student, Eudemus of Cyprus.)[4] The dialogue in the list of Sotion entitled ' Casandrus ' can hardly be by Diogenes if it refers to the Macedonian successor of Alexander, who did not come

---

[1] op. cit.   [2] Anth. Pal., vii. 64.
[3] op. cit., pp. 55 and 57.
[4] Stilpo is said to have written a dialogue entitled ' To his daughter '. —D.L., ii. 120.

into prominence till after Diogenes' death. But further speculation on the authenticity of the remaining works is not of great value ; the list we have inferred to be genuine includes all writings which later authorities explicitly quote for the sayings of Diogenes.

7. Professor Taylor reminds me that if Book V of the *Republic* were only known to us from similar sources we might imagine that it was ' in praise ' of Free Love, and that the attacks of Sextus Empiricus on ' shocking ' tenets of Zeno and Chrysippus merely show that the early Stoics were fond of discussing ' extreme ' cases.

8. ª The history of the word τῦφος is interesting. Primarily of course it simply means ' smoke ' or ' vapour '. The associated verb τυφόω, according to Liddell and Scott, is only used in the metaphorical sense ' to be puffed up ', with conceit. There are two implications in the metaphorical use of τῦφος—inflation, and obscurity. The second seems to have been the earlier usage ; for the Hippocratean writings described the delirium produced by fever as τῦφος : hence ' typhoid ' fever is a fever that darkens or ' clouds ' the brain. But the word is uncommon before fourth-century prose ; ὦ τετυφώμενε, ' deluded fellow ', occurs in the Hippias Major ; Aristotle calls the bewildered stage of drunkenness τῦφος ; Demosthenes in several passages uses τετυφωμένος to mean ' deluded, misled '. With the Cynics τῦφος became almost a technical term. The twofold implication was retained : the opponent of the Cynics was ' puffed up ' and arrogant (cf. the Cynic story of how Diogenes trampled on the fine carpets of Plato—' with conceit of another kind, Diogenes ', was the reply ; and the similar story of Antisthenes) ; all doctrines except the Cynic δόξαι were obscure and illusory. Menander makes Monimus say that the whole of supposition is an illusion. In our passage, τῦφος refers to the obscurity of false beliefs and illusory sense impressions.

ᵝ Reading περιρρύπος with Stephanus. Diels follows Rieske in reading περίρρυτος, which admittedly reproduces the wording of Homeric lines.

> Κρήτη τις γαῖ' ἔστι μέσῳ ἐνὶ οἴνοπι πόντῳ
> καλὴ καὶ πιείρα, περίρρυτος, etc.

but seems to have little force. περίρρυπος would be used παραπροσδοκίαν, like τύφῳ in the previous line, and is an apt reference to the well-known squalor of the Cynic life. Menander called Monimus ὁ προσαιτῶν καὶ ῥυπῶν.

ᵞ The pun of θύμος, ' Thyme ', and θυμός, ' strength ', is not to be accurately rendered in English. Perhaps one might say ' heart-sease '.

ᵟ Reading with Diels ἀθάνατον βασιλείαν ; Wilamowitz reads ἀθανάτων βασιλείαν, ' rejoicing in the rule of the immortals ', but this is not specifically Cynic and overlooks the rôle played by βασιλεία in Cynic conceptions. βασιλεία personifies the Cynic self-mastery, as opposed to the condition of a man dominated by Lusts, who is under a τυραννίς. The whole conception is well illustrated in the famous story of Heracles in Dio Chrysostom,[1] which Weber and François regard as based on Cynic originals. There Heracles is shown a great mountain with twin peaks, the one called βασιλείας ἄκρα and sacred to Ζεὺς βασιλεύς ; the other, ἄκρα τυραννική, was called Τυφῶνος ἄκρα ; Typhon as usual signifying illusion. On the first was enthroned βασιλεία, who is called μακαρία δαίμων, Διὸς βασιλέως ἔκγονος, and is attended by Δική, Ἐννομία, Ἐιρήνη, and Νόμος (who is also ὀρθὸς λόγος). On the Peak of Illusion was enthroned Τυραννίς, attended by Ὠμότης, Ὕβρις, Ἀνομία, and Στάσις. The Cynic, then, could well be said ἀγαπᾶν . . . βασιλείαν καὶ ἐλευθερίαν.

9. ᵃ Cf. Iliad, II. 783, εἰν Ἀρίμοις, ὅθι φασὶ Τυφωεύς ἔμμεναι εὐνάς. ἐν Μεγάροις is παραπροσδοκίαν for εἰν Ἀρίμοις. There is no mythological connexion of Typhon with Megara ; as in the passage already quoted from Dio Chrysostom, the Titan is the personification of Illusion. Perhaps the conception is based on the famous description in Pindar (Pyth., I. 29) of the monster confined beneath Etna, from which

ἐρεύγονται μὲν ἀπλάτου πυρὸς ἀγνοτάται
ἐκ μυχῶν παγάι · ποταμοὶ δ' ἀμέραισιν μὲν προχέονται
ῥοὸν καπνοῦ | αἴθωνα. κτλ.

Diels (Sillog. Gracc., ii. 193) quotes Aristotle (Rhet., 1412, d. 33) τὰ δὲ παρὰ γράμμα ποῖει οὐχ ὃ λέγει λέγειν, ἀλλ' ὃ μεταστρεφει ὄνομα. The point is twofold: (a) Stilpo pursued ἀρετή in verbal quibbles (his eristic studies), (b) and another object of his pursuit was not ἀρετή herself, but his mistress Νικαρέτη. The doubles entendres which Wachsmuth discovered in εὐνάς διώκειν and κατατρίβειν do not commend themselves to Diels. But κατατρίβειν was so frequently used sensu obsceno that the suspicion seems justified.

10. Diels hesitates to ascribe the passage to Crates ; ' vereor ', he says, ' ne ea quae congruenter cum Axiocho, p. 336D, exponuntur, a Cratete abhorreant. Illum enim nec tam Attice gesturum fuisse, ut Thebanum, nec tam molliter, ut Cynicum.' The first does not seem an important objection ; Crates passed much of his time at Athens and must have been perfectly familiar with Athenian customs. For the second, we shall see that with him the austerity of Diogenes was considerably relaxed. The parallel with the Axiochus is admittedly striking, but there is no evidence to prove that Teles is quoting that dialogue. The date of the Axiochus is disputed. Immisch gives 305–300 as a probable date, which Taylor quotes with the remark that ' it may be too early '. Chevalier argues that it is of Neo-Pythagorean origin and does not appear to be earlier than the first century B.C. ; the Budé editor, regarding the passage of the Axiochus as being a quotation from Teles rather than vice versa and further

---

[1] περὶ βασιλείας, I. 65.

relying on two other passages (366E : 367B) which show the influence of Bion of Borysthenes, dates it about the end of the third century. However this may be, it is probable that both our passage and that of the Axiochus have a common source in Prodicus. It is expressly stated in the Axiochus that ταῦτα ἃ λέγω, Προδίκου τοῦ σοφοῦ ἐστὶν ἀπηχήματα . . . φράσοιμ᾽ ἂν σοὶ ταῦτα ἃ μνημονεύσω. The famous story of Prodicus about the choice of Heracles, quoted in Xenophon's *Memorabilia*, seems to have formed the basis of much Cynic allegory (cf. Dio Chrys., 1. 65); and it is very possible that Crates might have adapted a familiar passage of Prodicus to the refutation of Hedonist theories. This would itself account for the ' non-Cynic softness which Diels discovers.

CHAPTER III

CYNICISM IN THE THIRD CENTURY B.C.

By the beginning of the third century B.C. Cynicism must have been a familiar phenomenon in the Greek world. In attempting to determine its influence during the Hellenistic period it is important to remember that it was a phenomenon which presented itself in three aspects. There was first the κυνικὸς βίος, the mendicant life, whose insignia were the wallet, the τρίβων and the staff. Second, there was the Cynic slogan, παραχάραττειν τὸ νόμισμα, with all it implied in the way of attack on established conventions and values. Finally, there was the κυνικὸς τρόπος in literature ; for the writings of Monimus, Crates, and Metrocles had established τὸ σπουδαιογέλοιον as the genus of Cynic writings, though one of its most familiar species, the diatribe, was a development largely due to Bion. Since Cynicism was never a school of philosophy in the strict sense, these diverse aspects were not inseparable ; hence we shall find men of widely different outlook and temperament described as ' Cynics ' ; hence, too, tendencies inherent in earlier Cynicism were found when developed to lead to very divergent conclusions. Doubtless many persons took up staff and wallet and imagined that by virtue of this alone they were the disciples of Diogenes, although to judge from the literary evidence there were not so many charlatans associated with Cynicism during this period as later in the Roman Empire. Again, the Cynic παραχάραξις attracted from time to time philosophers of the dogmatic schools who were particularly interested in stressing the gulf that separates the Wise Man from the standard of the normal world ; while the ridicule of accepted values was pushed to its nihilistic conclusion by such persons as Menippus, who became ' The mocker of human life '. The literary influence of Cynicism leads to the appearance of Cynic forms and ideas in writers who were very far from living the κυνικὸς βίος,

59

such as Leonidas of Tarentum, and, in Roman times, Lucilius and even Horace. It will be most convenient to deal first with the followers of the κυνικὸς βίος, the Cynics proper ; then with the influence of Cynicism on the philosophic schools ; finally (and more briefly, since it has attracted the attention of many scholars), something must be said about the literary influence of Cynicism.

The ' succession ' of Cynics given by Diogenes Laertius takes us two or three generations beyond Metrocles, i.e. well into the latter half of the third century.

The ' pupils ' of Metrocles were Theombrotus and Cleomenes ; Theombrotus had for a pupil Demetrius of Alexandria ; while Cleomenes instructed Timarchus of Alexandria and Echecles of Ephesus. Echecles also heard Theombrotus ; his own lectures were attended by Menedemus. . . . Menippus of Sinope also became famous amongst them.[1]

Nothing more is known of Timarchus, Theombrotus, and Echecles ; and of Cleomenes only that he wrote a book called παιδαγωκικός, which employed the legend of the ' Sale of Diogenes '. Cronert[2] was the first to point out that the passage of diatribe quoted by Stobaeus viii. 20 is almost certainly a fragment of Demetrius of Alexandria. The fragment gives independent grounds for dating the *floruit* of Demetrius *c.* 250 B.C., for the employment of personification shows the influence of Bion. It deals, in the manner of the choice of Heracles, with the struggle between good and evil instincts in the human soul : the style is lively, the sentences short, with frequent appeals to the ' imaginary adversary '.

Now if Courage and Cowardice were to take their stand beside the soldier in the battle-line, what contradictory advice do you suppose they would give ? Would not Courage bid him stand fast and guard his post ? ' But the enemy have opened fire.'—' Stand fast.' ' But I shall be wounded.'—' Be brave.' ' But I shall die.'—' Die rather than leave your post.' A stubborn council this, and bitter ; but the advice of Cowardice is indulgent, and full of loving kindness (φιλάνθρωπος). He is frightened, she bids him retire forthwith. ' My shield gets in my way.'—' Throw it away, then.' ' So does my breastplate.'—' Loosen it ' ; yes, truly a milder counsel than the former. So is it in other things—Continence says, ' Take nothing from a forbidden source. Go without food, without

---

[1] D.L., vi. 95. [2] Kolotes und Menedemos, pp. 46–7.

drink—but persevere, be strong.   And at the last, die, rather than live by crime.'   Incontinence says : ' Drink what you like, eat what is sweetest.   Your neighbour's wife is fair in your eyes ? Take her.   You lack money ?   Borrow.   You have borrowed, and are still in want ?   Don't pay anything back.   Your credit is not good for further borrowing ?   Then steal.'   Great indeed is the difference between them on this point ; yet who knows not, that the goodwill of Incontinence brings ruin to those who accept her, while that of Continence is as a saviour to man ?

Cronert [1] is also responsible for the fact that we are able to view Menedemus is a more sober light than that in which he is portrayed by Diogenes Laertius.

Menedemus [according to the latter] reached such a pitch of charlatanry as a miracle-monger that he used to go about dressed as a Fury, saying he had come from Hades as a scout (ἐπίσκοπος) of human wrong-doing, and that he was going to report on it to the nether-gods.   He was dressed in a long grey tunic, with a crimson girdle ; on his head an Arcadian hat (or πῖλος) with the twelve signs of the Zodiac wrought on it. . . .[2]

Cronert argues that Menedemus is here confused with some character (perhaps Menippus himself), from the Νεκυία of Menippus.   It is noteworthy that parallels to this passage can be found in two of Lucian's dialogues which are based on Menippus.   In the Χάρων ἤ ἐπισκοποῦντες Charon is brought up by Hermes to view the world of men ; in the *Menippus*, Menippus wears the πῖλος, and has gained admission to the underworld by the help of a Chaldaean astrologer ; the twelve signs of the zodiac are of course of an astrological significance.

This portion of the βίος can then be dismissed as fictitious, but there is no reason to doubt the statement that Menedemus was first a pupil of Colotes of Lampsacus, the Epicurean ; that later, becoming that very rare phenomenon, an apostate from Epicureanism, he came under the influence of the Cynic Echecles of Ephesus.   Two papyri from Herculaneum confirm this,[3] they show Menedemus in conflict with his former master on the question of Epicurean criticism of Poetry, when a spirited interchange of argument evidently took place.   The

[1] op. cit., p. 1 ff.

[2] D.L., vi. 102.   [3] Herc. Pap., Nos. 208, 1082.

controversy will be more relevant in the chapter on the relations between Cynicism and the philosophic schools.

We find no mention in Diogenes Laertius of Sochares, the subject of satirical epigrams of Leonidas of Tarentum, nor of Teles; while Bion of Borysthenes is classified as a follower of the Academy, and a quotation from Cercidas of Megalopolis is introduced into the *Life* of Diogenes without a definite statement that he was a Cynic. The lack of exact chronological data for the last three writers and for Menippus makes it a matter of some doubt as to their proper places in an account of Cynicism during the third century; but chronology will be approximately observed, and it will be most convenient to treat them in the order Bion–Menippus–Cercidas–Teles.

(a) Bion.

Approximately contemporary with Metrocles, and of great importance in the development of Cynicism, is Bion of Borysthenes. Diogenes Laertius, though admitting that he had Cynic connexions, includes him amongst the followers of the Academy; but there is an essentially Cynic spirit in the surviving fragments of his writings, and he played an important part in the development of the diatribe, so that he may properly be considered here.

'A strange creature,' is Tarn's opinion; 'few men in the third century are harder to judge, and probably few had more influence.' Bion's career is of interest as showing what the age had to offer to a man of humble birth who chose to make his living by his wits. He was the son of a fishmonger and a hetaira—a combination from which, as von Arnim penetratingly remarks, he may have derived that familiarity with vulgar phraseology which distinguished his style. But perhaps there was more than the argot of the fish-market to be learned at Borysthenes. In the time of Dio Chrysostom the town was remarkable for its devotion to Homer—'they are all enthusiastic admirers of the poet: most of the citizens know the Iliad off by heart . . . their poets refer to Homer alone in their writings.'[1] So it is possible that the young Bion was

---

[1] Dio Chrys., 36, 9. Prof. Rostovtseff tells me that recent archaeological finds at Borysthenes (Olbia) strikingly confirm Dio, for over a long period both papyri and inscriptions abound with Homeric personal names.

not wholly uneducated when his father's fraudulency caused the whole family to be sold into slavery.   At any rate he was handsome, and was bought by ' a certain rhetorician ' for obvious enough purposes ;   a fact which Bion's enemies pounced on, and which he hardly troubled to deny.   But the boy seems to have had brains as well as looks, and the rhetorical training which he got (presumably) during this period was to have an important influence on his style.   When his master died he left all his possessions to Bion.   ' I burned all his speeches,' [1] Bion says ; ' scraped everything together, and came to Athens to study philosophy.' [2]   We cannot say precisely when this was : but it seems to have been earlier than 314, for he is associated with Xenocrates.   In keeping with the custom of the age he went the round of the schools ;   the passage of Diogenes Laertius which gives his philosophical training has caused much controversy.   But perhaps the most likely account is that he first studied at the Academy under Xenocrates, then for a time lived as a Cynic, then studied with Theodorus ' the atheist ' and finally with Theophrastus.[3]

At some time in his career Bion ' taught ' at Rhodes : like the Sophists he went on lecture-tours round the Greek world : but the only other date we can determine with anything like certainty is for his visit to Antigonus Gonatas at Pella, which Tarn thinks must have been later than 276.   The date of Bion's death is unknown, though one may conjecture that it was between 260 and 250 ; tradition says that it took place at Chalcis, and, according to Favorinus, Antigonus himself attended his old counsellor's funeral.

[1] Hicks translates συγγράμματα as ' books ', but it is probably more technical than that—' written speeches '—if used of the works of a rhetor.   Cf. Isoc. 405c.

[2] These biographical details, up to the arrival at Athens, are from a letter which Laertius says was addressed by Bion to Antigonus Gonatas as an answer to his traducers.   Cronert doubts its genuineness :   but it is accepted by Hirzel, Hense, and Tarn :   also by Kiesling with the reservation ' haec si vera non sunt at ad veritatem ficta esse concedi debet '.   This is true ; the passage is marked by the φόρτικα ὀνόματα which Bion is described as using (τῷ ἀγκῶνι ἀπομυσσόμενος) : the use of quotation (ταύτης τοι γενεῆς τὲ καὶ αἵματος εὔχομαι εἶναι) : the sentiments are those of Bion (σκόπει δὲ μ' ἐξ' ἐμαυτοῦ).   Hense considers that the passage of Stobaeus (86. 13) on the same theme— a man's a man for a' that—derives from this letter.

[3] See Note I to Chap. III.

Bion's career and temperament were such as to earn him many enemies ; and their attacks have survived in the biography of Diogenes Laertius. Hense [1] finds that the life in Diogenes Laertius uses two sources hostile to Bion, one attacking his morals and way of life, the other a criticism of his style. The former is the more malignant, and since it contains charges of homosexuality similar to those found in the Life of Arcesilaus, he lends somewhat hesitating support to Wilamowitz' view that these derive from Aristippus περὶ παλαιᾶς τρυφῆς. Charges of homosexuality are of course the stock-in-trade of Greek scabrous gossip, but there remain indictments against Bion which do not come under this head, and which deserve more detailed examination. They are found in Plutarch and Stobaeus as well as Diogenes Laertius ; though the latter puts the case most concisely in his description of Bion as σοφιστὴς ποικίλος,[2] ' a most versatile sophist '. Certainly Bion followed the practice which originally brought the Sophists into disrepute—that of giving lectures for money. Diogenes Laertius says that he was πολυτελής ; and Stobaeus [3] quotes him as saying that there were three types of pupil, like Hesiod's three races of men ; the golden learned and paid, the silver paid but did not learn, the bronze learned but did not pay. Of course no follower of the Cynic way of life could charge high fees for his lectures and remain true to the ideal of Penury ; still, the mere charging for professional services cannot have carried the stigma that it did in the days of Socrates. A student at the Lyceum or the Academy needed a well-lined purse, as we have seen from the complaints of Metrocles ; the objection to Bion was not that he demanded a fee but that he had little to offer in return—that he was, in fact, a charlatan, both in his life and his writings. His manner of life is described as being πομπικὸς καὶ ἀπολαῦσαι τύφου δυνάμενος, ' showy, and able to derive pleasure from arrogance ' ; he was φαντασίαν ἐπιτεχνώμενος, ' one who devised methods of ostentation ' : ' extremely selfish ' ; above all, ' one who gave many openings to those who wished to rail against philosophy '. We know that Persaeus and Philonides [4] tried to dissuade Antigonus from inviting Bion to the court at Pella by stressing his lowly origin ; possibly they also urged on the king that Bion was no

[1] Tel., *Rel.*, lx.   [2] D.L., iv. 47.   [3] *Flor.*, 31. 97.
[4] D.L., iv. 47.

real philosopher, and are ultimately responsible for the charges we have been examining.

More value may be attached to the criticisms directed against the style of Bion, for, as Hense points out, the numerous writings of Bion would give ample material for a fair judgement ; it is furthermore possible to suggest that these criticisms derive from the Stoics of the second century B.C. and their theory of the Plain Style.[1]

The hostile references to Bion are embittered by the fact that through his association with Theodorus he was charged with being an atheist, which seems to have prejudiced Diogenes Laertius against him. Diogenes makes this the subject of one of his usual frigid epigrams—how Bion had denied the gods all his life, and how when he came to die at Chalcis he wore amulets and muttered charms ' as though the gods only existed when Bion graciously chose to recognize them '. For this pragmatic conversion he applies to Bion the particularly opprobrious term of λεμφός, ' scum '. Hense points out that there are not many examples of impious dicta related of Bion, and what there are are of the usual Cynic type, retorts to the priests of the mystery religions, doubts about oracles, and the like.

' Of all the many who flocked to his lectures ', says Diogenes Laertius, ' not one is named as his pupil.' This may well be true ; on the formal side of philosophy Bion had nothing new to offer. Eclectics are not the persons to start a new movement, their doctrines are generally hastily patched together to meet an emergency, and become obsolete when that emergency has passed. No direct trace remains of Bion's lectures ; and Laertius gives no formal list of his writings, he merely says that ' He left very many memoirs (ὑπομνήματα) and also sayings of useful application' (ἀποφθέγματα χρειώδη πραγματείαν περιέχοντα) ; while from a fragment of Philodemus we gather that one of his diatribes was called περὶ ὀργῆς. But it is a small change from the spoken lecture to the written diatribe which is designed for a larger audience than can be reached by word of mouth, and quotations from Bion in Teles are sufficiently numerous and detailed to enable us to form a clear picture of his methods. The most obvious point about Bion's philosophy is that it treats of ordinary

[1] See Note 2 to Chap. III.

human problems in a common-sense spirit, though for emphasis
employing all the devices of contemporary prose style. It
follows the spirit of the Socrates of Xenophon's *Memorabilia*,
or of Crates going from house to house to cure the dissensions
that arise in family life. The situations dealt with are those
that may confront any man, from the universalia of old age,
poverty, exile, slavery, the fear of death, down to the more
particular case of a nagging wife. The panacea is still αὐτάρ-
κεια-ἀπάθεια but with a difference ; for the blending of
Hedonist and Cynic doctrines adopted by Bion had evolved
an αὐτάρκεια quite different from the aggressive asceticism of
Diogenes, one best expressed by the famous simile of the
Actor. The actor's concern is to play adequately the part
assigned to him by the playwright ; but while doing that he
preserves the integrity of his own personality. Hecuba is in
reality nothing to him, however much his performance gives
an impression to the contrary. ' Just as the good actor plays
with skill the Prologue, the middle portion, and the dénoue-
ment of a play, so should a good man play well the beginning,
the middle, and the end of life.' It is the attitude represented
in the Spartan verses,

> οὔτε τὸ ζῆν θεμένοι καλὸν οὔτε τὸ θνήσκειν
> ἀλλὰ τὸ ταῦτα καλῶς ἀμφοτέρ' ἐκτελέσαι.

Circumstances being unalterable, the key to happiness lies in
our approach to them.

Bion says, just as the bites of wild animals depend on how you
hold them (e.g. get hold of a snake round the middle and you'll be
bitten, grasp it by the neck and you'll come to no harm), so
with circumstances, one's approach to them determines the amount
of pain that will be experienced. If you treat them as did Socrates,
there will be no pain : if otherwise, you will experience pain due
not to circumstances themselves, but to your own character and
false illusions. Hence we should not try to alter circumstances,
but to adapt ourselves to them as they really are, as do sailors.
They don't try to change the winds or the sea, but take care that
they are ready to adapt themselves to conditions. In a dead calm
they use the oars, with a following breeze they crowd on sail ;
with a head wind they shorten sail or heave to. Do you adapt
yourself to circumstances in the same way. You have grown old,
do not long for youth. Again, you are weak : do not hanker after
what belongs to the strong. . . . You are penniless, do not seek

the ways of the wealthy. . . .   Adapt yourself to conditions as sails to the wind. . . .[1]

The fault is always in ourselves

. . . If circumstances could speak, as we do, and had the power to state their case . . . would not Poverty say to the man reviling her, ' What is your quarrel with me ?   Have I deprived you of any good thing ?   Of prudence, or justice, or courage ?   Or are you short of any of the necessities of life ?   Well, are the roads not full of herbs, and the springs of water ?   Do I not offer you a bed wherever there is soil, and bedding wherever there are leaves ? Can you not make merry in my company ?   What, have you never heard an old woman singing to herself as she munches her barley-cake ? ' . . .   If Poverty spoke in this vein, what answer would you have to make ?   I think I should have nothing to say.   But we blame anything rather than our own bad training and disposition, age, poverty, our adversary, the day, the hour, the place. [2]

Avoidance of μεμψιμοιρία is essential to happiness, the recipe for which is simple.   ' If you can fashion a man who despises lusts, and is not oppressed by toils, who takes glory and obscurity alike and has no fear of death, then you have a man who can do anything without sorrow.' [3]   The first three of these qualifications may obviously be attained by the method of adapting oneself to circumstances ; for the last, a new set of similes is employed.   ' We regard death as the most dread of terrors ' but in reality it is nothing of the sort. . . .   ' The aged should quit life as gladly as would a tenant a tumbledown house.'

Just as we leave a house [says Bion] when the landlord, failing to get the rent, takes away the door or the slating, or closes up the well : so should we quit our bodies, when Nature, our landlord, deprives us of the use of our eyes, ears, hands, and feet. . . .   I do not remain behind : as a replete guest from a feast, so do I leave life, when the hour is come for ' passengers to board ship '.

It is possible that the piling up of similes in this passage is artificial, for after all what we have is Theodorus' epitome of Teles' version of Bion : but we can at any rate, when confronted with the famous similes of life as a Paneguris, as a feast, and of the aged body as a ruined house, appreciate the force of the adjective ποικίλος applied to Bion.

[1] 6. 3 ff.   [2] 4. 6 ff.   [3] 11. 7.

There is nothing new about the thought of the passages quoted : even the similes are sometimes old ones refurbished. It is significant, too, that the apophthegms ascribed to Bion so frequently parallel those quoted of earlier personages, especially Diogenes.[1]   It is likely enough that Bion would take some apophthegm of Diogenes, common currency amongst the Cynics, alter it to suit conditions, and pass the result off as his own.

' Bion mingled together every aspect of style ' ; the diatribe as he developed it employed all the devices of contemporary prose.   Hense [2] points out the care taken in the balance of syllables and their rhythm, the use of asyndeton and assonance, and of the ' conversionis figurae ' ; perhaps Bion learned these from the teacher of rhetoric who gave him his early education. Fiske notes the use of quotation, of χρεῖαι, of allegorical personification, of little scenes which appear to be influenced by the Mime, of stock-figures, animal similes, and character-sketches.   The latter show the influence of Theophrastus, the parallels with whom are interesting.[3]

In Fiske's judgement, ' Bion added nothing to the world's thought ' ; none the less, he is of great importance to Cynicism, and to a lesser degree to the development of Greek literature. The question of the influence of the diatribe as perfected by Bion on the satire of Lucilius and Horace has been fully discussed by Fiske, and is not especially relevant here.   For the Cynic movement, Bion has a double significance.   We have seen how Diogenes personified the Cynic conception of αὐτάρκεια, while Crates stands for that of φιλανθρωπία ; a third great ideal, that of the κοσμοπολίτης, finds its first real embodiment amongst the Cynics in Bion.   Diogenes and Crates, while professing the ideal of cosmopolitanism, had in fact kept to the great centres of Greek civilization, mainly, of course, to Athens.   But Bion, like the Sophists, travelled from city to city, and made prolonged stays at Rhodes and Pella.   The vagrant preacher, who became so important a figure in the Roman Empire, finds his prototype in Bion, the traditional accounts of whom remind us of the description of Whistler ' the scintillant tramp . . . exempt from human knowledge and human decencies '.   But Eratosthenes admitted

---

[1] See Note 3 to Chap. III.   [2] op. cit.
[3] See Note 4 to Chap. III.

that under his trappings Bion was sound ; and there is perhaps some justification for Bion's own claim, that what he brought to market was the wheat of philosophy, not the barley of rhetoric. Only, it was the philosophy of Hellenistic times, which we have defined as daily strength for daily needs. Bion, too, was the first Cynic to become court-philosopher ; Tarn thinks he may well have had much influence on Antigonus Gonatas, or, at least, that their viewpoints had a good deal in common. The Stoics played the rôle of King's counsellor more successfully than any other school ; the Cynic, if true to his profession, was too wedded to παρρησία to be amenable to all but the most tolerant of monarchs. Nevertheless, there were Cynics at court under the Empire ; here as elsewhere Bion anticipates the later Cynicism, rather than reflects the earlier.

On the world in general, Bion's influence has not been negligible.

> Dixeris egregie, notum si callida verbum
> reddiderit iunctura novum . . .

the simile of Man the actor on the stage of the world, of Life as a Feast which one should quit ' ut conviva satur ', the advice to trim your sails to the breeze, the story of the dying frog, ' this may be fun to you, but it's death to me '—have all passed into common usage. One is tempted to say that Bion, in a different way from that of Diogenes, fulfilled the command παραχάραττειν το νόμισμα. Similes and metaphors are indeed a kind of currency ; ' licuit semperque licebit, signatum praesente nova producere verbum ' ; some of the best issues, whose values have not depreciated, bear the impress of Bion.

(b) Menippus.

The name of Menippus is familiar, yet we have surprisingly little detailed information about him ; like the Cheshire cat, he has faded away to a grin. Ancient tradition is agreed that he was a slave ; according to Diocles [1] he was born at Gadara, and was in the service of a citizen of Pontus, but in some way obtained his freedom and lived at Thebes. Here he came under Cynic influence, most likely that of Metrocles. This

---

[1] D.L., vi. 99.

evidence shows that his *floruit* falls in the first half of the third century; we do not know when he died. The tradition that he was a moneylender and speculator in marine insurance is probably apocryphal, resting as it does on the always dubious authority of Hermippus. This account has led Zeller and other modern writers to speak of him as ' a degenerate Cynic ', but Varro refers to him as ' Menippus ille, nobilis quidem canis ', and Lucian ranks him with Antisthenes, Crates, and Diogenes as the most notable of the Cynics.

In the writings of Menippus the Cynic spirit of mockery of human values was all-pervading. Lucian [1] says that he went about κωμῳδοποιῶν καὶ γελωτοποιῶν ; Marcus Aurelius [2] calls him ' the mocker of mankind '. ' No serious treatises were produced by him,' says Diogenes Laertius, ' but his books overflow with ridicule ' ; there is no conflict here, as both Hicks [3] and Helm [4] suggest, with the description of him as σπουδαιογέλοιος in Strabo. [5] τὸ σπουδαιογέλοιον was a distinct literary genre ; Diogenes Laertius, or rather his source Diocles, means that all Menippus' works are thus comprised, there are no serious ethical writings, such as were perhaps some of the Dialogues of Diogenes, and certainly the Epistles of Crates. The comic genius of Menippus may well have stressed the γελοῖον, but to judge from the fragments of the *Sale of Diogenes* and those dialogues of Lucian which use Menippus as a model, an element of the σπουδαῖον was not absent. Very scanty fragments of Menippus survive, and it is a highly speculative proceeding to try to reconstruct his works from Varro or even from Lucian. Lucian was obviously attracted by the detached and satiric attitude of Menippus, so like his own ; he also found a ready vehicle for his thought in the adaptation of the dialogue for comic and satiric purposes, which was Menippus' chief contribution to literature. The classical theory of Imitation demanded that in handling a particular literary genre an author should conform to a more or less definite framework, but it offered plenty of scope for originality in detail. It is not therefore likely that from the dialogues of Lucian we can reconstruct in any detail the Menippean original. [6] To take

---

[1] *Bis. Acc.*, 33.   [2] vi. 47.   [3] *Diog. Laert.*, vol. ii, p. 103 (Loeb).
[4] Pauly-Wissowa, s.v. Menippus.   [5] xvi. 759.
[6] For an attempt to do this see R. Helm, *Lucian und Menipp.*, Leipzig, 1906.

one example, the *Sale of Diogenes* is generally conceded to have
influenced Lucian in writing his *Sale of Creeds* : but in detail
they must have differed widely, for we know that the work of
Menippus held up Diogenes to admiration, while Lucian
ridicules him together with the other philosophers. The most
that can be done is to gather a general idea of the subject and
spirit of the Menippean writings from the evidence of their
titles, and from the outlines of those dialogues of Lucian which
seem to have been influenced by them. ' The books of
Menippus ', says Diogenes Laertius,[1] ' number thirteen,' and
he gives a partial catalogue as follows : ' Νεκυῖα, Διαθῆκαι,
Ἐπιστολαὶ κεκομψευμέναι ἀπὸ τοῦ τῶν θεῶν προσώπου, πρὸς
τοὺς φυσικοὺς καὶ μαθηματικοὺς καὶ γραμματικούς, Γονὰς
Ἐπικούρου, τὰς θρησκευσμένας [ὑπ' αὐτῶν] εἰκάδας καὶ ἄλλα.'
How many books are thus comprised we do not know ; but
the titles of some of the works not in this list may be gathered
from other sources.

Diogenes Laertius [2] himself mentions a book called Διογένους
πρᾶσις ; and Athenaeus [3] speaks of a συμποσίον and an
Ἀρκεσιλάος.

The original of all Greek νεκυῖαι is of course Homer's
description of the descent of Odysseus to Hades in the eleventh
Book of the *Odyssey*. Literature has always been ready to
grant the Duchess of Malfi's wish

> Oh that 'twere possible we might
> But hold some two days' converse with the dead ;

In Greek literature stories of the Underworld had enforced
the loftiest lessons of philosophy, as in the myths of Plato, or
provided material for hilarious comedy, as in the *Frogs* of
Aristophanes. But for no purposes are they better adapted
than those of Satire ; and Menippus is one of a long line of
satirists who have taken a tour of the Underworld to describe
how there, where a truer standard of values prevails, their
enemies are faring very badly indeed. The Homeric parodies
of Crates seem to have touched on the Νεκυῖα, and, like the
Σίλλοι of Menippus' contemporary Timon of Phlious, to have
described the wretched state of his philosophical opponents in
the life to come. The Νεκυῖα of Menippus formed the model
for Lucian in several dialogues (such as the Menippus, or

---

[1] vi. 101.　　　[2] vi. 29.　　　[3] xiv. 27, 84.

Necyomanteia, the Charon, the Κατάπλους, and the Dialogues of the Dead), from which we may catch something of its spirit. From the evidence of a passage of Diogenes Laertius which Cronert clearly shows to be based on the Νεκυΐα of Menippus, it seems clear that the journey was made by Menippus himself by the aid of magic arts ; and that its avowed object was to consult Tiresias is likely both from the Homeric original and the presumable echoes of Menippus in Horace and Lucian. There was of course a description of our future state. Sceptre and Crown have tumbled down ; the only people to enjoy happiness are the poor man and the Cynic, who are free from Illusion in this world and the next. The Cynic does not shrink from inquiring too curiously, and we see Philip of Macedon cobbling old shoes in a corner, and are unable to distinguish the skull of a famous beauty from that of Thersites. To judge from the *Icaromenippus* of Lucian, and the fact that one of Varro's satires was called the *Endymiones*, it is possible that the Νεκυΐα included a tour of Heaven as well as Hell, and that the gods received scarcely more respectful treatment than had the dead kings and potentates.

The Διαθῆκαι (Wills or Testaments) may have been parody of the Wills of Philosophers ; or more probably pieces of humorous legislation like the decree proposed against the rich by Skull the son of Skeleton of the deme Cadaver in Lucian's *Menippus*,[1] and the resolution to exclude undesirable aliens from Olympus in the *Gods in Council*.[2]

The *Epistles composed as through from Gods* were Lucian's model for the *Letters of Cronos* ; the comic possibilities are many and obvious ; Lucian confines himself to satire on the importunate nature of human prayer, and the conflict between the rich and poor.

The *Sale of Diogenes* may be conjectured to have played an important part in the development of the Diogenes legend. Menippus, himself once a slave, was evidently concerned to show that slavery was something indifferent to the Wise Man. His ideal σοφός was, of course, Diogenes, and he must be turned into a slave in the way most probable at that time, by being captured and sold by pirates.[3] Fragments are preserved in the account of Diogenes Laertius. Diogenes was put up

---

[1] *Men.*, 20.   [2] *Deor. Con.*, 14.
[3] Possibly in imitation of the stories about Plato.

for sale in the market of Crete. Asked what he could do, he replied ' Govern men ', and told the crier to advertise that he was available in case any one wished to purchase himself a master. He was bought by Xeniades of Corinth, who was soon aware of what kind of purchase he had made, and put Diogenes in command of his estate and of the education of his sons.

Of the contents of the *Symposium* we only know that in it the ἐκπύρωσις of the Stoics was described as a dance.[1] Some form of philosophical conversation was held appropriate for the genre; it may well have taken the form of parody in this case. Hirzel's[2] suggestion that the encounter of Hipparchia and Theodorus described by Diogenes Laertius[3] derives from Menippus is interesting, but not very probable. The way in which the incident is mentioned, ' This story and countless others are told of the female philosopher,' suggests that it comes from a collection of χρεῖαι. Nor do we know how far the *Symposium* of Lucian, which shows the sages present behaving or rather misbehaving like so many Lapiths, is based on the work of Menippus.

The remaining works form an attack in the true Cynic manner on devotees of useless knowledge. ' Away with the learning of the clerks ! ' is the cry, natural scientists, mathematicians, and philologists are employed in wasting time and in little else. The schools of philosophy are also attacked; the *Arcesilaus* is presumably directed against the first head of the Middle Academy, whose devotion to dialectic would earn him the contempt of the Cynics ; while the *Birth of Epicurus* and *The School's Reverence for the Twentieth Day* are clearly attacks on the Epicureans.[4]

The literary importance of Menippus is that he developed for comic purposes two genres previously monopolized by Philosophy—the dialogue and the letter. True, such a development had been foreshadowed in some of the Platonic dialogues, notably the *Euthydemus* and the *Menexenus* ; but on the whole Dialogue had hitherto, as he complains in the *Bis*

---

[1] Athen., xiv. 27.   [2] *Der Dialog.*, p. 365, n. 3.   [3] vi. 97 f.
[4] In the Will of Epicurus (D.L., x. 18), the school was directed to meet on the twentieth day of the month in commemoration of Epicurus and Metrodorus. The custom was still observed in the time of Cicero.

Accusatus of Lucian, ' been a dignified person, pondering on the gods and on Nature and the Cycle of the Universe '. Now, however, his tragic mask has been snatched away, and one comic, satiric, and almost ridiculous thrust upon him. Worse still, he has become a hybrid, a centaur-like creature, neither prose nor verse, a strange phenomenon to all who hear him. (The complaint is, of course, directed against Lucian, but the main features of its indictment apply to Lucian's model Menippus.) In the *Menippus* the Cynic appears lisping in numbers, which had come from his association with Euripides and Homer in the Underworld, and it is some time before he can be called to his senses and prose. The mixture of prose and verse is found also in Varro, in the *Apocolocyntosis* of Seneca, and in Petronius, for all of which Menippus was, even if indirectly, a model.

One can only regret the loss of the writings of Menippus, our estimate of Greek humour would almost certainly have been increased had they survived. The claim made by Lucian, that he improved the Dialogue by giving good injections of Eupolis and Aristophanes, could probably be advanced for Menippus. For, like Aristophanes, his laughter ranged over Earth and Heaven and Hell : only it has lost a tone or two of geniality, it has become truly a mordant wit, that of the Cynic who γελῶν ἅμα ἔδακνεν. To Menippus the world was a vast madhouse ; as Diogenes had said, most men are so nearly lunatics that a finger's breadth would make the difference. Equally absurd are the trappings of wealth, the pedantry of learning, the vanity of beauty, and that most awful of all cosmic phenomena, the ἐκπύρωσις of the Stoics, is no more than a mummery. This is the way the world ends, not with a bang, but a—grimace.

(c) Cercidas

The connexion between Antigonus Gonatas and Bion shows the Cynic in contact with the man of affairs ; but what, if any, political result came of their relationship we lack evidence to decide. In Cercidas of Megalopolis, however, we have a man of Cynic leanings who played a very prominent part in the politics of his own city, and a not inconsiderable rôle on a larger stage. Cercidas is one of those figures whose personality has become definite in the light of the evidence of papyri.

Two Megalopolitan statesmen of that name were known, one
of whom lived in the fourth century, and was denounced by
Demosthenes [1] for having betrayed his country to the Macedonians, the other the friend of Aratus [2] who helped to bring
about the alliance between Antigonus Doson and the Achaean
League.   Which of these was the ἄριστος νομοθέτης καὶ μελιάμβων ποιητής of Stephanus of Byzantium [3] was uncertain ;
Meineke and Gerhard inclined to regard him as the older man.
That the writer of meliambic poems had Cynic leanings was
an inference from the fragment in praise of Diogenes of Sinope,
preserved by Diogenes Laertius.   Then in 1906 came the
discovery of an Oxyrhynchus papyrus, containing seven fragments, described as Κερκίδα κυνὸς μελιάμβοι, the meliambic
poems of Cercidas the Cynic.   Hunt [4] showed that the chronological evidence indicated the latter half of the third century
as the date of their author : Powell [5] that the Cercidas of that
date was the more likely to be described as νομοθέτης.   The
poems are, moreover, marked by obvious Cynic sentiments, in
some cases of peculiar relevance to current political events.
All the evidence, then, points to the conclusion that the Cynic
meliambic poet was also the friend of Aratus ; we thus have
a phenomenon unique at this period of history—a Cynic
politician.

   We first hear of Cercidas in the year 225.   It would here be
irrelevant to narrate the events which brought Aratus and
Cleomenes of Sparta face to face as rivals for the headship of
the Achaean League and supremacy in the Peloponnese.
Suffice it to say that the war between Sparta and the Achaean
League had at first found Aratus half-hearted, and the driving
force on the Achaean side had come from Sparta's old enemies,
Megalopolis and Argos.   But by 225 Cleomenes' policy and
his resources were obvious, and Aratus could be indifferent
no longer.   The year before Cleomenes had offered to come
to terms with the League, the condition being that he should
be made strategos for life ; had not a haemorrhage prevented
him from attending the League Council at Lerna, his terms
would probably have been accepted.   As it was, Aratus
secured their rejection, but his position, the work of years of

---

[1] *De Corona*, 295.   [2] Polyb., ii. 65.
[3] s.v. Μεγάλη πόλις.   [4] Ox. Pap., viii. 26 ff.
          [5] *Collectanea Alexandrina*, p. 201.

skilful, patient, and unscrupulous intrigue, was now really desperate. Luck had been on his side at Lerna ; but the troops of the Achaean League were no match for Spartans under a Cleomenes, as was shown at Hecatombaeon ; throughout the Peloponnese the masses were ready to rise for Cleomenes and revolution ; there was the threat of an alliance between Sparta and the Aetolians. Help could only come from one quarter ; Aratus, who had won his ascendancy by driving the Macedonians out of the Peloponnese, must bring them back again to retain it. The story of the negotiations which brought Macedon into the war, and the campaigns leading up to the decisive battle of Sellasia, are of absorbing interest, heightened by the good fortune that we have accounts written from opposite standpoints. The pro-Spartan history of Phylarchus seems to have been Plutarch's chief source for his *Life of Cleomenes* ; while Aratus' own memoirs are generally conceded to have been followed in the account of Polybius. Certainly the ingenious piece of special pleading with which the negotiations with Antigonus are justified is not unworthy of that politician.

Perceiving the Achaean League to be in desperate straits . . . [says Polybius (or Aratus)], and knowing that Antigonus was a man of energy, and of sense, and moreover of some pretensions to honour ; but knowing full well that kings always measure their friends and foes by the sole standard of expediency . . . Aratus determined to come to terms with the said monarch, pointing out to him what would be the most likely result of the political situation. . . . And he had to act in a very overt way, on many occasions being compelled to do and say things in public which were quite contrary to his real intentions, so as to keep his designs hidden by creating the exact opposite impression. Hence some things he has not written about even in his Memoirs.[1]

What masterpieces of dissimulation are thus withheld we can but speculate : but what is revealed is disingenuous enough.
 The Macedonian had to be approached : but how to do it ? The obvious answer was through Megalopolis, ever since her foundation anti-Laconian, and as a corollary the ally of whatever Northern power wished to curb the influence of Sparta in the Peloponnese. The Megalopolitans had borne the brunt of

[1] Polyb., ii. 48 ff.

the war against Cleomenes, so an appeal would come well from them, and Aratus had family friends there, Cercidas and Nicophanes, who would be well qualified to make it. So, on the suggestion of Aratus, Cercidas and Nicophanes proposed to the Megalopolitans that envoys should be appointed to seek the alliance of Antigonus, if they could first get the permission of the League. (No doubt it was a principle of the Achaean League that any alteration of foreign policy by one of its members must be with the consent of the League Council, but clearly this move suited Aratus well. He could sound the opinions of the Council on a Macedonian alliance, and if they were unfavourable, the odium would rest on Megalopolis.) The embassy was approved by the Megalopolitans, and in due course by the League Council, and Cercidas and Nicophanes went to the court of Antigonus. To him ' they said very little about the affairs of their own city, but spoke as Aratus instructed them ', that is, they urged on the King the advantages of an alliance between Macedon and the Achaean League at that particular moment. ' Aratus would see that good terms were offered : he would also tell the King just when his help was required.' Antigonus recognized that Aratus' summary of the political situation was true, and perhaps he, too, rejoiced at the prospect of alliance with one whose sole standard was expediency. At all events, he gave the envoys to understand that help from him could be looked for when needed. Nicophanes seems to have played the leading part in this embassy. Cercidas may have been chosen because he stood well at the Macedonian Court through his kinship with the pro-Macedonian Cercidas of the time of Demosthenes. The envoys then returned to Megalopolis, and in the spring of 224 reported their mission to the League. Megalopolis, they said, had obtained the goodwill of Antigonus, whose aid they could now count on. Thereupon Aratus, who had private information from Nicophanes of the King's attitude, rose to his feet. He was delighted to hear of the King's sympathy, but would it not be more honourable if they could win the war by themselves ? Macedon should only be brought in as a last resort. It was a masterly stroke : secure in the knowledge that Antigonus would come in when *he* gave the word, Aratus had covered his tracks from every one but the King and his friends, the envoys of Megalopolis ; the latter, if they had any sense of humour, must have found the Council of 224 very satisfying. But, as Aratus doubtless expected, the League soon proved quite incapable of resisting Cleomenes by itself ; the duress of events forced Aratus to sacrifice his quixotic sense of honour for his country's good. Antigonus was called in. But the troubles of Megalopolis were not over ; in 223 Cleomenes captured the city, though most of the citizens succeeded in escaping to Messene. What then happened is not quite clear, apparently Cleomenes offered to spare the city if the inhabitants would return as his allies. The terms were rejected, it is said at the instance of the young Philopoemen, and Cleomenes razed the city to the ground. Cercidas would seem to have been amongst those who escaped to Messene, for we next hear of him as commanding the thousand Megalo-politans, exiles who fought on the Achaean side at Sellasia. But the honours of that day were not to be with the higher officers among the Megalopolitans, but with Philopoemen, who saw the psychological moment to attack, and seized it in the face of their orders. Sellasia was decisive, Cleomenes fled into exile ; Aratus returned to the headship of the Archaean League ; and the inhabitants of Megalopolis to their ruined city. Over the refounding and rebuilding of the city there was much dispute and bitterness, and a reform party proposed to reduce the city to a size which could more easily be defended, and to provide for additional citizens by dividing up a third of the land of existing landowners. They met with strenuous opposition, and Antigonus appointed Prytanis, an eminent member of the Peripatetic school, as νομοθέτης.[1] The code he proposed caused violent controversy, and the dispute was not settled till 217, through the mediation of Aratus. It seems highly probable that this was the occasion on which Cercidas distinguished himself as νομοθέτης.[2]

There had been nothing of the Cynic cosmopolitanism about Cercidas' conduct in standing so resolutely by his country in her misfortunes, and in being so concerned about the right ordering of her own political affairs. Not for him the indiffer-ence of Crates, asked by Alexander if he favoured the restora-tion of Thebes after her fall, ' Why should it be restored ? Perhaps another Alexander would destroy it again.' [3] Cercidas

---

[1] *Pol.*, v. 93.   [2] See Note 5 to Chap. III.
[3] D.L., vi. 93.

had been a citizen of Megalopolis, not the fellow-citizen of Diogenes in the κόσμος. But in one very remarkable fragment [1] we see how his Cynic leanings influenced his political views.

(Why does not God) choose out Xenon, that greedy cormorant of the well-lined purse, the child of licentiousness, and make him the child of poverty, giving to us who deserve it the silver that now runs to waste ? What could prevent it (ask God that question, since it is easy for him to bring about whatever his mind resolves) that the man who ruins wealth by pouring out what he has or the filthy-dross-stained usurer, should be drained of their swine-befouled wealth, and the money now wasted given to him that has but his daily bread, and dips his cup at the common bowl ? Has Justice then the sight of a mole, does Phaethon squint with a single pupil, is the vision dimmed of Themis the bright ? How can one hold them for gods that lack eyes to see and ears to hear ? Yet men say that the dread king, lord of the lightning, sits in mid-olympus holding the scales of justice, and never nods. So says Homer in the *Iliad*. ' He doth incline the scale to the mighty of valour, when the day of fate is at hand.' Why then does the impartial balancer never incline to *me* ? ' But the Brygians, [2] dregs of humanity (yet I dread to say it), see how far they swing down in their favour the scales of Zeus ! What lords, then, what sons of Ouranos shall a man find, that he may have justice ? For Zeus, father of us all, verily is a father to some, to others but a step-father. Best leave the problem to astrologers ; I think for them it will be a light task to solve. But for us, let us have a care for Paean, and for Sharing—she is indeed a goddess—and Retribution that walketh the earth. While the godhead blows a favourable wind astern, hold her in honour ; but though mortals fare well, yet shall a sudden wind blow vaunted wealth and proud fortune away. Who then shall vomit them back to you from the deep ? '

Can we date this remarkable outburst against social inequality ? Tarn thinks it emanates from the period when the reforms of Cleomenes were arousing the oppressed classes throughout the Peloponnese. Cercidas, he says, ' is actually found preaching philanthropy and exhorting his fellows ' (i.e. the governing classes) ' to heal the sick and give to the poor while they had time, otherwise the social revolution might be

---

[1] Fr. 4 (Powell).

[2] Reading, with Knox, τὰ δ' ἔσχατα Βρυγία Μυσῶν. Powell reads τὰ δ' ἔσχατα βρυτία Μυσῶν.

upon them and their wealth taken away '.[1] But this seems to
miss the bitterness of the passage : Cercidas does not speak
of himself as one of the governing classes, but rather as one
oppressed by the unequal distribution of wealth. ' Why not
give to us the wealth that flows on useless expense ? ' and
again, ' Why does the impartial balancer never incline the
scales to me ? '

We know from Polybios that social distress was particularly
rife in Megalopolis about the time of the refounding of the
city after its destruction by Cleomenes, and I suggest that it
is to these years that we must assign the poem. Polybius says
that there was a party which proposed to force men of property
to contribute a third of their land to make up the numbers of
new citizens required ; and it is significant that the poem twice
refers to the division of superfluous wealth for redistribution
amongst the poor. The bitterness of the reference to Xeno
harmonizes well with the ' disputes, jealousies, and mutual
hatreds ' which Polybius says were rife amongst the Megalopolitans. If we accept Knox's attractive suggestion that τὰ
δ' ἔσχατα βρυγία Μυσῶν are the Macedonians, the nature of the
allusion (ἅζομαι δὲ θὴν λεγειν) is understandable. Cercidas,
who had played a leading part in securing the Macedonian
alliance, could hardly complain if its results were unsatisfactory. That Antigonus would do little for the reforming party
is likely enough, as Tarn says, Macedonia was always the
bulwark of law and order and the existing state of affairs.
The Peripatetics, too, were always more or less dependent on
Macedonian protection, and it is likely that the code of Prytanis, which caused so much dispute, unduly favoured the
wealthy. On this interpretation, the poem is not a warning
to the governing classes to mend their ways while there is time,
but a call to the party of reform not to wait for the vengeance
of Heaven to strike the rich, but to act themselves under the
inspiration of a new triad of deities, Paean and Sharing, and
Nemesis. The tone in which the false deities of popular belief
are assailed is essentially Cynic, as is the attack on luxury.
The three deities are especially interesting. As Hunt well
observes, the Cynics had a particular reverence for doctors,
they themselves were ἰατροί of men's souls, so the reference
to Paean is readily intelligible, it implies healing both physically

[1] Cambridge Ancient History, Vol. vii, p. 755.

and spiritually. What of Sharing (Μετάδως) ? Cercidas was
an enthusiast on the old poets, and doubtless knew the line of
Hesiod, ' Giving (Δὼς) is a good wench, but Thieving a bad
one, the bringer of Death '. Μετάδως would be a very suitable
deity for a party whose programme included land-distribution,
and one can understand the commendation θεὸς γὰρ ἄντα.
Νεμέσις κατὰ γᾶν is thus not named as a threat to the wealthy
that Cleomenes and the Spartans will be upon them, but perhaps a reminder to the party of reform that they have to fulfil
on earth the functions assigned to Zeus in heaven. As for the
wealthy, at present the winds blow fair, but let them beware
a sudden squall.

The other fragments of Cercidas can be more briefly dealt
with. Powell fragment 5 amplifies the saying of Euripides
—that Love has two breezes (δισσὰ πνεύματα πνεῖς "Ερως) to
enforce the Cynic maxim that the sexual instincts should be
gratified with as little trouble as possible. One should avoid
the *grande affaire* ; ' against whomsoever Aphrodite's son
loosens his left jaw, rousing the whirlwinds and hurricanes of
passion, their voyage is ever beset with unending turmoils of
waves '. The wise man will not embark on such a stormy
voyage when a calmer passage may be had. ' Take Aphrodite
that walks the market-place, she brings not repentance. She's
there whenever you like, whenever you want her, nothing to
fear or fret over. For an obol you may lie with her, and think
yourself son-in-law to Tyndarus.' Fiske [1] deals very fully
with the conception of ' Venus parabilis ' in the literature of
Epicureans, and with the obvious imitations of this passage of
Cercidas in Lucilius, and more especially in Horace, satire II.
He suggests with some probability that Cercidas' simile of the
stormy and the calm voyages of love is influenced by Epicurus'
contrast of the tempest of the soul (χειμὼν τῆς ψυχῆς), and the
calm of the soul (γαλήνη).

Another fragment,[2] much mutilated, appears to be an attack
on music as an enervating influence. Apollo is the god of
' races who dwell in the shade, of mortals benumbed by
pleasure, avoiding toil '. The offsprings of ' the lofty-tragic-
goddess (Music) ' are ' the Phrygian eunuch with puffed cheeks
and the Lydian harlot '. Cynic parallels are readily found.
Diogenes [3] would ' marvel that musicians should tune the

[1] *Lucilius and Horace*, p. 250 ff.   [2] Powell, fr. 6.   [3] D.L., vi. 27.

strings of the lyre, while leaving discordant the disposition of their souls ', and Bion ' in general made sport of music and geometry '—we have as a sample his attack on Archytas ' born of the strings, happy in his conceit, skilled beyond all men to awake the bass note of discord '.[1]

Powell fragments 8 and 9 are joined by Knox ; the general sense is clear enough, the Stoics of Cercidas' time are attacked as having degenerated from the standard of Zeno. The text is in very bad condition, particularly fragment 9, so that there are many doubtful readings.[2] Knox's restoration of fragment 9, lines 1–7, suggests an attack on the preoccupation of the Stoics with dialectic, and their neglect of discipline. ' Petti-fogging lawyers they, babbling pitiful nonsense, and whetting well their pointed tongues, no habit of discipline blunteth, nor fatigue, its bitter edge.' Fragment 8 explicitly alludes to ' Sphaerus ' as one of these degenerates ; this is almost cer-tainly Sphaerus of Bosporus, the philosophic adviser of Cleo-menes of Sparta. In the list of his writings given by Diogenes Laertius are works on Similars, on Definitions, on Contra-dictory Statements, on Predicates, on Ambiguous terms, and a *Handbook of Dialectic* in two volumes, besides treatises on ' physical ' subjects, such as the sense-organs, and minimal parts ($\pi\varepsilon\varrho\grave{\iota}$ $\grave{\varepsilon}\lambda\alpha\chi\acute{\iota}\sigma\tau\omega\nu$). All such occupations would come within the sphere of $\tau\tilde{\upsilon}\varphi o\varsigma$ to the Cynic. Throughout the two fragments is evidence that the erotic practices of Sphaerus and his associates are unfavourably contrasted with the ' $\check{\varepsilon}\varrho\omega\varsigma$ $Z\alpha\nu\omega\nu\iota\varkappa\acute{o}\varsigma$ ' ' the love of a Zeno '.

Fragment 2 quotes an animal proverb. ' Remember what the wrinkled tortoise said, " Truly home is dearest and best ".' Whether these lines can be linked on to fragment 5, as Knox suggests, is highly doubtful. The tortoise ' happy in its thick shell ' might well typify the Cynic $\grave{\alpha}\pi\acute{\alpha}\theta\varepsilon\iota\alpha$; Gerhard quotes Plutarch for the tortoise as a symbol of $o\grave{\iota}\varkappa o\upsilon\varrho\acute{\iota}\alpha$ and $\sigma\iota\acute{\omega}\pi\eta$, and suggests that its affection for its home typifies Diogenes' attachment to his tub ! But perhaps we are here dealing not with that sagacious animal, but with the other tortoise who rashly desired to quit his lowly station and see the wonders of the upper air, and who came to a bad end.[3] The animal

---

[1] D.L., iv. 52. [2] See Note 6 to Chap. III.
[3] Cf. Aesop's Fables : The eagle and the tortoise : quoted by Powell.

is thus warning us from the wisdom of experience, against the folly of μεμψιμοιρία.

Fragment 1 is the encomium of Diogenes quoted in Diogenes Laertius, hailing him as ' rightly named the offspring of Zeus, and the Heavenly Dog '. Fragment 3 apparently assails those addicted to τρυφή. ' How can they see wisdom standing close at hand . . . men whose heart with mud is filled, and with lees whose stain may not be washed away ? '

Cercidas was the inventor of the meliambic measure ; from a statement in Athenaeus it appears that he wrote iambics also. Knox [1] maintains with great force that the iambic verses contained in two second-century papyri, Londinensis 155, and Heidelberg Pap. 310, form part of a moral anthology compiled by Cercidas. The Cynic sympathies of the author at least of the Heidelberg fragment are unmistakable, and it is likely enough that some such anthology, which would fulfil the same use as a collection of χρεῖαι, would be compiled by a Cynic. The ideas underlying these fragments, and the parallels throughout Greek literature, are fully discussed by Gerhard ; [2] their spirit is akin to that of the diatribes of Teles, together with which they will be briefly considered.

There is no evidence to decide how long Cercidas lived after the νομοθεσία of 217 ; Powell fragment 7 is his address to his soul when on the threshold of old age. It is the declaration of a man who had enjoyed his life, and certainly Cercidas had had a full one. He had been in contact with great political figures of the day, had negotiated with Antigonus Doson, and seen from the inside the subtle workings of the policy of Aratus, he had been present on that July day at Sellasia when Sparta fought one of her greatest battles and suffered, in effect, her final defeat. Of all this there is no direct mention ; his thoughts are on the delights of literature, and of the frugal life.

Oft will a man unwillingly close his eyes in surrender, though not beaten ; but thou didst have an unshakeable heart [3] within thy breast, and one unconquered by all the cares that attend flesh-

---

[1] *The First Greek Anthologist*, Cambridge, 1922.
[2] *Phoenix von Kolophon*, Leipzig, 1909.
[3] Of the perseverance shown by the Megalopolitan exiles after the sack of the city ?

wasting luxury. No good thing evèr escaped thee, ever within thy affections were all the cublings of the Muses. Thou hast been a hunter, my soul, of all the Pierian maids, and a most keen tracker. But now are a few white hairs round the fringes of thy cheeks. . . .[1]

' Thou wast a hunter, my soul, of the Pierian maids ' . . . whether it refers to his own works, to his enthusiasm for literature in general, or more narrowly to his industry as an anthologist, it is an odd reversal of the epitaph of Aeschylus, who says nothing of his glory as a tragedian, but only that he fought at Marathon. Yet here is no reference to Sellasia. Cercidas' devotion to literature passed into tradition. ' He ordered Books I and II of the *Iliad* to be buried with him,' we are told ;[2] and Aelian[3] describes how

A man from Megalopolis in Arcadia, Cercidas by name, being about to die, told his sorrowing kinsmen that he gladly departed this life, for, he said, he had hopes of meeting Pythagoras amongst the philosophers, of the historians Hecataeus, of musicians, Olympus, and of poets—Homer. So saying, he gave up the ghost.

In the Apology, Socrates declared himself ready to meet a hundred deaths, if he might meet Orpheus and Musaeus, Hesiod and Homer.

The name of Cercidas was gratefully remembered by his fellow-citizens ; and in Stephanus of Byzantium the notice under Megalopolis reads, ' that is where Cercidas came from, that excellent lawgiver and meliambic poet '. Gregory Nazianzen refers to him as ὁ φίλτατος, and his verses were echoed by Lucilius and Horace. In the years after 240 Megalopolis produced a succession of noteworthy men, the far-seeing tyrant Lydiades, Philopoemen, ' the last of the Greeks ', and the historian Polybius. To their company one must admit Cercidas, ' ἄριστος νομοθέτης καὶ μελιάμβων ποιητής '.

(d) Teles

It is a curious turn of literary fortune that Teles, apparently a fourth-rate writer of little originality, known in no reference

---

[1] Knox takes the passage to refer to the compilation of the anthology, the ' cublings of the Muses ' were the improving passages ; Cercidas congratulates himself on his diligence, he never missed a reference (τῷ τιν διεφεῦγε καλῶν οὐδὲν ποκα).

[2] *Apud. Phot.*, 190 (151 Bekk).   [3] *Hist.*, xiii. 20.

of earlier date than Stobaeus, should be represented by larger fragments than Crates, Bion, and Menippus, whose works were admired and frequently alluded to in classical times. Teles comes down to us in extracts made by Stobaeus from an ἐπιτομή made by an otherwise unknown Theodorus [1]— there may have been other middlemen involved in the process. The fragments are edited and the date and sources of Teles discussed in Hense, *Teletis reliquiae* ; he has also occupied the attention of Wilamowitz [2] and Cronert.[3] As a result of these studies it is known that Teles was a Megarian schoolmaster who flourished in the second half of the third century ; the one reference which can be definitely dated shows that the diatribe περὶ φυγῆς was composed later than 240,[4] and delivered to an audience of youths at Megara ; Teles has a Megarian name, his writings employ certain Doric forms, and he alludes to himself as παιδαγωγός.[5] The seven fragments are diatribes ; four on such familiar Cynic themes as Exile, Self-Sufficiency, Poverty and Wealth ; that entitled περὶ περιστασέων is a warning against μεμψιμοιρία ; while two have a polemical purpose, being respectively directed against the Hedonist doctrine that Pleasure is the End, and the popular view that outward appearance is the true criterion of justice (περὶ τοῦ δοκεῖν καὶ τοῦ εἶναι).

A literary judgement of Teles must be based on the evidence we possess, and can only be unfavourable. It is of course always possible that this evidence does him much less than justice ; it is uncertain whether his diatribes were published as delivered or from the notes of an auditor, and in all ages it is the fate of lecturers to be remembered for their jokes rather than for their matter. But in six of the seven fragments, if we take away borrowed passages and anecdotes, Teles himself is represented by little more than a few connecting sentences. This may be due to the successive " cuttings " of Theodorus, Stobaeus, and whatever other epitomators took a hand in it ; but it implies at least that Teles' own work was less interesting than what he quoted. A further difficulty is

---

[1] Conjectured to have been a Cynic of the time of the revival of Cynicism in the first century A.D. But definite evidence is lacking.
[2] Antigonus von Karystus, *Exkurs. Der kynischer prediger Teles.*
[3] *Kolotes und Menedemos*, pp. 37–47.
[4] 16. 3.   [5] 16. 13.

that Theodorus (presumably) maintains an annoying running commentary to ensure that his reader is missing nothing— 'You see the joke?' he asks anxiously, and again, on the bravery of Spartan women, 'What woman of our day would have acted thus?' These comments are not always easy to distinguish from what may have been Teles' remarks to his class, e.g. 'Would any of us have gone to sleep in such circumstances?' (of Socrates' fortitude in prison). But in the first diatribe there is less extraneous matter than in the others and some judgement can be formed of Teles' style.

A. They say it is better to seem just than to be just. Well, is it better to seem good than to be good? B. Hardly. A. Again, are actors esteemed for seeming to be good, or for being good? B. For being good. A. And do men become accounted good harpists by seeming to be good harpists, or for being good? B. For being good. A. And in general, do men become successful in all things rather by seeming to be good, or by being good? B. By being good. A. By the presence of that quality success is assured, rather than by its absence ; so that it does seem a better thing to be good than to seem good, and the just man is good, not he who appears to be just. . . .

And so on. However edifying this may have been to the youth of Megara, it is deficient in both literary and logical virtues.

But, like many bad authors, Teles is of interest in reflecting the literary tastes of his audience. His great heroes are Socrates, Diogenes, and Crates ; and Cynic literature is freely quoted, especially Bion. There are references to οἱ ἀρχαῖοι, presumably the older Cynic authors, and explicit quotations from Crates and Metrocles, though it cannot be decided whether he got them at first hand, or, as Hense maintains, through Bion, or through books of χρεῖαι.[1] Socrates he knows at best through the Xenophontic tradition ; the allusion to the *Phaedo* [2] can hardly be at first hand, for it is coupled with a magnificent howler about the last words of Socrates which argues a very dubious source. Stilpo is naturally drawn upon as an eminent Megarian philosopher. Of quotations from the poets the great majority are from Homer, in all ages the school-

---

[1] 35. 4. There is one definite allusion to the Κράτητος ἀπομνημο- νεύματα of Zeno.
[2] 11. 15 ; 12. 1.

book of Hellas. The only gnomic poet quoted is Theognis.
Of the tragedians Euripides is quoted six times, Sophocles
once, Aeschylus not at all ; there are several quotations from
unknown authors. The Old Comedy is not quoted, and the
New Comedy represented by Philemon and not Menander.
Finally there are references to mythological characters such as
Heracles, Cadmus, Tantalus, Oedipus, and Perseus, to familiar
historical personages, Aristeides, Lysander, Callias, and to
contemporaries, Ptolemy, Antigonus, Chremonides. Several
admiring references to Sparta imply that her valorous conduct
on such occasions as her resistance to Pyrrhus maintained
during the third century the Spartan reputation for ἀνδρεία.
The taste catered for is clearly a popular one whose chief
interest lay in the didactic aspect of literature.

Whatever our disparagement of Teles as a writer, we can
but be grateful that these fragments have been preserved ;
without them we should know little of third-century diatribe
or of Bion.

(e) Educational Theory
The Cynics had always laid great stress on παιδεία though
Teles is the only known case of a Cynic schoolmaster. During
the third century Cynic works on education appeared in which
Diogenes was depicted as the ideal παιδαγωγός ; two such
books known to us were the Παιδαγωγικός of Cleomenes [1]
and the Διογένους πρᾶσις of Eubulus.[2] The fragment preserved from the latter is of especial interest, for it outlines a
curriculum supposed to have been adopted by Diogenes in
educating the sons of his master Xeniades of Corinth. ' After
their other studies he taught them to ride, to shoot with the
bow, to sling stones and hurl javelins. He also took them out
hunting.' . . . Such exercises were presumably recommended
as involving πόνος, and it is interesting to be told that ' in
the wrestling-school he would not permit the master to give
them full athletic training, but only sufficient to keep them
in colour and in good condition '. The Cynics deprecated
specialization in athletics and several apophthegms directed
against athletes were attributed to Diogenes.[3] ' He would

---

[1] D.L., vi. 75.
[2] id., ib. 30, presumably Eubulus was himself a Cynic.
[3] id., ib. 27, 33, 49, 68, &c.

wonder that men would strive to out-do each other in digging and kicking, and yet no one strove to become a good man ' : ' Athletes are so stupid because they are built up of pigs'-flesh and bulls'-flesh ' ; a victory at the Great Games was won over slaves, the Cynic's victory over men. The point was, of course, that the athlete's abounding energy might be better directed. The boys' intellectual development was to be secured by ' making them learn by heart many passages from the poets, historians, and the works of Diogenes himself ; and he would try every short cut to improve their memories '. We see from the quotations and historical allusions in Teles that the poets and historians were esteemed for their didactic value, they provided λόγοι χρηστόι. As for behaviour, ' he taught them to wait on themselves, to eat plain food, and to drink water. They were made to crop their hair, and wear it unadorned, and to go about lightly clad and barefoot; in the streets they were to be silent and not to stare about them.' The educational programme thus fostered on Diogenes is a compound of various existing systems, interpreted in a Cynic spirit. The ordinary Greek elementary education (τὰ γράμματα) forms its backbone, augmented by features derived from Sparta (hunting) and from the Persian system described by Xenophon in the *Cyropaedia* (shooting with the bow, riding). The regimen is that of the Cynic αὐτάρκεια, but the aim of the system is not to produce little Cynics, as παιδαγωγός in the literal, ἰατρός in a figurative sense, the Cynic labours not on behalf of his movement but of mankind.

The papyri [1] dealing with the theme of αἰσχροκέρδεια are on the same literary level as the diatribes of Teles. They are obviously part of an anthology ; Knox's theory that the compilation is due to Cercidas is attractive and probable. Addressed to a certain Parnos, who ' lends a ready ear to ennobling verse ',[2] they are an expression of disgust at an age of shameless commercialism whose keynote is the line of Sophocles,

Faith withers, and Faithlessness comes to flower.

---

[1] Londinensis 155 ; Pap. Bod. MS., Gr. F. 1, Heidelberg Pap. 210. I follow Knox in regarding them as connected.
[2] On Knox's reading.

The author announces his own intention of abiding by ' That old rule of simplicity, to be no slave of luxury, nor of the stomach's pleasures '. Though Business Ethics have driven Faith and Justice from the earth, and Zeus and the gods of popular belief are apparently impotent, the righteous man can live in the knowledge that a day will come . . . ' for I see many who grow rich on shamelessness, yet their wealth all vanished as though it had never been '. There follows a remarkable outburst.

> ἔστιν γὰρ ἔστιν, ὃς τάδε σκοπεῖ δαίμων
> ὃς ἐν χρόνῳ τὸ θεῖον ὂν καταισχύνει,
> νέμει δ' ἑκάστῳ τὴν καταίσιον μοῖραν

The deity in question is, one may conjecture, Nemesis ; Theophrastus, asked what powers govern human life, answered Ἐνεργεσία καὶ τιμωρία, divinities also recognized by Democritus.[1] To enforce the warning against αἰσχροκέρδεια an iambic poem of Phoenix of Colophon is cited ; it deals with profiteers where ' houses are fair and noble and worth a fortune, but they themselves would be no bargain at three obols a head '. Gerhard's very full discussion of these fragments shows how the ' commonplaces ' and similes they contain are those regarded as especially appropriate to the theme of αἰσχροκέρδεια ; and Fiske points out the parallels in Horace, Satires, i. 1.

NOTES TO CHAPTER III

1. The data are as follows.   Diogenes Laertius includes Bion amongst the adherents of the Academy, after Arcesilaus (ἐχομένως Ἀρκεσιλάῳ). He speaks of him as one of the pupils of Crates the Academic (iv. 23) ; then in the biography of Bion comes the following passage : οὗτος τὴν ἀρχὴν μὲν προῄρητο[2] τὰ Ἀκαδημαϊκά, καθ' ὃν χρόνον ἤκουε Κράτητος· εἶτ' ἐπανείλετο τὴν κυνικήν ἀγωγήν, λάβων τρίβωνα καὶ πήραν. καὶ τί γὰρ ἄλλο μετεσκεύασεν αὐτὸν πρὸς ἀπαθείαν ; ἔπειτα ἐπὶ τὰ Θεοδώρεια μετῆλθε διακούσας Θεοδώρου τοῦ ἀθέου κατὰ πᾶν εἶδος λόγου σοφιστευόντος· μεθ' οὗ Θεοφράστου διήκουσε τοῦ περιπατητικοῦ. This certainly seems to imply a sequence, but as it stands it involves some confusion, for, as Zeller points out, Crates was not head of the Academy till c. 276 B.C.   He thinks Crates the Academic is confused with Xenocrates or with Crates the Cynic, and von Arnim in Pauly-

---

[1] See Powell, op. cit., p. 206.
[2] παρῃτεῖτο Hunt followed by Hicks.

Wissowa agrees.[1] Gomperz on the other hand refuses to attach any significance to the Laertian chronology, further remarking that there is no reason why Bion should not have heard the Academic Crates before he was scholarch. In this he is followed by Hense, who gives a quotation (from the *Acad. Phil. Ind. Herc.*, xvi. 62, 30) which makes Bion one of the pupils of this Crates.

But the order Cynic–Theodorus (whom Zeller believes to have visited Athens in 306)–Theophrastus involves no chronological difficulty ; furthermore, a passage of Laertius [2] definitely associates him with Xenocrates, who died in 314. Again, the reading παρῃτεῖτο deserves more attention than it has received from Gomperz and Hense. Hicks [3] adopts it and translates ' Bion at the outset used to deprecate the Academic doctrines, even when a pupil of Crates '. If we accept Zeller's view that Crates the Academic has been confused with Xenocrates, this difficulty is resolved. D.L., iv. 10 shows Bion ' mocking ' at Xenocrates. ' Xenocrates, when mocked by Bion, refused to reply, saying that tragedy does not deign to answer the banter of comedy.' The anecdote which follows is perhaps not without significance. To an unnamed person who wished to attend his lectures, Xenocrates said, ' Go away, you give philosophy nothing to catch hold of.' Bion joined in the Cynic deprecation of astronomy and grammar and similar ' useless ' pursuits ; [4] it is perhaps not wholly fanciful to suggest that he may have been the ill-prepared student in question. Of course, Bion *may* have heard Crates lecture before he became scholarch. Crates was on the most intimate terms with Polemon, head of the Academy from 314 to 276 ; Bion was probably in Athens for the greater part of this time. But in any case the doctrines of the Academy seem to have had little or no effect on Bion's thought.

2. The relevant passage of Diogenes Laertius runs as follows—ἦν 'δὲ καὶ θεατρικὸς καὶ πολὺς ἐν τῷ γελοίως διαφορῆσαι, φορτικοῖς ὀνόμασι κατὰ τῶν πραγμάτων χρώμενος. διὰ δὴ οὖν τὸ παντὶ εἴδει λόγου κεκρᾶσθαι φασι λέγειν ἐπ' αὐτοῦ τὸν Ἐρατοσθένην, ὡς πρῶτος Βίων φιλοσοφίαν ἀνθινὰ ἐνέδυσεν.

This passage has engaged the attention of Wachsmuth,[5] Hense, and Fiske, and their interpretations leave its meaning fairly clear. The chief point of difference between them is the exact value to be attached to θεατρικός : Wachsmuth thinks it refers to the little mime-like scenes, the προσωποποΐα, which Bion frequently employed ; Hense more broadly refers it to the whole stylistic method of Bion, which was more adapted to the stage than to the works of philosophy, ' theatricus enim mihi audit philosophus qui philosophatur πρὸς ὄχλον καὶ θέατρον qui in speciem laborat risum captans . . . magnoque intervallo separatur ab illo cui alter philosophus satis magnum theatrum est.' [6] Fiske follows this interpretation, further adducing

---

[1] s.v. Bion. [2] iv. 10. [3] Loeb edition. D.L., 1. 429.
[4] Stob., 2. 1. 30 ; 3. 4. 32. D.L., iv. 53.
[5] *Sill. Graec.*, p. 76. [6] *Tel. Rel.*, lvii–lix.

the sensationalism of Bion's methods, as exemplified by the story of the sailors at Rhodes.[1] The phrase καὶ πολύς . . . χρώμενος he ' refers to the diction of Bion, which was absolutely realistic.' Finally the mixing of ' every style of diction ' clad the works of Bion in flowery garments (ἀνθινά) unbecoming the σεμνότης of philosophy. These criticisms suggest the standard of the Plain Style formulated by the Stoics Diogenes of Babylon and Panaetius, which, as Fiske [2] shows, go back to the Peripatetic doctrines of τὸ πρέπον, a probability increased by the fact that the criticism about the ἀνθινά seems to have been made in the first place by Theophrastus.

The five merits of style, according to Diogenes, were pure Greek ('Ελληνισμός), conciseness (συντομία), clearness (σαφηνεία), appropriateness (τὸ πρέπον), and distinction (κατασκευή).[3] Panaetius developed this theory, in particular enlarging the concept of τὸ πρέπον ' from the field of aesthetics to the field of ethics '.[4] From Cicero we gather that Panaetius repudiated the Cynic παρρησία as an offence against decency. ' Cynicorum vera ratio tota est eicienda : est enim inimica verecundiae, sine qua nihil recte esse potest, nihil iucundum.' [5] The φόρτικα ὀνόματα of Bion were doubtless included with the ' obscena verba ' of Diogenes in this condemnation. The phrase καὶ πολύς . . . χρώμενος, taken as a whole, suggests a charge of βωμολοχία, scurrilous jesting, which Cicero, again following Panaetius, describes as ' illiberale, petulans, flagitiosum, obscenum.' [6] The ' theatrical ' nature of Bion's style was inappropriate for philosophy, and hence offended against τὸ πρέπον ; the φόρτικα ὀνόματα violated the canon of 'Ελληνισμός, which does not employ ' the language of the streets ' (μὴ εἰκαία συνηθεία), and of κατασκευή, which is λέξις ἐκπεφευγυῖα τὸν ἰδιωτισμόν. The inference is therefore that these criticisms of Bion's style come from a period when the adherents of the Stoic theory of the Plain Style were rejecting the παρρησία of the Cynics for the εὐτραπελία of the Socratic writers. If this is so, the source from which Diogenes Laertius derives this portion of the life of Bion will probably be of the first century B.C. or later ; unless we regard him as deriving directly from Panaetius a likely guess would be Diocles.

3. As in the following examples : (a) Stob. 11. 20. 7. ' Bion says that astronomers were ridiculous for pretending that they know all about the fish in the sky, though they neglect the fish on the beach.' Similar remarks are attributed to Diogenes, who ' would marvel that astronomers would look at the sun and the moon, and neglect matters close at hand '.[7] Again, ' a certain astronomer was exhibiting a map of the heavens in the agora—here, he said, are the eccentric stars—

---

[1] D.L., iv. 53
[2] For a full discussion of the plain style see Fiske, op. cit., reference in Index *sub* Panaetius.
[3] D.L., vii. 59.   [4] Fiske, op. cit., p. 73.   [5] *de Offic.*, i. 148.
[6] ib., i. 128.   [7] D.L., vi. 28.

" Don't lie," said Diogenes, " the eccentrics are not there but here "
(pointing to the spectators).'¹ Astronomers, in fact, had been used
as examples of πολυπραγμόνες ever since the Thracian servant-girl
jeered at Thales.² (b) Another variation on the theme of πλανώμενοι.
' Bion said that grammarians who busy themselves on the wanderings of Odysseus are heedless of their own ; nor do they discern
that they are themselves astray on this very point, i.e. that they are
wasting their time on valueless pursuits.' ³ With this compare the
story that Diogenes ' would wonder that men should study the woes
of Odysseus, when they are ignorant of their own '.⁴ Wilamowitz
thinks that the similarity of these dicta of Bion and Diogenes is
explained by their occurrence in books of χρεῖαι ; notably that
compiled by Zeno, and that the names have got mixed. Hense
accounts for the confusion by the familiar habit of the ancients of
quoting without acknowledging their sources.

4. The date of the *Characters* is taken to be 319 or earlier ; if we
take the statement of Diogenes Laertius that Bion studied under
Theophrastus after he had heard Theodorus, we get a date for their
association some time after 306. The delineation of character-types
had in the meantime been perfected by the poets of the New Comedy,
especially by Philemon and Menander, the latter also the pupil of
Theophrastus. That Bion was interested in the analysis of character
is confirmed by the apophthegms which appear in Laertius as well as
by passages in Teles generally assumed to be quoting Bion ; in
almost every case a parallel can be found in Theophrastus. Thus,
Bion retorts to an ἀδολέσχης—τὸ ανὸν σοὶ ποισω, ἐὰν παρακλήτους
πέμψῃς καὶ αὐτὸς μὴ ἔλθῃς.⁵ 'Αδολεσχία is the subject of one
of the Theophrastean character-sketches, κ' ἂν ὑπομένη τις' αὐτοῦ
μὴ ἀφιστάσθαι (παρασείσαντα δὴ δεῖ τοὺς τοιούτους τῶν ἀνθρώπων καὶ
διαραμενον ἀπαλλάττεσθαι). Again, Bion says of a wealthy miser,
' He has not acquired a fortune, it has acquired him ' ; and ' Misers
take care of their property as though it belonged to them, but get
no more benefit from it than if it belonged to others '. Of the
μικρόλογος Theophrastus says, ' των μικρολόγων τὰς ἀργυροθήκας ἔστιν
ἰδεῖν εὐρωτιώσας, αὐτοὺς δὲ φοροῦντας ἐλάττω τῶν μηρῶν τὰ ἱμάτια.
Of the other Theophrastean types, we find in Bion references to
the ἀλάζων, δεισιδαίμων, μεψιμοιρῶν. The βάσκανος of D.L. 51
may be compared with the κακολόγος of Theoph. xxviii ; and the
definitions of virtue, courage, prudence, &c., are in the vein of the
definition which Theophrastus always prefixes to his character-
sketches.

5. This is the view of Croiset,⁶ von Hiller,⁷ and Tarn.⁸ Gerhard⁹
and Powell,¹⁰ however, urge that this νομοθεσία more probably took

---

¹ Stob., 2. 22. ² Theaet., 174a. ³ Stob., 5. 4. 53.
⁴ D.L., vi. 27. ⁵ id., iv. 50. ⁶ *Journal, d. Sav.*, 1911.
⁷ *P.W.*, s.v. Megalopolis. ⁸ *C.A.H.*, Vol. vii, p. 755.
⁹ in *P.W.*, s.v. Kerkidas. ¹⁰ *Collect. Alex.*, p. 201.

place after the abdication of the tyrant Lydiades, i.e. some time later than 235 ; Powell thinks that Cercidas may have been given supreme authority for the purpose. Unfortunately the coinage of Megalopolis gives no help ; but (1) the only occasion on which we are expressly told of a νομοθεσία in Megalopolis at this period is the year 217. (2) Lydiades would seem to have been the most prominent man in Megalopolis, even after he abdicated as a tyrant, down to his death at the battle of Ladoceia. (3) The tone of the references to Cercidas as ἄριστος νομοθέτης imply that the code he drew up was successful. If he had so distinguished himself as a lawgiver after the abdication of Lydiades, why was there so much discontent and civil discord at Megalopolis in 221 and the following years ? On the other hand, Polybius says that the νομοθεσία of 217 *was* satisfactory, ' the terms on which they composed their differences were engraved on a stone and set up beside the altar of Hestia in the Homarium ' ;[1] (4) Polybius also implies that the code of Prytanis was rejected, and the final settlement was due to the influence of Aratus. Cercidas was the friend of Aratus, he had commanded the Megalopolitan contingent at Sellasia, what more likely than that Aratus appointed him as νομοθέτης for his native city ?

6. The sequence of thought does seem intelligible, always admitting that the uncertainty of the readings makes any interpretation highly conjectural. For (1) on Knox's emendation, the first lines of fr. 8 are to be taken thus, ' What driver of a team of four horses brightly sparkling in the sun, would use to spur them a goad fitted for oxen's flanks ? '[2] (2) 8, lines 8–15, though fragmentary, contain unmistakable attacks on Sphaerus and his associates. ' This is the pathway trodden of villains. . . . O Stoic Callimedon (not alone is Scylla the harlot evil . . .),[3] if thou dost yield aught to Sphaerus (Σφαίρῳ γὰρ αἴ τι . . . προβάλῃς) . . . this leads not to virtue . . . thou art a hunter after boys (ἰχνεύεις)[4] . . . it bears a harvest of madness.' (3) Fragment 9, lines 11–16, describe the ' love of a Zeno '. ' When thou shalt find a youth, formed in perfect harmony, then shalt thou find equal desire, temperate (κ' ἀστάθευτον : Powell) and sweet. This is the love of man for man, this the love of a Zeno.'

The ἔρως Ζανωνικός was notoriously homosexual, as his enemies were not slow to point out. But Zeno's views on the subject were evidently akin to the theory of sublimation through sexual love developed in the *Phaedrus* ; ' they say the wise man will love those youths who by their countenance show a natural disposition to virtue. Thus Zeno in the *Republic*.'[5] So with the ' image of a youth ' described by Zeno, together with the physical characteristics we find

---

[1] v. 93.
[2] Reading ποτ' αἰολώπολον υ—— ὠμοπληζιβουσόῳ μύωπι χρῆσθαι ἀνδρὶ τέθριππον χρέων ; πολλοῦ δεήσαι
[3] Powell, restoration suggested by Wilamowitz.
[4] Thus Powell.   [5] D.L., vi. 129.

postulated ὀρθὸς νοῦς πρὸς τὸν λόγον, ὀξύτης καὶ κατακωχὴ τῶν ὀρθῶς εἰρημένων . . . αἰδὼς μὲν ἐπανθείτω καὶ ἀρρενωπία.[1] We have then two types of love contrasted, one that of Zeno, which is ἀστάθευτον (Powell aptly quotes Hor. *Od.* ii. 19. 28. ' Me lentum Glycerae torret amor meae '), the other that of Sphaerus, which is ' a pathway trodden of villains ', bringing an evil harvest. One thinks at once of the δισσὰ πνεύματα ἔρωτος of the fragment previously considered, the ' temperate love ' would be the ' calm voyage governed by the rudder of persuasion ', the love of Sphaerus the κωματίας διόλου πορθμός. What then of the charioteer and the goad ? I suggest that they are an adaptation of the famous simile of the *Phaedrus*, which compares the soul of man to a charioteer and his double yoke of horses. (That we are here dealing with a four-horse team is no great objection.) The voyage of love is now made in a chariot instead of a ship, and the violent breezes which provide a stormy passage are here symbolized by the ox-goad, obviously a goad too heavy to apply to a team of spirited horses.

[1] von Arnim, *Stoic. vet.*, fr. 1, 246.

CHAPTER IV

CYNICISM AND THE PHILOSOPHICAL SCHOOLS IN THE THIRD CENTURY

FOR the sake of clearness the relations between Cynicism and the philosophical schools were not discussed in the last chapter. The problem deserves a chapter to itself, which may well be prefaced with a recapitulation of the aspects Cynicism presented. First, then, Diogenes and Crates were living examples that ἀπάθεια, in one form or another the End of all the Hellenistic philosophies, could be attained, at least through the frugality of the κυνικὸς βίος. Second, the Cynic παραχάραξις emphasized in an extreme form the cleft between the Wise Man and the accepted values of the age, a cleft which also figured in most of the new systems. Third, by the middle of the third century Cynicism had evolved a type of literature, τὸ σπουδαιογέλοιον, which offered definite genres both for popular exposition and for satire.

We shall find that the influence of Cynicism was most potent during the lifetime of Diogenes and Crates, and rapidly declined later. This is readily explicable : Cynicism was then a novel phenomenon represented by men of striking personality : further, the age was eminently one of the founding of new philosophies. By the middle of the third century the several schools had taken on their individual shape : a hundred years later only the Stoics, Epicureans, and the New Academy were of any importance. Of these, the New Academy had no point of contact with the Cynics ; the Stoics accepted them more or less as poor relations : the Epicureans were uncompromisingly hostile. This chapter is therefore mainly concerned with the period c. 340–250 B.C.

(a) The philosophical school with which Cynicism first came in contact was that of Megara ; for a time close relations seem to have existed between that school and the circle of Diogenes. Pasicles, the brother of Crates, was a pupil of Eucleides of

95

Megara : [1] Stilpo [2] himself for a while came under the influence of Diogenes, and in his turn gave instruction to the Cynic Philiscus of Aegina.[3] One of the Dialogues of Diogenes bore the name of the Megarian Ichthyas, while Stilpo named one of his works after Metrocles. The influence of Diogenes is discernible in the ethics of Stilpo, who made ἀπάθεια the end of philosophy, and stressed the self-sufficiency of the Wise Man, who would remain unaffected by the loss of his worldly goods ; knowing that wisdom and knowledge could not be taken from him. Teles,[4] teaching the Cynic doctrine that exile is a matter of indifference to the wise man, cites as an authority a passage of Stilpo. Like Diogenes, Stilpo urged the necessity of philanthropy, in its widest sense ; Demetrius the Fair is said to have been greatly impressed by his lecture περὶ εὐεργεσίας.[5] He joined in Diogenes' attacks on popular religion : and apparently practised the ἐγκράτεια which was a feature of their life. ' The intimates of Stilpo ', says Cicero,[6] ' describe him as a man naturally inclined to wine and women : and in doing so they are rather praising him than the reverse. For, they add, none ever discovered him indulging these inclinations '—and he concludes with the well-known story of Socrates and the phrenologist. It was probably through Stilpo that a diluted version of Cynicism influenced Menedemus of Eretria, who was called by his enemies κύων καὶ λῆρος.[7] λῆρος evidently refers to his skill in controversy, κύων probably to his habitual παρρησία, perhaps also the frugality of his well-known suppers, upon him the influence of Cynicism was not of much weight. But Stilpo's ethics undoubtedly joined on to his logical studies and his doctrine of the One Good to form a coherent individual system, though we lack evidence to reconstruct it in detail. What is apparent is that his devotion to logic brought down on him the inevitable Cynic ridicule ; and Crates in his Παίγνια attacked Stilpo for ' wasting his time on the verbal pursuit of ἀρετή '.

(b) Stilpo's influence, however, was short-lived ; Cynicism was to contribute to a more enduring system, that of Zeno of Citicum. After landing at Athens in 314, Zeno attached himself to Crates the Cynic ; the reason for the attachment

---

[1] D.L., vi. 89. [2] id., ib. 76. [3] *Suidas*, s.v. Στίλπων.
[4] Teles περὶ φυγῆς. [5] D.L., xi. 116. [6] de fato, 5. 10.
[7] D.L., iii. 140

is clear, Zeno recognized in Crates the ideal σοφός after the pattern of Socrates. How long their association lasted is not known, later Zeno passed on from Crates to the more scientific teachings of Stilpo and Polemon. But the contact with Crates had lasting influence on Zeno's philosophy, and indeed on Stoicism as a whole. The core of the Stoic system is admittedly ethics ; the core of Zeno's ethics is the simplified version of the Socratic teaching preserved by Diogenes and Crates, as a brief examination of his doctrines will show.

The ' End ' (τέλος) of Zeno's system is defined in the famous formula ' Life in accordance with the law of Nature ' (ὁμολογουμένως τῇ φύσει ζῆν) ;[1] here Zeno is borrowing and expanding the τέλος of the Cynics, which is ' Life in Accordance with virtue ' (κατ' ἀρετὴν ζῆν).[2] The Cynics regarded ἀρετή as κατὰ φύσιν, but the φύσις of Zeno is an altogether deeper conception and ὁμολογουμένως τῇ φύσει ζῆν meant obedience to Universal Law, much as did Heracleitus' precept, δεῖ ἕπεσθαι τῷ ξυνῷ.

The Cynics, like Zeno, adopted the Tripartite division of things into ' Good, Bad, and Indifferent ' (ἀγαθά, κακά, and ἀδιάφορα) ; Zeno went beyond them in introducing a further Tripartite division of things ἀδιάφορα. With wealth and good birth classed as προηγμένα (preferables), poverty, slavery, and death as ἀποπροηγμένα (not preferables), the way was clearly open for a pragmatism very different from the uncompromising morality of the Cynics, though such a course was not followed by Zeno himself. We have seen from the fragments of Crates how Cynicism emphasized the contrast between the σοφός, safe in the Island of Pera, and the rest of mankind storm-tossed on the sea of Illusion. The contrast is preserved in Zeno's division of mankind into σπουδαῖοι and φαῦλοι, of whom the former are uniformly happy, the latter uniformly miserable. For him, as for the Cynics, Virtue is independent as regards happiness, and once won cannot be lost ; the σοφός is impeccable, and worthy of the love of his equals. As already remarked, the σοφός of the Stoics is a development along lines laid down by Socrates ; Zeno would

---

[1] The evidence is on the whole in favour of the view that τῇ φύσει was included in the definition of Zeno, and was not a later addition.
[2] D.L., vi. 104.

come in contact with another version of the Socratic teachings in his studies at the Old Academy under Polemon. Antiochus and Cicero, indeed, charged him with having taken his entire ethical system from the Academy ; [1] but it is clear that Zeno himself never admitted this. His own acknowledgements were paid to Crates, as is shown by the fact that he wrote the Κράτητος ἀπομνημονεύματα—᾽Απομνημονεύματα formed a recognized literary genre, the *Memorabilia* of a master written by a pupil. Moreover, that the Stoics themselves admitted that they received the Socratic teaching via Cynicism is to be inferred from the reaction in the direction of Cynicism which we find in Ariston of Chios, and from the canonization of Antisthenes and Diogenes as Stoic saints.

The simplicity of the Cynic life was also copied by Zeno : ' after their pattern did Zeno of Citieum live his life '.[2] This statement cannot be accepted in all its implications ; Zeno never adopted the staff and wallet, for he never practised the wandering mendicancy of a Diogenes ; he seems also to have avoided the Cynic ἀναίδεια, which Diogenes displayed partly for purposes of advertisement. But he wore the τρίβων, followed the frugal Cynic diet, drank cold water ; his temperance passed into a proverb at Athens, and is amply confirmed by the comedians.[3] ' A single loaf of bread his food, figs his dessert, water his drink ', says Philemon ; ' truly this man teaches a novel philosophy—to go hungry ; yet he gets disciples.' That his disciples were required to copy his own frugality is the inference from the lines of Timon, ' Meanwhile he gathered around him a swarm of poverty-stricken creatures, surpassing all in beggary, the most worthless people in town ' [4] —a description which recalls Aristophanes' abuse of the companions of Socrates.

The ancient authorities agree that in at least one of Zeno's works—the *Republic*—there was clear trace of Cynic influence. From the taunt that it was written ἐπὶ τῆς τοῦ κυνὸς οὐρᾶς one can suppose that it was published shortly after he had left Crates for Stilpo, and still showed that he ' had not let go of the dog's tail '.[5] This agrees with the statement of the Stoic apologetic quoted in Philodemus, that the book was written

---

[1] de Fin., IV, *et alia*. [2] D.L., vi. 104.
[3] id., vii. 27. [4] id., ib. 16.
[5] D.L. says he wrote it while a disciple of Crates.

when Zeno was still an imprudent young man.[1] The Cynic παραχάραξις appeared in the book in its treatment of incest, cannibalism, and unnatural vice as not ' opposed to nature ' ; and the *Oedipus* and *Thyestes* together with the *Republic* of Diogenes formed fine material for the attacks of the enemies of Stoicism.[2] The teachings of Diogenes about the abolition of currency, temples, law courts, and gymnasia were adopted by Zeno, as was the famous ' community of women ' ; but in making Ἔρως as the bringer of ὁμόνοια, the ruling deity of the ideal community,[3] Zeno was going beyond the Cynic ideas, possibly to conceptions introduced by Alexander. In the *Republic*, again, Zeno joined in the Cynic deprecation of the Greek ' liberal education ' (τὰ ἐγκυκλία μαθήματα) : it is suggested that in connexion with the *Republic* Zeno published a series of works made up of the ' Homeric Problems ', ' On the Hearing of Poetry ', ' On the Greek System of Education ', as educational treatises, outlining an alternative curriculum, in which the allegorical interpretation of Homer evidently figured large.[4] This is a feature which can hardly have been borrowed from Diogenes or Crates : Diogenes, as we have seen, allegorized the story of Medea, but elsewhere he deprecates the wasting of time on Homeric exegesis, a practice apparently never indulged in by Crates. Zeno's source here is pretty certainly Antisthenes.

To sum up, Zeno incorporated in his system the σοφός of the Cynics : provided a logical and scientific theory which showed this ethical ideal in its relation to the macrocosm ; and by the doctrine of the προήγμενον made possible for his followers a way of life that would avoid the Cynic narrowness and fanaticism. Cynicism was, therefore, introduced into the Stoic system by its founder, and a Cynic element formed a left wing—the ἀνδρωδεστάτη Στωική [5]—in the school throughout its history. Of its occasional reactions against the neglect on the part of official Stoicism of the practical aspects of philosophy for the theoretical, the most powerful took place in the generation immediately following Zeno, and gave rise to the heresy headed by that interesting figure, Ariston of Chios.

---

[1] Herc. Pap., No. 339 (P), Col. xv.
[2] See Note 1 to Chapter IV.
[3] von Arnim, op. cit., *Stoic. vet. fragmenta.* 1. 263.
[4] Stein, *Logik und Erkenntnis. der. Stoa.*, n .689.   [5] D.L., vi. 14.

(c) Ariston left the Stoic school while Zeno was ill, and came for a time under the influence of Polemon. This must have been earlier than 276,[1] but perhaps Ariston did not open a school of his own till after the death of Zeno, i.e. probably not till after 260 ; he lectured in the Cynosarges, as Antisthenes had done. The teachings of Ariston represent a protest against the additions with which Zeno had encumbered the simple Socratic ethics he had taken from the Cynics. Two of Zeno's branches of philosophy, Logic and Physics, were rejected by Ariston ; Logic, he said, had nothing to do with us, while Physics is far beyond our ken.[2] Dialectical reasonings he likened, in one of those comparisons for which he had a gift, to spiders' webs, their workmanship is admirable, but they serve no useful purpose.[3] Philosophy's sole concern is with Ethics ; and in that sphere too Ariston tried to simplify the system of Zeno. He rejected the tripartite division of things ἀδιάφορα, reaffirming the Cynic doctrine that everything between virtue and vice is completely indifferent.[4] Moreover, Zeno had extended the category of things κατὰ φύσιν to cover the προήγμενα ; Ariston contended that none of the ἀδιάφορα, health, disease, wealth, poverty, &c., is by nature either desirable or undesirable, they are only to be judged κατὰ περίστασιν—according to individual cases. He showed, for example, that for the σοφός occasions might arise on which he would prefer to die of disease than to live.[5] The ethical system of Ariston posited a different τέλος from that of Zeno ; instead of ' a life lived in harmony with Nature ' we are commended to ' a life of complete indifference to everything between virtue and vice '. To illustrate this precept he borrowed Bion's simile of the Actor : the wise man will be like the good actor who, whether cast as Thersites or Agamemnon, will play his part well.[6] To continue with the simile, the business of philosophy was to produce the good actor, not, according to Ariston, to coach him in separate rôles. For he rejected not only Logic and Physics, but also one branch of ethics, the ὑποθετικὸς καὶ παραινετικὸς τόπος.[7] This study, according to Seneca, ' dat propria cuique personae praecepta nec in universum componit hominem ' ; it gave advice on the

---

[1] D.L., vii. 160.   [2] von Arnim, op. cit., 1. 351.   [3] id., ib.
[4] id., ib. 360.   [5] id., ib. 361.   [6] D.L., vii. 160.
          [7] von Arnim, op. cit., 50. 358.

conduct of marital affairs, on the management of servants, and so on ; Cleanthes in particular seems to have devoted attention to it. Such precepts were rejected by Ariston as improper for philosophy. They were too numerous and too particular to be embraced under the ' laws of Philosophy, which should be brief and universal '. For, says Ariston,

consider the case of one giving precepts on marriage. He must advise separately the husband who has wedded a virgin, and he who has a wife who has known sex before marriage, he must provide rules for living with (a) a rich wife, (b) one without a dowry. Must he not also cater for, (c) a barren woman, (d) a prolific one ; (e) a mother, (f) one who is a step-mother ? . . .

This was a field of study fitted rather for the nurse and the schoolmaster : in any case it was superfluous for the σοφός who having grasped the central principles of ἀρετή would necessarily act virtuously in individual cases.

Ariston also differed from Zeno in his definition of the nature of ἀρετή.[1] Zeno, by taking over the ' four cardinal virtues ' of Plato, and regarding them as at once inseparable and distinct from one another, had become involved in logical difficulties. Ariston maintained that virtue is by nature one, an ἐπιστήμη ἀγαθῶν καὶ κακῶν, and the separate ' virtues ' such as Courage, Justice, &c., that ἐπιστήμη operating in a particular sphere.

Ariston resembles the Cynics not only in his teachings on ἀδιαφορία, and the uncompromising way in which he concentrates all the philosopher's powers on the pursuit of ἀρετή, but also in his earnest description of philosophy as ἄσκησις καὶ μάχη, and his insistence on the fact that by nature we have neither country nor lands nor possessions. We are told that he fell away from his own ideals ; but none the less he was an important figure in his day. His pupil Eratosthenes, indeed, thought it miraculous that a single city should contain at the same time philosophers of such eminence as Ariston and Arcesilaus ; but Strabo in citing the remark adds that therein Eratosthenes showed how foolish his judgement was, that he should praise a man who left no successors rather than the disciples of Zeno.[2] But Ariston had at least one quality Zeno lacked, he was a most persuasive speaker, and was nick-

[1] See Note 2 to Chap. IV.
[2] See von Arnim, op. cit., i. 338.

named ' The Siren '.[1]   He also had wit, as shown by his
description of Arcesilaus as a chimaera, ' Plato in front and
Pyrrho behind, in the midst, Diodorus ', and his remark that
those who wasted their time on the ἐγκυκλία μαθήματα, and
never studied Philosophy, were like the suitors of Penelope,
who spent their time seducing the maids and never came at
the mistress.[2]   For a while his school seems to have attracted
more pupils than did the Stoa proper : and indeed it is possible
that Chrysippus deserves to be called ' the second founder of
Stoicism ' as much for maintaining the school against the rival
attractions of Ariston as in repelling the attacks of the
Epicureans and of Arcesilaus.   But though the Ethics of
Ariston were more scientifically formulated than those of the
Cynics, yet his system resembled theirs in that it depended
largely on the personality of its leader, and lacked a comprehensive theoretical background which might ensure its survival.
Consequently we hear nothing of it after the first generation of
his pupils, amongst whom are known the names of Miltiades
and Diphilus.

Meanwhile, the development of the orthodox Stoic teaching
under Cleanthes and Chrysippus had been tending to lay less
emphasis on the Cynic element in Stoicism.   True, both
retained the Cynic features of Zeno's *Republic* ; [3] but Chrysippus, in admitting that ἀρετή can be lost, and that there is
some profit to be derived from the ἐγκυκλία μαθήματα, is
dissenting from Zeno and the Cynics.[4]   But above all the
great development made by Cleanthes in Physics, in Logic by
Chrysippus, had introduced into Stoicism a complexity little
to the Cynic taste.   We have already seen the attacks made by
Cercidas on the dialectical studies of Sphaerus and his
followers ; if, as Helm thinks, the *Symposium* of Menippus
was a model for that of Lucian, it would seem that the Stoics
were there especially made mock of ; in any case it is likely
enough that they came in for their share of satire poured forth
on all the dogmatic schools by Menippus in the works πρὸς
τοὺς φυσικοὺς καὶ μαθηματικοὺς καὶ γραμματικούς.   It is
interesting to learn that there were apparently retorts from
the Stoic side ; for Hermagoras, a pupil of Persaeus, wrote a

---

[1] D.L., vii. 166.   [2] von Arnim, op. cit., 1. 350.
[3] Philodemus περὶ Στωικ ; cf. Cronert, op. cit., p. 53 ff.
[4] D.L. vii. 127, 129.

dialogue called *Anti-Cynic* (Μισοκύων).[1] Official Stoicism indeed became increasingly opposed to Cynicism ; an opposition which culminates in Panaetius. From the fragment of Philodemus [2] we see how the Middle Stoa tried to explain away the offensive passages of Zeno and Diogenes—' Zeno was only a young man when he wrote that . . .' ' Anyway, Diogenes didn't write the tragedies, they are the work of certain wicked persons.' . . . Diogenes and Antisthenes were still Stoic saints, and were accepted as such by Posidonius. But the new Stoicism was determined to have no truck with Cynicism in its own day ; ' Cynicorum vero ratio tota eicienda est.' The expulsion was never achieved ; there were still two parties in the School as regards Cynicism. The controversy is preserved by Cicero, who says that some Stoics held Cynicism to be proper for the σοφός, should chance lead him into it, others that it was wrong in any circumstances.[3] The anti-Cynics are presumably Panaetius and his school ; a representative of the other party was Apollodorus of Seleucia, whose *floruit* was apparently in the middle of the second century B.C. He maintained that ' the σοφός will play the Cynic : for Cynicism is a short cut to virtue.' [4] The same party held that the σοφός, once a Cynic, would remain so.[5] The Stoic street preachers in Rome during the latter half of the first century B.C. were, as we meet them in Horace's *Satires*, Cynic in all but name and tunic ; the Stoics always used Cynic literary genres for what may be called their exoteric teachings. Thus the Cynic element, present in Stoicism from its foundation, was maintained throughout the three hundred years we are considering, and indeed the noblest conception of Cynicism ever formulated was to come from the Stoic Epictetus.

(*d*) The philosophic doctrine to which Cynicism was most opposed was that which posited Pleasure as the End ; later stories contrast Diogenes and Aristippus as the respective extremes of asceticism and hedonism. But between Diogenes and the elder Aristippus there was probably never any contact, and we know too little about the life of the younger Aristippus to know whether he can ever have met Diogenes. It is however certain that Hedonist doctrines were attacked by the early Cynics ; we have already seen how Teles' diatribe περὶ

---

[1] Suidas. [2] Cronert, op. cit., p. 53 ff. [3] de Fin., iii. 20, 68.
[4] D.L., vii. 121. [5] Stob., 238.

τοῦ μὴ εἶναι τέλος ἡδονήν quotes Crates to prove that the happy life cannot be judged by a favourable balance of pleasures. But the doctrines of Aristippus were greatly modified by later Hedonists such as Anniceris, Hegesias, and Theodorus, and their systems had much in common with Cynicism, particularly as regards contempt for accepted values. Scholars who accept the ' successions ' given by Diogenes Laertius explain this *rapprochement* on the grounds of a ' family likeness between the minor Socratic schools ' ; [1] but Cynicism never was strictly a Socratic school, as we have tried to show, and, moreover, the ' Cyrenaic ' succession as given by Diogenes Laertius is notably open to suspicion.

A more probable explanation is simply that both the asceticism of Diogenes and the sensualism of Aristippus were modified at a later period, and we have in Theodorus of Cyrene an instance of contact between Cynicism and Hedonism. Theodorus was a teacher of Bion at Athens shortly after Bion had been a disciple of Crates, and it is very likely that he came under the influence of Crates himself.

Theodorus [2] was an aristocrat of Cyrene, and had an eventful life. He was twice exiled from Cyrene ; the fact that throughout his career he seems to have been on friendly terms with Ptolemy the Lagid points pretty certainly to the anti-Egyptian risings in 322 and again in 313 as the occasions. Both times he took refuge in Greece : and during his second period of exile, some time between 313 and 306, we find him lecturing at Athens and also at Corinth. At Athens his notorious ' Atheism ' got him into trouble, and he was only saved by the influence of Demetrius of Phalerum from having to appear before the Areopagus on a charge of impiety. Even thus he was expelled from Athens, and seems to have gone to the court of Ptolemy. The king evidently thought well of him, for later he sent him on an embassy to Lysimachus, but to judge from the stories of his conduct on that occasion, diplomacy does not appear to have been one of Theodorus' strong points. [3] Later he returned to Cyrene, once again in Egyptian hands, and was held in high honour by its ruler, Magas, a brother of Ptolemy.

The philosophy of Theodorus rejected, with the Cynics,

---

[1] As does Zeller.   [2] Cf. D.L., 11. 98 ff.
[3] Cic., *Tusc.*, 1. 43. 102 ; D.L., 11. 102.

the principle that Pleasure (ἡδονή) is the End ; his reasons were probably those of Hegesias, that Pleasure is not always in our control. As an improvement on Aristippus' opposition of ἡδονή and πόνος he suggested χαρά and λύπη ' cheerfulness and grief ', both states of mind depending respectively on wisdom and folly (φρόνησις and ἀφροσύνη). ' Cheerfulness of mind ' had been of course a characteristic of Crates : though we are not expressly told that this practical example had any influence on the thought of Theodorus. The indispensability of intelligence for the production of this mental cheerfulness led Theodorus to insist as strongly as did the Cynics on the gulf dividing the Wise (—the σοφοί or φρόνιμοι) from the rest of mankind, who are mere fools (ἄφρονες). The wise man is completely self-sufficient, and the standards which govern the ἄφρονες cannot be applied to him. It was this doctrine which caused Theodorus to be described later as an inciter of his pupils to theft, adultery and sacrilege. Actually his position was like that familiar in the last century—Hell is an excellent thing for the working-classes, but there is no need for *us* to believe in it. The wise man will commit such actions ἐν καιρῷ, on occasions, of which of course he will be the judge, for they are not by nature αἰσχρά, though the opinion that they are αἰσχρά is of value in keeping in order the foolish (ἕνεκα τῆς τῶν ἀφρόνων συνοχῆς). Theodorus probably discussed these actions much as did Diogenes and the Stoics ; he is said to have complained that his pupils misunderstood him, perhaps they were more lenient in their interpretation of the clause ἐν καιρῷ. The self-sufficiency of the wise man would of course recognize no ties of patriotism ; and Theodorus expressly said that it was a good motion which resolves that the wise man will not fight for his country.[1] With Diogenes he affirmed that his true country was the Universe ; he even went beyond the αὐτάρκεια of the Cynic Sage by denying the necessity of friendship. The nature of the ' atheism ' which was the best-known feature of his philosophy cannot be determined from the references. Cicero says that he totally denied the existence of the gods ;[2] Clement of Alexandria[3] that he only denied the gods of popular belief. ἄθεος would of course be used at both positions. Diogenes Laertius, though admitting that he had read Theodorus' book *On the*

[1] D.L., ii. 98.   [2] *de Nat. Deor.*, 1. 2.   [3] *Paed.*, xv. A.

Gods, does not definitely say which was his view ; but implies that it was the second.[1] Though we cannot take literally Laertius' statement that ' Epicurus borrowed most of what he wrote on the gods from Theodorus ',[2] we can see how ' atheism ' was necessary for Theodorus' philosophy. The wise man cannot be self-sufficient if his αὐτάρκεια is liable to disturbance from the gods, an external agency over which he has no control. Theodorus, like Epicurus, was concerned to deliver mankind from ' the fear of Heaven '.

Theodorus of all the Hedonists most closely approached Cynicism ; the system of Hegesias, though joining in the deprecation of external goods, denies that self-sufficiency can be attained even by the wise man. Moreover, there is no record of direct relations between Hegesias and any follower of Cynicism.

(*e*) Of the Hellenistic schools of philosophy that of Epicurus adhered most faithfully to the teachings of its founder and kept the strongest hold on its adherents. Converts to Epicureanism were numerous and apostates few—for, said its opponents, men may become eunuchs, but eunuchs can hardly become men.[3] One of the precepts of Epicurus, enunciated in his book *On Lives*, is that the Wise Man will not beg, nor live as a Cynic ;[4] he is said to have described the Cynics as ' the enemies of Hellas '.[5] This hostility was probably due to the repugnance Epicurus felt to the Cynic ἀναίδεια ; certainly the life of the Epicurean Sage avoided the Cynic παραχάραξις of established law and convention. For their part, the Cynics attacked the Epicureans for their doctrines of ἡδονή and for the elaborate physical and logical aspects of their system ; two books of the satires of Menippus were expressly directed against the Epicureans and their reverence for the festival of their founder.[6] Polystratus, an Epicurean of the later part of the third century, wrote a book called περὶ ἀλόγου καταφρονησέως which attacked amongst others the ' sect of the Cynics, who profess themselves to be

---

[1] He says Theodorus completely rejected the δόξαι (popular beliefs) of the gods. The story about the remark of Lysimachus' minister, Mithras, ' It seems you do not recognize kings either, Theodorus ', suggests that Theodorus was ἄθεος in the second sense.
[2] D.L., ii. 97. [3] id., iv. 43. [4] id., ix. 119.
[5] id., ib. 8. [6] id., vi. 101.

ἀπαθεῖς '; while in the περὶ φιλοσοφίας he describes them as ' acting and speaking utterly at random ', the companions of Bion, he says, may well be called dogs, for they go sniffing round everything improper. The Epicurean system offers the true philosophy, not a life of vagrancy.[1] The Cynic Menedemus was one of the few whose tracks are seen leading out of the lions' den of Epicureanism, and a personal controversy raged between him and his former Epicurean master Colotes of Lampsacus. Menedemus apparently attacked the Epicurean deprecation of poetry ; Colotes replies that Menedemus does not understand the Epicurean position, and interprets all too literally the saying of his own ally Zeno. The dispute was apparently a lengthy one. Colotes attacks Menedemus in the book *Against Plato's Euthydemus*. Menedemus, he says, ' keeps on bringing up reproaches against us '; ' even the Stoics are beginning to get tired of him '; ' they walk up and down in the Stoa saying that Menedemus will not give up his childish, foolish, trivial, and contemptible arguments.' Colotes also attacked Bion in a controversial essay entitled ' That life is impossible on the systems of other philosophers '. Epicurean polemic against the Stoics made great play with the Cynic features of Stoicism ; and Philodemus,[2] castigating the immorality of the *Republic* of both Zeno and Diogenes, exclaims against ' those accursed beings who choose to live the lives of dogs '.

(*f*) The Cynic spirit of antagonism to the dogmatists found an ally in Timon of Phlius, and it is not surprising that in his satiric writings Timon should have followed Cynic models. Wachsmuth [3] points out that his Σίλλοι are clearly an imitation of Crates ; who himself parodied the Νεκυία of Homer's *Odyssey* and showed the wretched state of the philosophers in Hades. Incidentally it is noteworthy that none of the fragments of the Σίλλοι attack any Cynic, though the Stoics and especially Zeno come in for abuse. Timon was also following Crates in his use of the iambic metre for purposes of satire ; and in the numerous ' tragedies ' he composed he may have been influenced by those of Diogenes. Indeed, were it not for his exposition of the philosophy of Pyrrho, we

---

[1] Cronert, op. cit., p. 36.
[2] περὶ τῶν Στωικ. Col. viii, Cronert, op. cit., p. 63.
[3] *Corp. poes. Graec. lud.*, Vol. ii, Introd.

should class Timon with Menippus as the outstanding literary representatives of the Cynic nihilism.

NOTES TO CHAPTER IV

1. We have said in dealing with Diogenes that these charges are probably not to be pressed, and the caution applies even more emphatically as regards Zeno. Probably the ' shocking ' passages in question amounted to little more than an argument that in certain hypothetical cases even incest and cannibalism would be permissible ; e.g. Chrysippus [1] seems to have argued that if a Wise Man and his daughter were the sole survivors of some catastrophe which fell on mankind incest would be permissible, ' for the preservation of the human race '. To say that the Stoics ' recommended ' cannibalism is absurd.

2. As the difference is not dealt with fully by Zeller, and is definitely muddled by von Arnim in *Pauly-Wissowa*, it may be worth while to examine the evidence here. I begin with the statement of Diogenes Laertius that ' Ariston did not admit the existence of many virtues called by many names, but treated it according to the theory of relative modes ' (κατὰ τὸ πρὸς τί πως ἔχειν).[2] The ' theory of relative modes ' is illustrated by a passage of Plutarch [3]—Ariston said that ' virtue is by nature one . . . but in relation to separate cases becomes many, as though for example our sight were called " whitesight " when it saw white objects, " blacksight " when it saw black objects, or something of the sort. So virtue, when determining what should be done and what should not, is called φρόνησις ; in controlling desires, and appointing a limit and a season for pleasures, it is called σωφροσύνη, &c.' This illustration is borne out by a passage of Galen ; [4] but Galen says that Ariston called ἀρετή an ἐπιστήμη ἀγαθῶν καὶ κακῶν ; Plutarch that he called it ὑγίεια. The last phrase is clearly incomplete, ὑγίεια as such was reckoned by Ariston amongst the ἀδιάφορα.[5] The ὑγίεια must have been that of the logical portion of the soul, a necessary condition for the functioning of the ἐπιστήμη ἀγαθῶν καὶ κακῶν ; Cleanthes adopted a similar theory in his account of the ἰσχὺς ψυχῆς induced by τόνος.[6] But it is evident that von Arnim is wrong in asserting that Ariston found the essence of ἀρετή to be φρόνησις. In none of the passages which deal with his views of ἀρετή does φρόνησις ever appear to be equated with it ; it is always ἀρετή functioning in a particular sphere. That the equation was made by Apollophanes,[7] a pupil of Ariston, is no evidence for Ariston's own position. And as a matter of fact this is apparently precisely the point on which Ariston joined issue with Zeno. For

---

[1] von Arnim, *Stoic. Vet. fr.*, iii. 743. [2] D.L., vii. 160.
[3] See von Arnim, op. cit., i. 375. [4] id., ib. 374.
[5] id., ib. 361. [6] id., ib. 563. [7] id., ib. 406.

Zeno's views on the nature of ἀρετή we are dependent on two passages of Plutarch ;[1] but they indicate that Zeno was involved in difficulties of logic. Apparently he adopted the four ' cardinal virtues ' of Plato, regarding them as at once inseparable and distinct from one another ; and attempted to define ἀνδρεία, σωφροσύνη and δικαιοσύνη as φρόνησις operating in different spheres. Ariston was clearly trying to provide a more logical definition of ἀρετή. The point on which he differed from the Megarians is not clearly brought out by Diogenes Laertius ; he agreed with them that ἀρετή was ' one called by many names ' but added the qualification κατὰ τὴν πρὸς τί σχέσιν.[2] That is, the Megarians presumably held that δικαιοσύνη, φρόνησις, &c., were equally valid synonyms for ἀρετή ; Ariston that they could be only used as ' accidental aspects ' of ἀρετή.[3] Ariston's views of the nature of ἀρετή clearly imply a deprecation of the παραινετικός τόπος of ethics : once the ἐπιστήμη ἀγαθῶν καὶ κακῶν is acquired the virtuous performance of individual acts is assured.

---

[1] id., ib. 200, 201. [2] Galen, *Hipp. et Plato*, vii. 1.
[3] The comparison with the phraseology of Herbart is made by Zeller.

CHAPTER V

CYNIC INFLUENCE ON HELLENISTIC
LITERATURE

To complete the survey of Cynicism in the Hellenistic period it remains to give some account of the development and influence of the literary κυνικὸς τρόπος. Literary forms, like animals, survive by adapting themselves to environment; the evolution of the κυνικὸς τρόπος is in the main an attempt to adapt the ' Socratic ' forms of popular philosophical propaganda to the requirements of the Hellenistic age. The conversation and character of Socrates had given rise to the Socratic dialogue, in the hands of Plato perhaps the supreme achievement in prose form. The spirit of irony of Socrates, and the brilliant fancy of Plato, had introduced into it an element of the γέλοιον in the shape of parody and myth. A less serious form of composition was the συμποσίον ; and the *Memorabilia* of Xenophon was the first work in a genre which was to gain great popularity in the third century and later. Finally, the epistle had been used for philosophical exposition by Plato, Isocrates, and Aristotle. Such were the traditional literary forms for philosophical propaganda available at the end of the fourth century. The first literary productions of the Cynics seem to have been predominantly ' serious ' (σπουδαῖον) : Diogenes used the dialogue and epistle ; the tragedies of Crates ' bore the most solemn stamp of philosophy ', while his epistles ' were written in a style closely resembling that of Plato '. [1] But it was soon found that the style suited to the intelligentsia of Athens was far above the heads of the audience to which the Cynics addressed themselves. Diogenes himself discovered that ' when he spoke in earnest on serious subjects, none stayed to hear him, but when he began to whistle, a crowd soon gathered '. [2] The common people, unlike the eager young companions of Socrates, had

[1] D.L., vi. 98.   [2] id., ib. 27.

neither the leisure nor the inclination to ' follow the argument
wherever it might lead, not caring how many digressions were
made, provided that truth was attained in the end '.[1]   They
wanted the lessons of philosophy presented ready digested, and
in an easily remembered form ; their tastes are fairly represented
by the collection of aphorisms, none of them more than three
words long, inscribed on a stone at Cyzicus, about the year
300 B.C.[2]   Clearly for such an audience simplicity was all—
φευκτέον ἡ τρηχεῖα παραίνεσις.   Primarily to cater for their
needs were evolved those literary forms which comprise the
genus of τὸ σπουδαιογέλοιον ;   the prose forms of which
were mainly the adaptation and popularization of ' Socratic '
literature ; while in verse the influence of the old gnomic
poetry, of the Mime, and of Comedy, are all discernible.

Of the prose genres the most highly developed was the
Diatribe.   Διατριβή was of course originally synonymous
with διαλόγος as describing the conversations of a philosopher,
in the Apology Socrates says the Athenians are condemning
him because they cannot bear τὰς ἐμὰς διατριβὰς καὶ τοὺς
λόγους.[3]   It is probably in this sense that the writings attributed to Aristippus were called διατριβάι ;[4] diatribe as a
literary genre appears to have been the work of Bion.   We
have seen the chief characteristics of the diatribe as he developed
it—its use of allegory, anecdote, and quotation, its appeals to
an imaginary adversary, &c.   It is obviously a popularized
form of the dialogue ; as the diatribe is not a ' zetetic ' argument but an exposition, there is only room for one main speaker,
and the other characters of the dialogue are dispensed with,
or combined in the ' imaginary adversary '.   The definition of
Hermogenes is worth quoting—διατριβὴ ἔστι βραχέος διανοήμα-
τος ἠθικὴ ἔκθεσις ' Diatribe is a moral exposition of some brief
topic'.[5]   After Diogenes the Cynics abandoned the ' serious '
dialogue, though, as we have seen, the form was adapted for
comic purposes by Menippus.

The ἀπομνημόνευματα was a genre obviously suited to the
purposes of the Cynics, and a closely allied form is the
ὑπομνήματα.   In theory these two forms are distinct, the
ἀπομνημονεύματα being the sayings, acts, &c., of a master
collected by a pupil, while the ὑπομνήματα is the scrap-book

[1] *Theaet.* 172D.   [2] *J.H S.*, xxvii.   [3] 37D.   [4] D.L., ii.
[5] Rhet. Graec. III, p. 406w.

of a writer or philosopher. We are told of Bion that he left many memoirs . . . and expecially maxims having a useful application (ἀποφθέγματα χρειώδη πραγματείαν ἔχοντα) and the χρεία, which formed the basis of the ἀπομνημονεύματα and the ὑπομνήματα, was one of the chief weapons of Cynic propaganda. The χρεία is, on the definition of Theon, ' σύντομος ἀπόφρασις ἢ πρᾶξις μετ' εὐστοχίας ἀναφερομένη εἴς τι ὡρισμένον πρόσωπον ',[1] i.e. an anecdote with a moral, attached to the name of a well-known person (with the Cynics, of course, notably Diogenes). Though the χρεία was not a Cynic invention, it was one of their favourite forms, being introduced into diatribe and even verse with great frequency. Being short, easily remembered, instructive, and yet popular, it was admirably adapted to their needs, and played a large part in education, as we see from the ' Wiener-Diogenes Papyrus ' and the later Papyrus Bouriant.[2]

The epistle, used as a serious form by Diogenes and Crates, was turned to comic purposes by Menippus ; and the first-century *Letters of the Cynics* are the chief contribution known of Cynics of that period to τὸ σπουδαιογέλοιον proper.

The συμποσίον was used by Menippus and Meleager, similar were the συμποτικοὶ διαλόγοι of the Stoic Persaeus.

For the Cynic propaganda verse was also employed. It had of course always been one of the staples of Greek education— Lucian says that ' The sayings of wise men and the great deeds of old and moral stories are set to verse that they may be easily remembered ' ;[3] we have seen that τὸ εὐμνημονεύτον was aimed at in the Cynic curriculum. Theognis, Simonides, and Aesop had been popular in the circle of Socrates ; and both tragedians and comedians had claimed to be the instructors of the public—' πολλὰ μὲν γέλοια μ' ἐιπεῖν, πολλὰ δὲ σπουδαῖα ', says Aristophanes.[4] But as a model for gnomic and satiric verse it was necessary to go back beyond the fifth century to such writers as Theognis, Hipponax, and Archilochus. Crates was the first of the Cynics to revive the old measures : the iambic, appropriate to satire from the time of Archilochus,

---

[1] Prog. 6.
[2] Cf. also Sen., ep. 336, '. . . pueris sententias ediscendas damus et has quas Graeci chrias vocant, quia complecti illas puerilis animus potest. . . .'
[3] Lucian, *An.*, 21.　　　　　　　　　　[4] *Frogs*, 339.

appears in several fragments, notably in the ἐφημερίς : elegiacs are used for the ' Hymn to Euteleia ' and the parody of the epitaph of Sardanapalus : hexameters appear, naturally enough, in the parodies of Homer. The early Stoics followed the example of Crates, and we have iambics associated with Zeno, Cleanthes, and Ariston, while hexameter is used by Cleanthes in his famous ' Hymn to Zeus '. Cercidas, as we have seen, invented a new metre, the ' Meliambus ' ; the verses of the London and Heidelberg Papyri περὶ αἰσχροκέρδειας employ the choliambic measure.

The great quantity of moralizing verse which characterizes the Hellenistic age cannot all be put down to the account of the Cynics, though it is safe to say that Cynic influence gave the first impetus to that literature. And it is noteworthy that this gnomic poetry exhibits the same features as the moralizing prose of the diatribe, the χρεία, and the ἀπομνημονεύμα. It abounds with quotation and parody, with anecdotes, and with examples taken from the familiar figures of the past. Heracles, Odysseus, Socrates, and Diogenes were the stock heroes of the prose literature : verse adds new figures to the gallery. Hipponax, a wanderer, a beggar, and noted for his mordant wit, was obviously well suited to appear as ' Anima naturaliter Cynica ' ; so were the slave Aesop and the barbarian sage Anacharsis. Poetic χρεῖαι and aphorisms could be fathered on to the Seven Wise Men, one of several examples that might be quoted is the anonymous epigram (*Anth.*, ix. 366.)

> Learn of the Seven Sages the city, the name, and the precept.
> First Cleobulus of Lindus, who tells us that ' Measure is best ' ;
> Cheilon, ' Know Thyself ', declared in the valley of Sparta ;
> ' Keep thy temper in hand ', the Corinthian sage Periander.
> ' Naught in excess ' is the word of Pittacus from Mitylene ;
> Solon of Athens has said, ' See thou consider the end.'
> ' Most men are mad ' 'twas declared by Bias the wise of Priene.
> ' Put not thy name to a pledge ', warns us Milesian Thales.

For didactic purposes the verse of the older writers and philosophers were parodied ; a Hibeh papyrus of 280–240 B.C. brings us some thirty lines of the *Epicharmea* of Axiopistus (?) [1] ; parodies of Phocylides, Xenophanes and Pythagoras were also in circulation in Hellenistic times ; and both Gerhard and Wachsmuth conjecture that the collection

---

[1] Pap. Hibeh, i. i ; Powell, op. cit., 219.

which has come down under the name of Theognis includes Cynic additions.

The κυνικὸς τρόπος in literature was, as has been said, not necessarily connected with the κυνικὸς βίος ; and the popular philosophy of the Hellenistic age has so many features in common with Cynicism that it is difficult to decide where Cynic influence begins and ends in the case of individual writers of the period. For example, Gerhard [1] identifies Sotades of Maroneia, the ' cinaedologus ', with a Cynic of that name mentioned in a story by Gregory of Nazianzen. The story derives from a late source, and the incident there told of Sotades and Ptolemy is elsewhere related of Diogenes and Alexander.[2]   However, once the identification is made it is easy to find the Cynic ἀναίδεια in his obscene verses, and the Cynic παρρησία in his attack on the marriage of Ptolemy Philadelphus and his sister Arsinoe.   But of course obscenity was not a monopoly of the Cynics, and if Sotades was true to the Cynic παρρησία in attacking a king, he was false to the Cynic παραχάραξις in rebuking incest.   More convincing evidence for Cynic influence on Sotades is the fact that he wrote a *Descent to Hades* [3] as did Crates and Menippus ; further, it seems likely that his poems contained moral precepts, for such occur in verses quoted under his name by Stobaeus.[4] One may therefore conjecture that Sotades at least came under the influence of the κυνικὸς τρόπος, as we have seen was the case with Timon of Phlius.   The same may be said of Chares,[5] whose verses on the avoidance of gluttony read like Crates, and were actually assigned to the Cynic by Bergk.   But in claiming Phoenix of Colophon as a Cynic in the full sense of the term, Gerhard is certainly rash.   The story of Ninos and the lines on αἰσχροκέρδεια are not necessarily Cynic, and when the ' Chough-bearers ' is described as a Cynic begging-song one must withhold assent, if not admiration.   These are, however, minor figures ; the influence of Cynicism is discernible in one of the greatest of Hellenistic authors, Leonidas of Tarentum.   Though one cannot with Gerhard regard pessimism [6] and contempt for death [7] as specifically Cynic, it must be admitted that Leonidas approaches the Cynic εὐτελεία

---

[1] op. cit., p. 245.   [2] 36.   1000B.   [3] Suidas.
[4] Powell, op. cit., p. 240.   [5] id., ib. p. 223.
[6] As in A.P., viii. 472.   [7] As in A.P. vii. 731.

in his description of his wandering frugal life in the following poem.

> Vex thyself not through all thy wanderings,
> through all thy vagrant course from land to land
> Vex thyself not, if but there be to hand
> A hut, a fire for warmth, and simple things
> For food—a cake, kneaded from trough of stone
> Relished with mint or thyme, or salt alone.[1]

He shows an interest in the Cynics, writing on the death of Diogenes, and on an unworthy follower of his ; and expands into an iambic epigram Bion's remark that the road to Hades is an easy one, for it can be travelled with the eyes closed.[2] His sympathy for the common people is well known, he sings of the fisherman, the neatherd and the aged weaver.   And in one of the most striking of his epigrams an echo of Simonides is turned into what Geffcken [3] justly calls a diatribe in verse :

Countless the years, O man, that have been ere ever
thou didst see the light, countless the years that will be when thou
   art in Hades :
What measure of Life is left thee, but as it were a pin's point, or
   aught that may be more meagre ?
Short verily is thy span of life, and even thus not sweet, but more
   bitter than Death the enemy. . . .
Consider, O man, as day followeth day, how sorry is all thy strength,
   and live a frugal life :
Ever be mindful in thy dealings with mortals, that thy nature is
   a thing compounded of straw.[4]

The influence of the κυνικὸς τρόπος on Hellenistic moralizing verse was powerful, though its limits cannot always be precisely determined.   In later times, too, the Cynic writers of the third century B.C. were still a potent force.   The diatribe, in a particular, became an important literary genre, and the influence of Bion thus affected not only the diatribes of Seneca, Musonius, and Epictetus, but also the sermons of Dio Chrysostom, and, at a later period, of Synesius, Themistius, and Gregory of Nazianzen. [5]   The old view of satire as a purely Roman production has long been abandoned ; and Fiske shows how marked is the influence of Bion's diatribe in Lucilius and Horace.   Menippus, again, was the model of Varro in his *Satirae Menippeae*—thus indirectly influencing

---

[1] A.P., vii. 736.   [2] Stob., 120g.   [3] *Leon von tar.*, 131.
[4] A.P., vii. 472.   [5] vide Wilamowitz, *Ant. von. Kar. exkurs Teles.*

Petronius and Seneca—and is of course of great importance for Lucian. It may be conjectured that the Cynic χρεῖαι influenced similar Roman compilations, and it is certain that as school-books they were widely used throughout the Greek-speaking portion of the Roman Empire. A detailed account of these developments falls outside the scope of this book. Here we are only concerned to note how in ' τὸ σπουδαιογελοίον ' the Cynics evolved from the ' Socratic ' literary forms and from the old gnomic poetry a powerful and many-sided instrument for popular philosophical propaganda, and that the κυνικὸς τρόπος was a fertile influence successively on Hellenistic, Roman, and later Greek literature.

NOTE TO CHAPTER V

1. Only a brief account would here seem necessary : the extant fragments of Cynic literature have largely been discussed in connexion with individual authors : and besides the ground has been covered by the research of Geffcken, Fiske, Wendland, above all, Gerhard, as well as by the standard histories of Alexandrine literature. This chapter is simply a general summary of the κυνικὸς τρόπος as a whole.

CHAPTER VI

CYNICISM IN THE SECOND AND FIRST
CENTURIES B.C.

IN the life and literature of the third century the Cynics had
played a prominent part, but after about 200 B.C. strangely
little is heard of them. Cynic literary genres as perfected by
Bion and Menippus certainly influenced Roman satire ; but
there are very few references to Cynicism as a still observed
ἔνστασις βίου till the revival in the first century of our era.
Zeller indeed supposed that the movement entirely died out,
and that the revival alluded to was really a rebirth of Cynicism
out of Stoicism. This is certainly not the case ; we do possess
evidence that Cynicism continued during the second and first
centuries B.C., though it was obscure and unimportant. Before
setting out this evidence it is pertinent to suggest causes for
Cynicism's lengthy eclipse.

A consideration of the history of the movement itself during
the third century reveals one set of causes. The Cynics were
so called as the followers of Diogenes of Sinope ; the founder
of Cynicism was a man of outstanding personality, and he had
a worthy pupil in Crates. But of course a succession of such
' originals ' was not to be expected, the next hundred years of
Cynicism failed to produce a man of the θαυμαστὴ πειθώ[1]
of Diogenes. Bion was a brilliant figure, but there was in him
too great a discrepancy between precept and practice to win
many converts, and Menippus does not seem to have ' taught '
at all. The decline in personality from a Diogenes to a Teles
is obvious. Now a school of philosophy with a definite
theoretical background, like a well-organized state, can survive
and even prosper without men of genius ; Epicureanism is not
marked by a man of any real distinction between Epicurus and
Lucretius. But Cynicism had never had such a background :
its appeal lay in the character of its adherents. Moreover, as
the first of the new ' philosophics of retreat ', Cynicism as

[1] D.L., vi. 75.

represented by Diogenes and Crates, had attracted men of such intellect as Zeno, Stilpo, and Menedemus. But by the end of the third century the essential features of the Cynic system, the αὐτάρκεια and ἀπαθεία enjoyed by its σοφός, were to be found without the Cynic squalor in Stoicism and Epicureanism, which also gave a comprehensive theoretical background. The weakness of Cynicism lay in its inability to give an account of itself (λόγον διδόναι); now that its adherents could not command the ' persuasive charm ' (ἴυγξ) of a Diogenes, it could make no appeal to the intelligence. Cynicism thus became a ' popular ' philosophy ; the philosophy of the proletariat as it has been called, and the description will serve provided one avoids the implications such a phrase would carry to-day. Moreover, the Cynic himself was becoming a familiar rather than a remarkable figure, and his ἀνάιδεια ceased to shock ; we now regard a communist orator as part of the furnishings of Hyde Park rather than as a forerunner of the Red Dawn.

But an even more potent set of causes for the eclipse of Cynicism were those produced by the great shift in the centre of gravity of the civilized world to Rome. The ultimate fusion of Greek and Roman culture achieved in the Roman Empire tends to obscure the fact that many features of the older civilization were not to the taste of the Rome of the Republic. ' Captive Greece took captive her proud conqueror'; yes, but truth has been sacrificed for effect. Rome only took what she wanted from Greece, and she did not want Cynicism, at least as an ἔνστασις βίου for some time to come. Philosophy had to meet the tastes of the Roman aristocracy with their traditions of ' gravitas ' ; such men as Scipio Aemilianus or Laelius would have regarded Cynicism as offensive vulgarity. They found what they wanted in the modified Stoicism of Panaetius and Posidonius, a nice blend of Stoic ἀρετή and Roman ' virtus '. One of the achievements of Panaetius was to purge Stoicism of the Cynic features which had marked it under Zeno and Chrysippos ; how hostile the new Stoicism was to Cynicism can be gathered from the reflection of its criticism in Cicero.[1] For indeed, Cynicism had

---

[1] e.g. *De Officiis*, 1. 148. ' Cynicorum vero ratio tota est eicienda : est enim inimica verecundiae, sine qua nihil rectum esse protest, nihil honestum.'

flourished in a ' Zeitgeist ' very different from that which now prevailed at Rome. The age of the Diadochi had been one of a growing distaste for politics, and politics at Rome in the last days of the Republic ran a course whose very turbulence is a tribute to their vigour ; it had seen the decay of the city-state and the spread of cosmopolitanism, while Roman nationalism was still vigorous ; its keynote was a ' world-weariness ' which was not felt at Rome till the end of another hundred years of civil war and bloodshed. Admittedly certain features of the Hellenistic age which had provided material for the preachings of Cynicism, a great increase in luxury, and gross inequality in the distribution of wealth—were just as prevalent in Republican Rome. But Rome had her own contrast to those in the ' antiqua virtus ', without calling on the material of the Cynics. Why cite Diogenes as an example of virtuous poverty when Cincinnatus and Cato lay to hand ? Again, no need to go back to the mythical labours of Heracles to emphasize the virtues of πόνος, they could be demonstrated by the ' proles Sabella ' and their hard life in the fields. It is worth noting that in *Satires* 2. 2, Horace, in enunciating educational precepts which are in the familiar Cynic-Stoic tradition, places them on the lips of that exemplar of Italian peasant virtue, the farmer Ofellus.[1] Rome had her own ideology in these matters—' malo unum Catonem quam trecentos Socratas '— and there is no reason to suppose that in the Republic Diogenes would have commanded a much better rate of exchange.

For all these reasons, Cynicism was known at Rome mainly as a literary phenomenon, as an examination of the evidence shows. The references to Cynicism in the Roman Comedy [2] do not justify the assumption that it was a familiar thing at Rome, for Plautus and Terence derived their material from the New Comedy of Greece, in which such references were frequent. Nor can we assume with Hirzel [3] that Varro had an ' early phase of Cynicism ' because he wrote ' satirae Menippeae '. Admittedly he is called ' Cynicus Romanus ', but the reference is to his imitation of Cynic Satire : he is the ' Romani stili Diogenes '. [4] As Cicero makes him say, ' he did not so

---

[1] Cf. Fiske, op. cit., pp. 379 ff.
[2] Cf. Plautus Stichus, 5. 4. 22 ; Pers., 120–5.
[3] *Der Dialog.*, 441, note 2.   [4] Tert., *Ap.* 14.

much translate Menippus as imitate him ' ; [1] it was a Romanization of a Greek literary form, much as were the satires of Lucilius and Horace. Street preachers were familiar enough in Rome towards the end of the first century B.C., as we gather from Horace's references to such persons as Fabius, Crispinus, and Stertinius. The discourses of these men were Cynic διατριβάι in their improvisatory nature, in their use of stock exemplars and similes, and in the lessons they inculcated—avoid μεμψιμοιρία, live simply, know that virtue is independent of externals in regard to happiness, satisfy your sexual desires with as little trouble as possible.[2] There is nothing to distinguish them from the Cynics of Hellenistic times as far as their creed goes, but they call themselves Stoics ; they resemble the Stoics who ' differ from the Cynics only in dress ' alluded to by Juvenal. But that the κυνικὸς βίος was not wholly unknown at Rome is to be inferred from an allusion in one of the mimes of Laberius to the ' Cynica haeresis ' ; ' sequere in latrinum, ut aliquid gustes a Cynica haeresi ' ; [3] which suggests that the audience would be familiar with the Cynic ἀναίδεια. Still more significant is a passage of Cicero's *Academica* (1–2) where Varro is discussing the possible variations of philosophical sects. All sects of philosophy, he says, may be followed, ' according to the Cynic, or to the conventional, garb and rationale ' (' habitus et consuetudo '), which does suggest that the Cynic ' habitus et consuetudo ' were known at Rome. A person with a more genuine claim than that of Varro to the title of ' cynicus Romanus ' was Marcus Favonius, the devoted adherent of Cato the younger. Born about the year 90, he makes stormy entrances on the political scene from the candidature as tribunus plebis in 61 to his capture by Octavian after Philippi. Cynic at least are his παρρησία and his fierce opposition to luxury ; it was during his aedilship that Cato gave the famous games at which expenses were so ruthlessly reduced, and we hear of a speech of his in support of a sumptuary law. The most characteristic story about him is that in Plutarch's *Brutus*. Before the battle of Philippi Brutus and Cassius were on bad terms ; a meeting was held to compose their differences. The meeting was in private, and to judge from the angry voices heard by those

---

[1] *Acad.*, 1. 8.   [2] See Fiske, op. cit., index.
[3] *Compitalia*, fr. 3.

outside the tent, it was anything but friendly. None had the courage to intervene but Favonius. ' A man ', says Plutarch, ' more impetuous and frenzied than reasonable in his devotion to philosophy,[1] but amusing enough, if you could tolerate his impertinence.' Brushing aside the attendants, Favonius burst into the tent, in true Cynic style with a line of Homer on his lips, ' Listen to me, young men, for I am your elder in years.' Brutus thrust him out with the trite pun which one would expect from him. ' You call yourself a Cynic, Favonius, but you are really a dog.' But at dinner that night Favonius turned up uninvited, and sat down between the now reconciled leaders : there was much wit and learning shown in the conversation, we are told. The Cynic παρρησία also appears in Favonius' attacks in the Senate on Ptolemy Auletes, in his opposition to the Triumvirs, and his abuse of Octavian for his brutal treatment of the prisoners taken at Philippi. But in his devotion to the cause of the Republic, in good days and in bad, and in his attempts to bring back the ' antiqua virtus ' of a bygone Rome he was the follower of Cato rather than of Diogenes.[2]

Cynicism did, then, apparently succeed in gaining a footing in Rome during the first century B.C., though it appears in an altered form and is of no great importance. The evidence for its survival in the Greek world during this period is equally scanty, though less ambiguous. One name is indeed mentioned as that of a Cynic, and a surprising name it is ; that of Meleager of Gadara, weaver of the famous *Stephanus*, and author of some of its most graceful and sensuous pieces. Yet the tradition is unanimous ; the Cynic in Athenaeus' *Deipnosophists* permits him to be called ὁ πρόγονος ὑμῶν and ὁ κυνικός ;[3] Diogenes Laertius classes him with Menippus ; and Meleager[4] himself speaks of the σκηπτροφόρος σοφία on which he had prided himself, but which is now overmastered by Love. Meleager was presumably born about 135, for his *floruit* is given c. 96 B.C. He tells us himself the main details of his biography ; he was born at Gadara (' in Syria, but Attic

---

[1] Plut., *Brutus*, 34. One thinks of Agricola, who but for his mother's care might have become ' more learned in philosophy than was proper for a Roman and a gentleman '. Tac., *Ag.*, 4. 4.

[2] Cf. Plut., *Brut.*, 34 ; *Caes.*, 21 ; Dio Cassius, 38. 7 ; 39. 14.

[3] 157*b* ; 502*c*.   [4] *Anth.*, xii. 101.

for all that ', he claims), passed his early manhood at Tyre, and finally went to live at Cos.   Since he lived to a ripe old age, his death probably took place *c.* 50 B.C.   His earliest literary venture was to write satires after the manner of his fellow-countryman Menippus—χαρίτες he calls them, and says ' they rival with the Muses' aid the Graces of Menippus '. Only a fragment of them is preserved, in which it is claimed that Homer was a Syrian, ' for the Syrians do not eat fish, nor does Homer allow his heroes to do so, though the Hellespont abounds with them '.[1]   He also followed Menippus in writing a *Symposium*;   another work on a Cynic theme was that entitled Λεκίθου καὶ φακῆς σύγκρισις.[2]   The last-named was presumably a humorous description of the Cynic diet, whose range was comprised in the choice between Lentil soup—thick or clear.   As is to be expected, there are few traces of Cynicism in the poems of Meleager contained in the *Garland*, though an expression of the Cynic cosmopolitanism is found in the epitaph he composed for him, ' If I am a Syrian, what wonder in that ? Stranger, we are citizens of one city ; the universe : one Chaos is the begetter of all mortal things.'   From the evidence of the epigrams it is clear that Meleager was no follower of the κυνικὸς βίος as defined by Diogenes, he was a Cynic after the persuasion of Teles, who in enunciating the principle ' There must be no indulgence in luxury ', added the saving clause, ' unless circumstances are favourable '.[3]   Circumstances seem to have favoured Meleager ;[4] but there is evidence that that asceticism still survived amongst the Cynics.   Diocles of Magnesia, the friend to whom Meleager dedicated the *Garland*, had a particular interest in Cynicism and was evidently one of Diogenes Laertius' chief sources of information about it. In one passage based on Diocles the reference seems to be to Cynics of Diocles' own day.   After discussing the individual Cynics, Diogenes Laertius gives some account of ' their common doctrines ' (τὰ κοινῇ ἀρέσκοντα αὐτοῖς).

They hold that we should live frugally, eating food for nourishment only and wearing nothing but the τρίβων, and they despise wealth and high birth and fame.   Some of them live on vegetables and

---

[1] Athea., 157*b*.   [2] id., ib.   [3] Tel., *Rel.*, p. 41. 6.
[4] Ermatinger, in *Virchow. Samm.*, N.F. 13, calculates that ' he mentions 14 persons of both sexes, in terms of amorous passion '.

drink only cold water, and are content with any kind of shelter, or with tubs, as Diogenes had been. . . . [1]

That the ' Cynicus habitus ' at least was known in Greece in the Augustan age is to be inferred from an epigram of Antipater of Thessalonica [2] on a degenerate Cynic.

They cry shame on you, the wallet, and the stout staff of Diogenes of Sinope, meet weapon for a Heracles, and the doubled cloak bespattered with filthy mud, protection against bitter showers, they are befouled by hanging from your shoulders. Truly Diogenes was the Heavenly Dog, but you the dog of the dust heap. Put off these weapons that are not yours ; the lion's array is not for bearded goats.

Apart from the works of Meleager, there is little evidence of literary activity amongst the Cynics of this period. Berlin Papyrus, No. 13044, is dated by Wilcken [3] as *c.* 100 B.C. and is an echo of Onesicratus' description of the Gymnosophists. Alexander, however, does not receive favourable treatment, he is the τύραννος finally discomfited by the wisdom of the Gymnosophists, who wear the cloak of the Cynics. There is little or no literary merit about the fragment, it is a popularized version of the theme of an encounter between Cynic and tyrant : a theme later elaborately treated by Dio Chrysostom. The first half of the first century B.C. is apparently the date of the ' Wiener Diogenes Papyrus ', a collection of anecdotes, most of which are in Laertius' account of Diogenes. The so-called ' letters of the Cynics ' date in part at least from the Augustan age.[4] They purport to come from Antisthenes, Diogenes and Crates, but as von Fritz [5] shows, evince no sign of acquaintance with the works of their supposed authors, their knowledge of whom derives from the accounts built up by the χρεῖαι and the fictitious Diogenes-literature of the third century and later. Frequently they are merely elaborations of familiar Cynic anecdotes, e.g. the story of how Diogenes learned to dispense with his wooden drinking-cup ; others again are dialogues— narrated in a letter. The remarkable 28th epistle of Diogenes is addressed to the Greek race as a whole, and is a bitter polemic against the general standards of contemporary civilization.

[1] D.L., vi. 104.   [2] *Anth.,* xi. 158.   [3] Berlin, *Ak. Sitz.,* 1923.
[4] Capelle, *De Cynic. epistulis. Gott. Diss.,* 1896.
[5] *Diog., von Sin.*

From the number of references to tyrants and the misery of their lot in the epistles it is likely that many of them were composed in the Early Roman Empire. The purpose of the epistles may well have been, as Capelle suggests, to provide propaganda for the revival of Cynicism in the first century A.D. The absence of any individual character makes it hard to date them, but their anonymity is a true reflection of a period when the ' Cynic philosophy ' resembled nothing so much as an hereditary collection of well-worn gramophone records.

This completes the examination of the evidence for the survival of Cynicism during the last two centuries before Christ. We have seen that it did little more than gain a footing at Rome, and was presumably unknown elsewhere in the West ; in the Eastern half of the Mediterranean world it survived in obscurity, attracting far less attention than had been the case in the third century. Though Cynic writings of the best period still exert a considerable influence on literature, little new literature is found coming from the movement. Surveying the state of Cynicism at the end of the Augustan age, we should not be inclined to predict for it a revival and at least another five hundred years of life. But history was repeating itself, at least, in so far as it ever does ; that is to say that the conditions which had proved favourable for the growth of Cynicism after the death of Alexander were being reproduced in the early years of the first century A.D. The Imperial system, though an enormous gain in efficiency of administration, had taken the interest out of politics ; there was a great increase in cosmopolitanism ; finally, luxury was more rampant than ever, and philosophy, even Stoicism, had compromised with it. There was a demand for a simpler, practical creed, which Cynicism was to meet. The ' lion's array ' of Diogenes would again find worthy wearers ; Cynicism was to be, not reborn, but revived.

CHAPTER VII

DEMETRIUS. THE 'PHILOSOPHIC OPPOSITION' IN THE FIRST CENTURY A.D.

THE first name heard of after Cynicism's long period of obscurity and anonymity is that of Demetrius.[1] If no Cynic of the previous two hundred years stands in so clear a light, it is but another indication of how during this period interest focuses on Rome. Men may have followed the Cynic life with commendable, if not equal, austerity in Greece or in Asia Minor, but their names have not survived because they lacked Roman admirers. Demetrius carried on his propaganda at Rome, and aroused the interest of the Roman nobility, whose influence is paramount in the Latin literature of the period. If, then, he appears as an isolated phenomenon, this is probably misleading.

Demetrius would seem to have been born earlier than A.D. 10 ; nothing is known of his family or his earlier years. We first hear of him as attracting attention in Rome during the reign of Caligula [2] ; for Seneca says that he has heard from Demetrius' own lips how the Emperor had offered him 200,000 sesterces, which he had refused. ' It would have cost him his whole Empire ', the Cynic would add, ' to induce me to change my way of life.' From this passage von Arnim [3] deduces that already Demetrius was noted for the ' anti-monarchical radicalism ' that he showed under Nero and Vespasian. This assumption would appear to read more into the passage than is warranted ; and a more probable explanation is that the story of Demetrius' poverty and asceticism, which were remarkable even by Cynic standards, had provoked Caligula's erratic curiosity to discover whether such virtue was indeed proof against the temptation of wealth. The language of Seneca supports this view : the Emperor is trying

---

[1] See Note to Chap. VII.   [2] Sen., *de ben.*, vii. 11.
[3] In *Pauly-Wissowa v.* sub Demetrius, 91.

' aut honorare aut corrumpere Demetrium ', who rejects the gift with scorn as being ' not even worth refusing ' (' ne dignam qua non accepta gloriaretur '). Moreover, had Demetrius really been a troublesome opponent, it is unlikely that attempts to silence him would have stopped at unsuccessful bribery.

The next references belong to the early years of Nero, and show Demetrius as a well-known figure in Rome, unsparing alike in his own asceticism and in attacks on the luxury of the age. He was probably in Rome thenceforward till the death of Thrasea Paetus in 66 [1] ; in addition to his connexions with the curious coterie that surrounded Thrasea, he was cultivated by Seneca, alike when minister of Nero and in retirement. After the death of Thrasea he appears to have been banished from Rome and to have lived in Greece,[2] but he must have

---

[1] Philostratus has a story that he taught at Corinth during some part of this period ; that there he came under the influence of Apollonius of Tyana, whom he followed to Rome, but shortly afterwards (we are to infer) was expelled by Tigellinus for attacking the Thermae of Nero as useless and demoralizing extravagance. The details of this story do not bear examination. The Thermae were built in 60, but Tigellinus did not come into power till 62, and since Philostratus says that the attack was delivered on the completion of the Thermae, it must have taken place (if at all) after their rebuilding in 66. But in the *Epistles to Lucilius*, composed between 57 and 64, Seneca refers several times to Demetrius in a way which suggests he was then in Rome, and in the *De Providentia*, which is generally dated A.D. 62, says definitely that he has just been in his company (' a quo recens sum ', *de Prov.*, 3, 3). It is certain that Demetrius was with Thrasea Paetus at his death in 66, and hardly questionable that he had then been in close touch with him for several years. A visit of Demetrius to Greece between the years 57 and 66 is therefore unlikely, at least, it is hardly conceivable that he could have been there long enough to gather about him a crowd of disciples, as Philostratus suggests. He may well have been banished just after 66, but for more serious reasons than an attack on the Thermae ; Nero was very tolerant of such criticism. And it is a comment on the value of Philostratus as evidence that he does not mention Demetrius' connexion with Thrasea ; though he can give a detailed account of how the Cynic's ' pupil ' Menippus escaped in the nick of time from being married to a vampire.

[2] It must be admitted that the evidence on this point is scanty. Epictetus quotes him as being undismayed when threatened with death by Nero, which suggests most naturally that proceedings were taken against him after the death of Thrasea. Philostratus, as has been said, states that he was banished for criticizing the Thermae, and further states that he met Musonius engaged on digging Nero's

returned to Rome soon after the end of Nero's reign, for we find him opposing Musonius Rufus in the prosecution of Egnatius Celer. In vituperation at least he was the most prominent of the philosophers who opposed Vespasian, and was expelled from Rome in 71. Of his later life little is known ; but it seems likely that he lived in Greece, to judge from the stories of his encounter with Vespasian and his influence on Demonax. Philostratus represents him as living at Dicae-archia in Italy during the later years of Domitian, with what truth is unknown.

The teaching of Demetrius, at least so far as it can be recaptured from the references in Seneca, seems to have been in the familiar tradition of the austerer Cynicism. The insistence on the practical aspect of philosophy, and the consequent depreciation of theory and of scientific speculation, contempt for the unconverted mass of humanity, complete suppression of desires, attacks on the luxury of the age—all are in the well-known vein of the gospel according to Diogenes. For the opponents of convention had standardized both the manner and the matter of their assault into a conventional form, which demanded of its expositors no originality of thought, but rather, at best, unimpeachable asceticism and sufficient wit and rhetorical power to hold the attention of an audience. The only passage whose thought does not quite harmonize with that of traditional Cynicism is one where Demetrius professes complete and unquestioning resignation to the Will of God. Resignation, indeed, the older Cynicism had counselled, but rather resignation to Fate ; and one cannot but suspect that the religious colour of the passage may be due rather to Seneca than to Demetrius. Even if it is true for Demetrius, it is probably a borrowing from contemporary Stoicism. The apophthegms quoted by Seneca bear evidence of Demetrius' powers of expression ; that which calls a life which has never borne the attacks of Fortune a Dead Sea, is perhaps the most striking. But for us Demetrius is chiefly interesting not for his teaching or for a few striking

Isthmian Canal. Chronologically there is no objection to these stories ; the Thermae were completed in 66, the Canal begun in 67. The story in Lucian (*adv. indoct.*, 19), which shows Demetrius at Corinth, does not help, as it cannot be assigned specifically to the years 66–9.

phrases, but rather for the appearance he makes in Roman history.

The association of Demetrius with Thrasea Paetus and his circle is the most valuable piece of evidence for the so-called ' philosophic opposition ' which is such an interesting feature of Roman politics in the second half of the first century A.D. The precise nature and extent of this opposition have been very variously estimated. Dio Cassius says that Thrasea and Soranus were killed, not for what they did but for what they were; a point which Tacitus makes in his own way by telling how Nero, as the culmination of his Reign of Terror, deter- mined to attack Virtue Incarnate in the person of Thrasea Paetus. Boissier,[1] in saying that the opposition was ' plus morale que politique ', also implies that its persecution was the revenge of outraged vice on virtue. But, as Henderson justly remarks,[2] ' a mere dislike of arrogated superiority in morals is not quite an adequate explanation of a rigorous treatment ' ; and one remembers that similar rigour was employed by Vespasian and Domitian. The circumstances of the attacks made on the Stoic opposition by the three emperors are very similar ; in each case a prominent Roman aristocrat of Repub- lican sympathies was put to death, and Cynic and Stoic phil- osophers were banished from Rome. This differentiation in the punishment accorded to the two elements of the opposition shows how the authorities estimated the relative degree of political danger they represented ; and any analysis of the opposition must recognize its twofold nature. For, though the Roman aristocrats might be in agreement with their Greek philosophical directors in allegiance to Stoic ethical doctrine, they cannot have taken their political views from Zeno or Diogenes. Thrasea, Helvidius Priscus, Paconius Agrippinus and the rest, represent a resurgence of the old Roman aristo- cratic spirit which found its true embodiment in Cato, and it was an essentially Roman tradition, and not Stoicism, which governed their political outlook. Admittedly the mind of a Cato is an ' anima naturaliter Stoica ' ; but the Roman Republic, though idealized by Panaetius, was always different from a Stoic commonwealth. Early Stoicism had defined the best constitution as being a blend of kingship, oligarchy, and

[1] *L'Opposition sous les Césars*, p. 103.
[2] *Life and Principate of the Emperor Nero*, p. 295.

democracy; but the insistence on the Stoic paradox of the βασιλεία enjoyed by the σοφός made it especially sympathetic to the idea of the philosopher-king. This sympathy for βασιλεία is especially marked in the Stoics of the first century A.D. Nature herself, according to Seneca, first conceived the idea of a king, as we see from the example of bees and other insects.[1] The Roman emperor must recognize that he holds the most sacred and most responsible of all positions, he has been chosen as the viceroy of God on earth.[2] Musonius Rufus regarded a king as 'Law Incarnate, the contriver of good government and harmony (ὁμόνοια), the emulator of God, and, as He is, the father of his subjects'.[3] So too Dio Chrysostom[4] described to Trajan the majestic spectacle of the Peak of Kingship, also called the Peak of God, where Basileia sits throned, attended by Justice and Good Government, Law and Peace. Chrysippus had said that the σοφός will live with kings, and Seneca declares that he above all others will feel gratitude to the monarch who makes it possible for him to enjoy leisure, to control his own time, and to live in a tranquillity uninterrupted by public employments. To such a man, the emperor will seem a god . . . 'deus nobis haec otia fecit'. And Epictetus[5] acknowledges the debt the world owes to Trajan for the gift of peace, though insisting that peace of the soul can only be won through philosophy. Against monarchy as such, Philosophy had no objection to urge; if it criticizes, the criticism must be directed against the monarch himself. For according to the Stoic paradox, the σοφός is a king in his own right, understanding the art of government, though his kingdom is not of worldly things. As for the Cynic, he is schoolmaster as well as king, the παιδαγωγός of the human race, whose duty is to advise or admonish all who stand in need of correction, even though it be the Emperor himself. So the Cynic Isidorus reproached Nero, with the well-worn Cynic taunt that 'he knew well how to sing the ills of Nauplia, but disposed ill of his own goods'.[6]

From Stoic-Cynic doctrine, then, there was no menace to

[1] de Clem., i. 19.
[2] 'Electus sum, qui in terris deorum vice fungerer.' de Clem., i. 2.
[3] fr. viii. 8. 1.   [4] Or., i. 74, 75.   [5] Epict., lxxiii. 10.
[6] Suet., Nero, c. 39.

10

monarchy, but authority must always claim to judge a movement by its fruits. There were, at the beginning of Nero's reign, those who regarded Philosophy as a potential source of danger : there was some opposition to Seneca's acting as tutor to Nero, on the grounds that the Stoic system was most unsuitable for the education of princes.[1] In 64 Seneca found it necessary to protest against the view that ' The faithful adherents of Philosophy are rebellious and fractious persons, ever deriding kings and officials and those responsible for the conduct of public affairs.'[2] The protagonists of this view, one of whom was Tigellinus, must have felt that their case was greatly strengthened by the evidence of the Pisonian conspiracy. The record of Stoicism, viewed from the official standpoint in the early months of 66, could only have seemed a bad one. Rubellius Plautus, a possible rival for the principate, first banished to Asia and then executed, had been a prominent member of the sect ; his teacher, Musonius Rufus, was exiled shortly after the Pisonian conspiracy, which had implicated other distinguished adherents of Stoicism in Seneca and Lucan. Henderson[3] stresses the complete change in Nero's attitude to the nobility after the Pisonian conspiracy ; for the previous ten years he had treated them with marked clemency, now he regarded the nobility with distrust and the Senate with hatred. Such is the necessary preface to a consideration of Nero's attack on that eminent noble, senator, and Stoic, Thrasea Paetus.

The attack was, of course, not unexpected. Thrasea had incurred Nero's displeasure some years earlier, though there had been an attempt at a reconciliation. It is improbable that the reconciliation was sincere ; and we have evidence that for several months before his trial Thrasea had been living in daily expectation of exile or death.[4] The actual evidence on which he was condemned is dismissed by Furneaux[5] as ' flimsy ' ; but he rightly insists that no evidence

---

[1] de. Clem., ii. v. 2.   [2] Sen. Epist. Mor., 73.   [3] op. cit., p. 288 ff.
[4] Epictetus [1. 1. 26 ff.] tells how he remarked to Musonius Rufus, ' I would rather be put to death to-day than exiled to-morrow.' Musonius was banished late in 65 or early in 66, the trial of Thrasea was held in July 66. Coming from Musonius' pupil the story is trustworthy.
[5] Tacitus, Annals, Vol. ii, p. 81.

can have been produced of another conspiracy of which
Tacitus says nothing, for the trial was held in the Senate,
and Tacitus presumably derives his information from official
reports. We may be confident, then, that the Tacitean
account represents the substance of the case against Thrasea,
and indeed it is hard to see why some scholars have tried to
look outside it to find the reasons for his condemnation. I
do not, of course, suggest that his accusers, Capito Cossutianus
and Eprius Marcellus, were animated by any concern for
the welfare of the state ; they were Nero's creatures, and
were chiefly concerned to earn the handsome reward they
might expect if a conviction was secured. That being
admitted, it can hardly be denied that they produced a strong
case.

The gist of it is, Thrasea was setting himself up as the ' dux
et auctor ' of a system which was opposed to the Imperial
authority : his prestige among his followers was enormous,
and was elsewhere attracting widespread attention : there was
the possibility (hinted at but not directly mentioned by the
prosecution) that the more impetuous of his followers might
attempt to assassinate the Emperor. There the accusers were
content to rest their case, and it is odd that modern scholars
should so often have asked more of them. Their dissatisfaction, one may suggest, arises from failure to estimate
correctly the Emperor's position, above all, his exposure to
assassination. Boissier, for example, belittles the importance
of Thrasea's opposition on the grounds that his political
activities consisted in doing nothing.[1] But non-participation
and passive resistance are the most effective weapons against
an Imperial system, as a far more liberal Empire than that of
the Caesars has recently experienced. Idealism, no doubt,
would prefer that Thrasea should have headed a party in the
Senate and have worked for a majority with the object of
finally deposing Nero senatus consulto. But such methods
were completely impracticable in the Rome of the Emperors
and there were in any case quicker ways of getting rid of a
rule that depended on the life of a single man. But though
modern historians have doubted the force of the case for the
prosecution, it was fully acknowledged by Thrasea and his
party. For them, the question was not how to effect a defence,

[1] op. cit., p. 102.

but simply whether or not Thrasea should appear in the Senate on the day of the trial.[1] Conviction they regarded as inevitable, but it was felt that a better moral could be pointed by absence : and Thrasea's last act of non-participation was to stay away from his own trial. He was condemned to death, and it is hard to see how the verdict could have gone otherwise ; for though in private life he may have been the embodiment of virtue, that was from the official point of view entirely irrelevant.

His associates, Helvidius Priscus and Paconius Agrippinus, who had ' not as yet dared to emulate the contumacy of their leader ', were banished from Italy, a relatively mild punishment. Demetrius, Thrasea's philosophic guide, was probably banished shortly after the trial ; and about this time or a little earlier a similar sentence was passed on Cornutus, the teacher of Lucan—no doubt occasioned rather by his profession of the ' intempestiva sapientia ' of the Stoics than by any too outspoken criticism of Nero's literary abilities. Barea Soranus, whose trial took place on the same day as that of Thrasea, is not explicitly named as one of the latter's ' satellites '. But he was a prominent Stoic, and enjoyed the intimacy of Musonius Rufus ; he was condemned, like Musonius, on the score of his old associations with Rubellius Plautus. By the end of Nero's reign the Stoic opposition was muzzled, for all its most prominent members had either been put to death or else exiled.

After the death of Nero the exiles appear to have flocked back. Musonius and Helvidius Priscus were recalled by Galba ; before the end of 69 Demetrius was probably again in Rome. During the next few years the opposition had more scope for political action than had been the case under Nero ; the disorders of the ' Year of the Four Emperors ' gave the Senate a political importance it had not enjoyed since the establishment of the Principate, and of the surviving members of Thrasea Paetus' coterie, both Arulenus Rusticus and Helvidius held important offices, being praetors for the years 69 and 70 respectively.[2] Again, Vespasian was at first tolerant, till the intransigeance of the opposition forced him to severe measures. Unfortunately, our evidence for the opposition to Vespasian is scanty. Tacitus stressed the importance of

[1] *Annals*, xvi. 25, 26.   [2] Tac., *Hist.*, iii, 80 ; iv, 53.

the career of Helvidius Priscus ' which won him much glory
and much hatred ', and gives a character sketch as a prelude
to the frequent appearances he is to make ; but the Histories,
as we have them, break off before his opposition to Vespasian
has become acute, and even the account of its early stages
contains a most annoying lacuna at a critical point. The narrative of Dio Cassius is also much abridged ; and Suetonius,
the only authority for the fate of Helvidius, says little of his
policy. The impression of the opposition that can be derived
from these authorities is that it was directed by Helvidius,
who began with two main objects in view, to exact revenge
from the ' delatores ' responsible for the deaths of Thrasea
and Barea Soranus, and to secure a greater share of political
importance for the Senate in general and for himself in
particular. His impetuosity and ambition brought him increasingly into conflict with Vespasian, thus driving him to
an embittered opposition to the monarchy which finally became
so vocal that the reluctant Emperor had to get rid of him.[1]

Helvidius' first act in the principate of Galba was an attempt
to bring the arch-informer, Eprius Marcellus, to justice. The
possibility of a trial caused great excitement in the Senate,
some warmly approved of it, others were themselves too
deeply involved to feel easy about the outcome of investiga-
tions into the ' delatores '. Moreover, Galba himself was in
insecure occupation of the throne, and could not afford to face
a major split in the Senate. He therefore prevailed on Helvidius to drop the case against Marcellus for a time ; it was in
fact not taken up till some months later, under Vespasian.

When the attack on the delatores was taken up again, as a
preliminary trial of strength it was decided to fly at lesser game
than Eprius Marcellus.[2] The obvious object of attack was the
notorious Egnatius Celer, the betrayer of Barea Soranus. He
was not a senator, nor one of the great ' delatores ', so that his
fall was unlikely to involve any one else, moreover he was
manifestly guilty. The case was clearly one in which the
Emperor could safely let public feeling have its way, and feeling
was overwhelmingly opposed to Celer. The prosecution was
conducted by Musonius Rufus, the defence, surprisingly

---

[1] Our chief authority for what follows is Tacitus. *Vide Hist.*, iv,
c. 5–11 ; 40–4 ; 53.
[2] *Hist.*, iv. 10 and 40.

enough, by the Cynic Demetrius. Tacitus says that Demetrius
appeared to be acting ' ambitiosius quam honestius ' in under-
taking the defence.[1] It is hard to see what he means, and one
is tempted to suppose he is indulging his penchant for discovering evil motives behind every action. Celer lacked the
skill or the nerve to defend himself, and however guilty, had a
claim to be represented : it is hard to say what ambition
Demetrius could be serving in thus championing an unpopular
case. The spectacle of Stoic and Cynic appearing in the Roman
courts as prosecutor and counsel for the defence is in itself
remarkable, and appears even more so when we consider the
charge on which Celer was tried. He was, of course, condemned, and men read in the enthusiasm which greeted his
downfall a favourable omen for the attack on those greater
personages, the ' delatores ' themselves. A measure was
passed in the Senate which required all members to take an
oath that they were personally innocent of any attack on the
life of a senator during the reign of Nero, and which requested
the Emperor to permit access to the Imperial archives, that the
names of the ' delatores ' might be discovered in each case.
The oath was taken with much prevarication and some perjury,
and the feeling against the delatores was becoming intense.
All who had suffered joined the attack ; and there was one
particularly stormy meeting of the Senate. Domitian was
present, and at the climax of a series of attacks Helvidius
fiercely denounced Eprius Marcellus.

So hostile was the temper of the Senate that the chief
' delatores ' found it prudent to withdraw ; in so doing,
Marcellus uttered the ominous remark, ' I leave you to your
Senate, Priscus, play the king in the presence of Caesar.'
The day was passed in bitter discord, the majority of the
Senate being for the destruction of the ' informers ', while a
' few strong men ' urged an amnesty. The House rose with
nothing decided, but the prospects for the overthrow of the
informers were never so bright. At the next meeting came
the reversal, with a display of the Emperor's power which was
all the more impressive from the moderation of its tone.
Before any one else was called on to give an opinion, Domitian
spoke in favour of an amnesty ; he was followed by Mucianus,

---

[1] Possibly ' acting more from desire for notoriety than desire for
good repute '.

who spoke to the same effect, in particular suggesting the abandonment of the case against the delatores. Mucianus' speech was couched in mild language, amounting almost to a plea, but it was obviously 'inspired'. Once the Emperor's wishes were known, the obedient Senate performed a complete volte-face, and the matter was dropped. It was a crushing blow for the policy of Helvidius Priscus, and it may well be that the headstrong bitterness of his later opposition to Vespasian was largely occasioned by the disappointment of that day.

At every point the Senate had failed Helvidius' hopes, but he did all that a single individual could to lessen the Emperor's prestige. As praetor he omitted the Emperor's titles on his edicts, on his return to Rome he greeted him merely by the name 'Vespasian', 'such was his disrespect for the Emperor on all occasions that he seemed to be almost depriving him of his status' ('cogere eum in ordinem').[1] As has been said, our evidence for Helvidius' actions at this period is scanty, we merely know that his opposition was daring and bitter, and that Vespasian showed remarkable tolerance. We hear of a scene in the Senate, when Helvidius opposed Vespasian, who left the House in tears with the remark, 'Either my son shall succeed me, or no one at all.'[2]

Rostovtseff makes the attractive suggestion that the point at issue was the succession to the throne, and that Helvidius had objected to the nomination of Titus as heir, and wished the next emperor to be chosen as the 'best man', in the Stoic-Cynic sense.[3] Opposition to the principle of hereditary monarchy may well have been a feature of Stoic-Cynic propaganda, and as Rostovtseff points out, Philosophy made a truce with the monarchy when the principle of adoption was observed, as it was from Nerva to Marcus Aurelius. But it seems hardly possible to doubt that Helvidius was a genuine Republican; his book in praise of Cato, his refusal to acknowledge the Emperor's titles on his edicts, his behaviour 'ut libera semper civitate usus', all point in that direction. More significant still are the reasons Dio Cassius gives for his final suppression.

[1] Suet., *Vesp.*, c. 15.   [2] id., ib., c. 25 ; Dio. Cass., lxv. 12. 1.
[3] *Social and Economic Hist. of the Roman Empire*, p. 519, p. 14. Elsewhere he appears to think that the remark referred to a conspiracy.

Vespasian hated Helvidius, not on account of his abuse of himself and his friends, but because he was a turbulent fellow who cultivated the mob and was for ever praising democracy and denouncing the monarchy. He banded men together as though it were the function of philosophy to overthrow the established order, insult those in power, and bring about a revolution.[1]

Helvidius was first punished by ' relegatio in insulam ', then by death, though at the last moment the Emperor tried to cancel the order of his execution.

The banishment of Helvidius and the expulsion of Stoic and Cynic philosophers from Rome presumably took place about the same time, i.e. between 71 and 75, and more probably in the early part of that period rather than the later. The expulsion was ordered at the instigation of Mucianus, and the reasons for it are stated in more general terms that those which led to the suppression of Helvidius.

Inasmuch as many philosophers actuated by Stoic principles, especially Demetrius the Cynic, were taking advantage of the name of philosophy to preach publicly many doctrines inappropriate to the age, and had thus subtly corrupted certain persons, Mucianus . . . denounced them at length and persuaded Vespasian to expel all such persons from the city.

The nature of these inappropriate doctrines is not stated, but it is tempting to believe with Rostovtseff that what the Cynics and Stoics were opposing was the principle of hereditary succession to the principate : such doctrines were certainly inappropriate so soon after Titus' nomination as ' Imperator designatus '. It is clear, too, that in their propaganda they vigorously assailed the Emperor personally, and his favourite Mucianus ; Mucianus had not the Emperor's tolerance of ' yapping dogs ', and his resentment shows through his denunciation of the Stoics.

They are full of empty boasting, and if one of them grows a long beard and elevates his eyebrows, and throws his τριβώνίον over his shoulder and goes barefooted he claims straightway wisdom and courage and righteousness, and gives himself great airs, though he may not know his letters nor, as the saying goes, how to swim. They despise every one, and call the man of good family effeminate,

---

[1] D.C., 65. 12.

the low-born poor-spirited, the handsome man a debauchee, the ugly person simple-minded, the rich covetous, and the poor greedy.[1]

The passage is interesting as showing how at this period Stoic and Cynic philosophers were practically indistinguishable, alike in their rationale and their propaganda. Demetrius and Hostilianus were the most prominent undesirables, and were treated with the harsher sentence of ' relegatio in insulam ',[2] the others being merely expelled from the city of Rome. Hostilianus withdrew, but Demetrius remained obstinate, continuing his abuse and propaganda. Vespasian wisely refused to honour him with martyrdom, and ultimately he was compelled to accept his sentence ; so far as we know, he never again returned to Rome. The expulsion of Stoics and Cynics was complete, but for one exception—Musonius Rufus, who appears to have been exempted by name from the decree. It is probable that the prestige he had gained from his successful prosecution of Celer made it unwise to take immediate action against him ; that his doctrines were not more acceptable than those of the rest of the sect is suggested by the statement that he was banished shortly after the decree of general expulsion.[3]

But by A.D. 75 some of the Cynics had got back again into Rome, and were fanning the popular opposition to the marriage of Titus and Berenice. One Diogenes entered the theatre when it was full, and denounced them in a long abusive speech. He got off with a flogging, but another member of the sect, called Heras, who, expecting no harsher treatment, ' gave vent to many abusive remarks ', was beheaded.[4] Rostovtseff suggests that the punishment of Heras is evidence that he directly attacked the Emperor himself.

The next occasion on which philosophy came into conflict with the Imperial authority was during the reign of Domitian. It is clear that there were two separate ' expulsions of philosophers ',[5] and it is reasonable to suppose that the first of these

---

[1] D.C., 65. 13.   [2] id., ib. 13.
[3] *Vide* Hense, *Musonii reliquiae*, p. xxxv.   [4] D.C., 65. 15.
[5] Furneaux (Tac., *Agric.*, note on c. 2) says that Eusebius is an only authority for the earlier exile. But Dio Cassius (67. 13. 2) speaks of ' the philosophers being again driven out ', i.e. the general expulsion which followed the prosecution of Rusticus and Herennius Senecio, clearly implying that measures had previously been taken against them.

was in 89, and in some way connected with the conspiracy of Antonius Saturninus. This conspiracy was for Domitian what the Pisonian conspiracy was for Nero ; henceforward he was suspicious of the nobility, and hag-ridden by a perpetual and well-founded dread of assassination. The suppression of the conspiracy was followed by the execution of many Roman nobles. These executions were carried out in a secrecy which made them even more formidable ; we know few names of victims, but it is likely that many of those mentioned by Suetonius as executed for trivial reasons were really implicated in the conspiracy of Saturninus. The measures taken against the philosophers are not clear. It is probable that their expulsion came about through connexion with the discontented and rebellious members of the aristocracy, as had been the case under Vespasian. But the decree of expulsion can hardly have been a general one, or if so it was not rigidly enforced, for in five years' time we find the philosophers back in the city again ; while it does not seem likely that any action was taken against the philosopher Artemidorus till the second expulsion.

The more severe storm broke in 94 [1] to suppress an opposition that was clearly becoming more vocal. The features of Domitian's rule which caused the aristocracy to hate him more than any previous emperor are well known—his abolition of the principle of dyarchy, and the consequent disappearance of the last vestiges of senatorial authority, his insistence on the cult of his personal divinity, all combined to transform the Roman Empire into an Oriental tyranny. All men were not content with preserving that ' fifteen-year-long silence ' which Tacitus says lay so heavily on his generation. The opposition came from the quarter in which one would naturally look for it : the survivors and descendants of those who had opposed Nero. Helvidius Priscus, son of the victim of Vespasian, produced an Atellane farce which apparently could be construed as a satire on the intrigue between the Empress Domitilla and the actor Paris ; the fact that the satire came from one of that name no doubt weighed heavily against him, and he was

[1] I follow the chronology of Otto (*Sitz. der. Bayer. Akad.*, 1919, 10, p. 43 ff.), who places the decree against the philosophers in the last months of 94, a position he defends (id., 1923, i., p. 4 ff.) against the attack of Baehrens (Hermes, 58 (1923), p. 109 ff.).

put to death. Shortly after his death appeared the two famous eulogies on the great Stoic martyrs, that on Thrasea Paetus by Arulenus Rusticus, who as a rash young tribune had proposed to interpose his veto on Thrasea's trial ; that on Helvidius Priscus by Herennius Senecio, from materials supplied by Helvidius' wife, Fannia. The publication of these books evidently attracted much notice, and inflamed the hostility already felt towards Domitian; accordingly the informers were unleashed, and in the issue the authors were put to death, and their books publicly and ignominiously burned.

In connexion with this affair came the decree of the Senate which expelled from the city all philosophers, ' mathematici ', and ' astrologi.' The philosophers were implicated, as they had been in the time of Vespasian by their connexions with the disaffected Roman aristocrats ; Artemidorus, one of the most prominent Stoics of the day, was the son-in-law of Musonius Rufus, and Epictetus had been Musonius' pupil.[1] The mathematici and astrologi were expelled because their revelations of the future served to encourage conspiracies against the Emperor's life. In some cases the rôle of ' philosopher ' and astrologer might be combined, as is clear from the story of Apollonius of Tyana. ' During the reign of Domitian ', says Philostratus, ' some philosophers fled for refuge to the Western Celts, others hid themselves in Scythia or Libya.'[2] This can hardly be taken as evidence for the results of the expulsion of 94 ; the only philosopher known to have visited Scythia is Dio Chrysostom, who had been banished from Bithynia twelve years earlier, and who only took up philosophy after his banishment. One suspects that the Western Celts and Libya

---

[1] It is highly probable that Epictetus withdrew to Nicopolis in 94, and that those who, with Robert (in *P.W.*, sub Epictetus), regard 89 as the occasion of his retirement from Rome are wrong. For (1) Aulus Gellius (cv. 11) definitely says that he retired as a consequence of the senatorial decree banishing philosophers ; (2) Pliny (*Ep.*, iii., xi. 1) connects the expulsion of philosophers with the prosecution of Herennius Senecio and Arulenus Rusticus, as does Tacitus (*Agr.*, c. 2).

[2] Phil., vii. 4. Throughout this section Philostratus' purpose is to contrast the cowardly action of other philosophers with that of his hero Apollonius. They fled for refuge to the ends of the earth, Apollonius (not a little fortified, it may be suggested, by his useful gift of being able to disappear at will) remained to confront Domitian.

are introduced as rhetorical antitheses to Scythia; and the statement of Pliny that he visited Artemidorus in a suburban villa near Rome shows that the clause of the decree which banned the philosophers from Italy was not immediately enforced. But Artemidorus seems to have been kept under some kind of surveillance, and it was dangerous for any one in authority to visit him. The teaching of Epictetus in Nicopolis, on the other hand, seems to have been in no way restricted. The statement of Dio Cassius that ' many persons were put to death on this same charge of philosophizing ' refers (if to any one, for no names are given) to Roman aristocrats; the only case we know in which a non-aristocrat was executed for this or similar reasons is that of the ' sophist ' Maternus, who was ' put to death for abusing tyranny in a practice speech '.[1]

Within two years after the expulsion of the philosophers Domitian was dead, and the ' period of tribulation for the human race ' was over. Under the mild and benignant rule of Nerva ' monarchy and liberty, previously irreconcilable, were joined together '. ' Libertas publica ', ' Roma renascens ', were more than legends on the coinage, they were true reflections of the spirit of the times. ' If Cato were alive to-day, he would be a monarchist ', is a statement which by itself can hardly carry much weight, coming as it does from one who was guilty of the grossest flattery under Domitian. But the chorus of approval is universal, the *Panegyricus* of Pliny and the speeches περὶ βασιλείας of Dio Chrysostom show how the nobles and the philosophers, the two disaffected classes in the time of Domitian, are enthusiastic in support of the New Model monarchy of Trajan. Philosophy, indeed, as we have already seen, had never opposed monarchy, but only individual monarchs, and Dio Chrysostom, describing the Stoic-Cynic ideal of βασιλεία, suggests that it finds an embodiment in Trajan.[2]

Pliny had been the friend of the Stoic aristocrats who

---

[1] D.C., 67. 12. Was Maternus a rhetorician of the ' Second Sophistic ' or a philosopher? Dion Cassius speaks of the Cynics who crept back into Rome after the expulsion in the reign of Vespasian as σοφισταί, but the account of the ' practice speech ' suggests that Maternus was really a rhetorician.

[2] Dio Chrys., 1. 55.

perished under Domitian, but he was probably not so much attracted by the ideal of Cato as repelled by the actions of Domitian. He and his kind were not Republicans, they knew a good emperor when they saw one, and were prepared to support him. The small and closely related group of irreconcilables which had successively opposed Nero, Vespasian and Domitian had been almost extinguished. Writing in A.D. 107, when Fannia, widow of the elder Helvidius Priscus, lay dying, Pliny laments that, 'though she leaves descendants, yet at her death an ancient house will seem to be extinct '.[1] This appears to imply that the descendants were mere children, and in any case none of them adopted the rôle of opposition to the Emperor which was almost hereditary in their house. The only descendant we know of the Stoics of Domitian's reign is that Junius Rusticus who was consul suffectus in 133, city-prefect in the reign of Antoninus, and the teacher of Marcus Aurelius. Fannia, that indomitable old lady, must have been the last of the Republicans. Henceforward, as Rostovtseff says, there was an alliance between the educated classes and the monarchy —an alliance whose undisturbed harmony led to the Golden Age of the Antonines. Philosophy and especially Stoicism enjoyed the imperial favour ; and although Cynicism, its companion in adversity, did not follow it to court in the second century, there is no sign of any general opposition of the Cynics to the monarchy.[2] Under Antoninus the principle was laid down that ' no one in the garb of a philosopher was ever to be punished '. Finally, with Marcus Aurelius the old dream of the philosopher king was at last realized.

NOTE TO CHAPTER VII

Authorities.—For the character and teaching of Demetrius the best authority is Seneca. His references to Demetrius may fairly be regarded as trustworthy ; he esteemed the philosopher highly, and

---

[1] Pliny, epist. vii.

[2] Dio Chrysostom says that in the time of Trajan the Cynics in Alexandria were to blame for outbreaks of rioting ; while Peregrinus inveighed against Antoninus in Rome, and was apparently concerned in an abortive rising in Achaea, as we shall see. But Alexandria always had politics of its own, which necessitated its being treated as a special case. Peregrinus, too, was not a person from whose actions it is safe to generalize.

was apparently very intimate with him throughout the years A.D. 51–65. Tacitus mentions Demetrius' connexion with Thrasea Paetus and the ' philosophic opposition '; his activities under Vespasian, and his banishment, are referred to by Suetonius and Dio Cassius. There are also several references to him in Philostratus' *Life of Apollonius of Tyana*, but, as will be contended, these are of doubtful value.

CHAPTER VIII

CYNICISM IN THE SECOND CENTURY A.D.

(a) General Character

The period between the death of Vespasian and that of Marcus Aurelius saw Cynicism numerically far stronger than it had ever been before. The fact is reflected in the literature of the period, for references to the Cynics appear in almost every author from Martial to Lucian—and nearly always they are uncomplimentary. By the early years of the second century the Cynics were numerous at Rome, and even more so in Alexandria ; a great crowd of them from all parts of the Greek-speaking world assembled for the ' apotheosis ' of Peregrinus at the Olympic games of 167 ; a few years later the humbler classes of artisan were turning Cynic in such numbers that Lucian professes alarm at the prospect of work being brought to a standstill. But, though Cynicism increased its numbers, there is no evidence that it widened its range ; as in the earlier period, the wanderings of the Cynics seem to have been confined to the Eastern portion of the Graeco-Roman world, apart from their appearance in Rome itself. To judge from his name, Crescens may have been a Roman, but otherwise all the Cynics known were of Greek extraction, and probably few of them could speak Latin. The Western half of the Empire was in any case an unpromising field for the Cynic, its inhabitants had little use for philosophers, and the climate was unsuitable for the vagrant, begging life. But we hear of Cynics in all parts of the Eastern provinces—they were numerous in Asia and Syria, Athens and Corinth appear to have been their favourite places in Greece : they were familiar in Epirus and Thrace ; even in the remoter parts of Pontus and Moesia the inhabitants knew that a man in a beggar's dress might be a ' philosopher '. But most of their ' teaching ' seems to have been done in the larger towns—the psychological background of Cynicism is that of a reaction against an overdeveloped urban civilization—and probably they were seen in the country only on their wanderings from city to city.

143

Yet of all these adherents of Cynicism we know only the names of some dozen men who were certainly historical figures, and for only four of those—Dio Chrysostom, Demonax, Oenomaus of Gadara, and Peregrinus—is the evidence sufficiently detailed to enable any real estimate to be made. There is evidence of a certain amount of Cynic literary activity during this period, though very little of it has survived. Several of Dio Chrysostom's orations were delivered while he was leading the κυνικὸς βίος; Oenomaus of Gadara was a prolific writer after the model of the older Cynics of the time of Diogenes; Peregrinus Proteus sent ' letters, testaments and codes to all the chief cities ' to be delivered after his immolation; some of the ' Cynic epistles ', particularly those which go under the name of Crates, may be as late as the second century. But on the whole literary production was not characteristic of the Cynics of this period; some few, such as Demonax, were perhaps averse to it because they felt obliged to concentrate all their activities on the practical side of their teaching, while many others were more or less illiterate. It seems likely that few men of striking personality were to be found amongst them; the more earnest members of the sect probably conformed more or less to the stock-figure represented by the impersonal ' Cynicus ' of the pseudo-Lucianic dialogue of that name. It is obvious, too, that as in the Hellenistic period, the κυνικὸς βίος did not involve adherence to an organized system of doctrine. Demonax and Oenomaus were thorough-going sceptics in all religious matters; the Cynicism of Peregrinus and his numerous followers was tinged with mysticism, and finally evolved a cult of its own; Peregrinus was for a time a member of the Christian community while leading the Cynic life; Crescens was an opponent of the Christians, and responsible for the martyrdom of Justin.

A feature of the growth of Cynicism during this period was the influx into the movement of a large number of charlatans. The most vivid picture of this aspect of contemporary Cynicism is that given in the *Fugitivi* of Lucian; the work was written shortly after the death of Peregrinus, when Lucian was especially hostile, and one would be inclined to suspect his account were it not that ample confirmation is to be found elsewhere. Juvenal, Martial, and Aelius Aristides speak in the same way of the Cynics; more important still is the fact that Dio

Chrysostom, who had himself lived the κυνικὸς βίος, inveighs against ' those who bring the name of philosophy into disgrace ', while Epictetus, for whom the ideal Cynic was the highest type of philosopher, speaks with contempt of contemporary representatives of the profession. The *Fugitivi* may therefore be accepted as evidence for one side of second-century Cynicism. The dialogue opens on Olympus, where Zeus and Apollo are discussing the suicide of Peregrinus Proteus. They are interrupted by the entrance of Philosophy, weeping, and complaining of her treatment on earth. She has been outraged, she complains, not by the vulgar mob, as in the days of Socrates, nor by the philosophers themselves, but by a race of half-breeds

whose dress and look and equipment is like my own, and who claim to be enrolled under my command, and give themselves out as the pupils and comrades and devotees of Philosophy. But their life is an abomination, full of ignorance and boldness and depravity, and of great insolence towards myself.[1]

She then narrates the story of her career on earth in discharging the task Zeus laid on her as the ' healer of mankind ' (cf. the Cynic conception of the ἰατρός). Beginning with the barbarians, she had forced the Indians to come down off their elephants and turn to philosophy : then came the sages of Chaldaea, Babylon and Egypt. Then she turned her attention to the Greeks, was the friend of the Ionian scientists, the foe of the Sophists, and at the death of Socrates was minded to leave the Earth altogether, but was persuaded to stay by the older Cynics, Antisthenes, Diogenes, Crates and Menippus. These reminiscences are interrupted by Zeus, who demands to be told of her present aggressors. They are, she says, a low type of humanity, mostly slaves and hirelings, whose lack of leisure deprived them of any acquaintance with Philosophy in their youth, her very name they had never heard. But when they grew up and saw the respect in which philosophers were held, and the licence of speech allowed them, and the influence they possessed, they considered Philosophy to be a ' potent despotism '. They had no means of learning the

[1] Cf. the remark of Dio Chrysostom in the first Tarsian oration, that there is nothing in their appearance to distinguish the Cynic charlatan from the true philosopher.

necessary and true attributes of the profession ; but on the other hand their trades were shabby and laborious, and offered a bare livelihood, and many found slavery insupportable. So summoning up boldness and ignorance and shamelessness, and practising new forms of abusiveness, they assumed the garb of a philosopher, and, like Aesop's donkey, thought they were the lion when they had put on its skin and brayed. . . .

The whole city is full of this roguery, especially of such as call themselves followers of Diogenes, Antisthenes and Crates, and enroll themselves under the sign of the Dog . . . the canine qualities they possess are barking, lasciviousness, theft, sexual licence, flattery, fawning on any one who will feed them. . . . We shall soon see wholesale desertion from the factories, when the workers realize how they have to toil and labour from morning till night, and wear themselves out to earn a pittance for their drudgery, while these quacks and charlatans live a life of plenty, demanding like lords and readily getting what they ask. . . . This is what they call the life of the Golden Age [1] when honey drops from heaven into their mouths. . . . Many of them seduce the wives of their hosts and lead them off to be philosophers too, quoting Plato's dictum that women should be held in common [2] . . . their behaviour at banquets, and their drunkenness would be a long story to narrate.[3] And this they do while reproving drunkenness, adultery, lechery and greed. No two things are more utterly opposed than their precepts and their practices. . . . And then, the greed of their mendicancy ! Some even make a fortune out of it, and then, good-bye to the wallet, cloak and tub ! . . . So the average man holds Philosophy in contempt, and thinks all its adherents are like the Cynics.

Moved by the plight of Philosophy, Zeus decides to take measures against this plague. To the great patron saint of the Cynics, Heracles himself, is assigned the task of rooting out the pest, a duty which he says will be even more unpleasant than cleansing the Augean stables. By way of a beginning, Heracles, Hermes and Philosophy go down to Thrace, to Philippopolis, where notable charlatans are to be found, three runaway slaves, accompanied by a woman. (The fact that a

[1] Cf. Maximus of Tyre, Diss. 36. The Cynic life is the life of the Golden Age.

[2] In Athenaeus, Cynic women are mentioned. One of them, Nicion, nicknamed ' Dog-fly ', was presumably a courtesan.

[3] Cf. what is said of Cynics at banquets by Lucian in the *Lapithae*, and by Athenaeus.

definite locality is named, and some details given of the career of the leader of this little group, one Cantharus, suggests that Lucian is referring to real persons.) Through the agency of the gods these runaways are handed back to their masters, having first been exposed as arrant quacks.

Cantharus and his friends are, I think, to be taken as typical of many of the new converts to Cynicism. It is easy to understand how the ' free life ' of the Cynic could attract those engaged in the generally oppressive and monotonous tasks of an artisan in the ancient world. To a slave the attraction would be still greater, and the rapid spread of Christianity, and such of the mystery religions as were open to them, amongst the slaves, shows how eager they were to embrace any creed which would lighten the monotony of their lot. Nor must one forget, amongst the possible converts to Cynicism, those people, numerous in any civilization, who are characterized by what has lately been called the ' escape-psychology '—the desire to emancipate themselves from all the restraints imposed by an ordered society. It was this temperament, allied with religious mysticism, that later produced the curious extravagances of the anchorites of the Thebaid. That the κυνικὸς βίος in itself offered exceptional scope to the debauchee is improbable. The general standard of morals in the Empire placed no undue restraint on the sensual appetites, and there was no need to have recourse to the Cynic ἀναίδεια for indulgence. The accusations of immorality against the Cynics are animated by disgust not so much at the practices themselves as for the hypocrisy of those who indulge in them. But, all in all, it is easy to see that, for those in humble circumstances, there was some inducement to turn Cynic. It offered freedom from restraint, change of scene, wide tolerance of behaviour, and a living (of a sort) without work. And one must remember that however ascetic the traditional Cynic diet seems to us, it was probably little plainer than the normal fare of the lower classes. Moreover, the slave or artisan turned Cynic would meet with the respect of his equals, however much he might be despised by the cultured. For Lucian is right in saying that the illiterate Cynics of his day were taking advantage of the high respect generally accorded to philosophy ; in this sense one may admit the description of Cynicism as the ' philosophy of the proletariat '.

From this general description of Cynicism during the period

I pass on to consider those individual Cynics of whom any record survives, especially Dio Chrysostom, Demonax, Oenomaus of Gadara, and Peregrinus.

(b) Dio Chrysostom

Alike to the student of the Roman Empire and of classical literature, the most attractive of these names is that of Dio Chrysostom. Here he is of interest as the most illustrious example of a man who lived the Cynic life ' under pressure of circumstance ' (κατὰ περίστασιν), a course which had been approved by the Stoics as proper for the σοφός and as one in which he would persevere unless circumstances again intervened and forced him to renounce it. Such a change of fortune did occur for Dio, and he abandoned the vagrant Cynic life to become the friend of Trajan, a person of great influence in the affairs of his native province in Bithynia, and a kind of unofficial but influential intermediary between the Roman government and the Greek states generally. Weber's description of Dio as ' cynicorum sectator '[1] is thus very inadequate, and indeed Dio drew on Stoic quite as much as on Cynic ideas, and was also influenced by Plato and even Aristotle. Since Weber's time, however, the researches of von Arnim[2] into the chronology of his writings enable us to gauge with some accuracy the limits of the influence exercised upon him by Cynicism. We are here concerned with Dio as seen from within these limits, and as affording evidence for the nature of Cynicism in his day. For a full-length biography the reader must be referred to von Arnim, and to Dill[3] for a short but brilliant account of his work as a ' philosophic missionary '.

Dio's birth and upbringing alike prepared him for a career very different from that which circumstances actually forced him to follow. He came from one of the wealthiest families in Prusa : and after his father's death his own sumptuous style of living, more particularly untimely expenditure on building at a period of famine, drew down on him the hatred and envy of his poorer fellow-citizens. He received a rhetorical training, and won considerable fame as a Sophist ; and his speech

---

[1] ' De Dione Chrysostomo Cynicorum sectatore.'
[2] Leben und Werke des Dion von Prusa, 1898.
[3] Social Life at Rome from Nero to Marcus Aurelius, p. 367 ff.

κατὰ τῶν φιλοσόφων shows that he shared the hostility felt by
the Second Sophistic towards the philosophers. His standing
in his native city and his reputation as a Sophist brought him
excellent connexions at Rome, he enjoyed the acquaintance
of Titus, and was intimate with his stepson Flavius Sabinus.[1]
He was an ardent Hellenist, and the Rhodian oration, delivered
shortly before his exile, shows him looking forward to a cultural
revival which should make the Hellenic cities the moral and
spiritual leaders of the Roman world. His brilliant prospects
were suddenly and completely destroyed by the execution of
Flavius Sabinus, who was suspected of conspiracy against
Domitian, in A.D. 82. His downfall involved Dio, ' as a friend
and a counsellor (φίλον ὄντα καὶ σύμβουλον). For this is a
habit of tyrants, and even as the Scythians bury with their kings
their cupbearers and cooks and concubines, so do tyrants add
many other innocent persons to the list of their victims.'[2] Dio
was sentenced to exile, a sentence which Emperius shows as
meaning banishment from (1) Rome and Italy, (2) his native
province of Bithynia.[3] The sentence was an imperial decree,
not a *senatus consultum*, like the expulsion of philosophers in
94, nor a judicial sentence, arising out of a prosecution. Its
term was intended to be ' in perpetuum ', as may be deduced
from the fact that ' it was not lifted till after Domitian's death,
when Nerva refused to endorse the " acta " of his predecessor '.

Severe though the sentence was, it did not force Dio to the
vagrant life which he chose to lead. Though he no longer
derived any support from his property in Prusa and was apparently without means, several cities made him an offer of citizen
rights,[4] and he could have made a living as a sophist in any
part of the Roman Empire other than Rome, Italy or Bithynia.
Von Arnim suggests that his *amour-propre* as a famous sophist
was outraged by the Emperor's action, at once unjust and
contemptuous, and that he determined to revenge himself by
carrying on a literary campaign against Domitian. Such a
course would draw down the Emperor's anger on any community which harboured him, and Dio would naturally hesitate
before establishing himself in any city when he knew that he

---

[1] von Arnim (op. cit.) makes a convincing case for Flavius Sabinus
as ' the person of the highest connexions ' whose fall Dio describes
as responsible for his own exile.

[2] Or. 13. 1.   [3] Emperius, *Dio von Prusa*, 1844.   [4] Or. 44. 6.

was a potentially dangerous guest. These considerations, however, are not mentioned in Dio's own account ; he leaves us rather to infer that he adopted the vagrant life on the advice of the Delphic god. ' Following the ancestral custom of the Greeks,' he says, ' I went to Delphi, and asked the god whether exile was a good thing or a bad.' [1] He must further have asked for advice on his particular case, for the reply was, ' Do the near-by thing with all earnestness, as though it were of the highest importance, till you come to the ends of the earth.' The advice, and the fact that it was followed, suggest that the question came from a man whose world had crashed about his ears. Dio was cut off from his family and his home, apparently for ever, his dream of leading a revival of Hellenic culture had to be abandoned, and he was no longer interested in the career of a sophist. The only advice which could help a man in his situation was that which the oracle gave ; Oenomaus, in his demonstration of the futility of all oracles, wisely says nothing about the response given to Dio.

During the next fourteen years Dio wandered through the north-eastern portion of the Roman Empire, and we hear of him in Greece, in Pontus, in Asia, and in Moesia. He supported himself from the humblest occupations, and was at different times a gardener, a bath-attendant, an agricultural labourer, and, frequently, a beggar.[2] Naturally he was brought into contact with the lowliest people, and he, who, as he tells us, ' had sat at table with kings and satraps ',[3] learned that greater hospitality and kindness were to be found in the homes of the poor. His life during these years damaged his health,[4] but it brought him a deeper insight into the lives of the poor than can be found in any classical author since Hesiod. Furthermore, as with Diogenes, it was through his exile that he was brought to philosophy. He calls himself ' a self-made philosopher ' (αὐτούργος τῆς σοφίας),[5] and describes the process in a passage which is interesting in itself and as evidence for contemporary views of the Cynics.[6] As he wandered from place to place, clad in rough clothes, he says that,

the people who met me judged from my appearance that I was a vagrant or a beggar, while some took me for a philosopher. So it

---

[1] Or. 13. 9.   [2] von Arnim, op. cit., p. 238 ff.   [3] Or. 7. 65.
[4] ib., 19 ; 40. 2.   [5] ib., 1. 9.   [6] ib., 13. 1 ff.

happened that by degrees, without any deliberate intention on my part—for I did not rate myself so highly—that I came to bear the name of philosopher. Now most of the so-called philosophers announce themselves, like the heralds at the Olympic games. But in my case it was a name given by others, and I could not for ever be contradicting them. And indeed I came to reap a benefit from the appellation. For many would come and ask me what were my opinions of Good and Evil, so that I was forced to meditate on these topics to be able to answer those who questioned me. Again, they would bid me stand forward and make a speech. . . . When I reflected . . . it seemed to me that all were, so to speak, devoid of wit, and that none knew what to do nor where to look to find release from the evils that beset him and from his own gross ignorance . . . that all were led astray in the same manner and nearly always by the same distractions—money, reputation, and bodily pleasures, and that none knew how to escape them and free his soul. . . . So I blamed them all, and especially myself. . . .

It was therefore as a Cynic that Dio was asked for advice, and it was as a Cynic that he replied, when he felt justified in so doing. The most important ethical discourses belonging to these years are Orations 6, 8, 9 and 10, in each of which Diogenes is the central figure.[1] The orations are all marked by what von Arnim rightly calls a ' radical Cynicism ', with emphasis on the familiar slogans of ἀναίδεια (Shamelessness), αὐτάρκεια (Self-Sufficiency), and ἄσκησις (Training). A series of shorter speeches, or διαλέξεις which von Arnim assigns to this period, deal with such subjects as φθόνος (Envy), εὐδαιμονία (Happiness), δόξα (Reputation), &c., and show Dio in the capacity of the ἰατρός (Doctor) healing the diseases of the human soul. His eagerness to fulfil another of the Cynic's functions—that of the ἐπίσκοπος (Scout) leads him towards the end of his exile into a most interesting venture. The period was one of arduous fighting on the Danube frontier against the warlike Dacians or Getae, who had just inflicted a defeat on the Romans and were causing much anxiety.[2] Dio was eager to ' see the state of affairs in the country ' and journeyed thither, no doubt with the same curiosity that again led him to the Danube in Trajan's reign, ' to see one side struggling for power and empire, and the other for their country and freedom '. The result of his stay in what later

---

[1] See Note 1 to Chap. VIII.   [2] von Arnim, op. cit., p. 302 ff.

became the Roman province of Dacia was *A History of the Getae* (τὰ Γέτικα), which unfortunately has not survived. Von Arnim makes the attractive and highly probable suggestion that he saw in the barbarous Getae men nearer to ' the life according to Nature ' than the over-civilized inhabitants of the Roman Empire, and that in their great leader Decebalus he found exemplified the Stoic-Cynic conception of the βασιλεύς as ' the shepherd of the people '.

According to Dio his activities during these years were characterized by an outspoken invective against Domitian.

> I had for my enemy no common person . . . but the so-called Lord and Master . . . whom I never flattered, nor attempted to deprecate his hostility, but I was quite openly incensed against him. The evils that confronted me I am not now going to write and speak about, for I have already written and spoken of them, and my speeches were delivered everywhere, and my books widely circulated.

At first sight these claims hardly seem to be borne out in the extant speeches, where, apart from the remarkable prophecy of Domitian's murder in Or. 66, the references to the Emperor seem veiled and indirect. Von Arnim, indeed, pointing out that Dio makes a clear distinction between his speeches and his writings, suggests that the denunciations on which the claim is chiefly based, have not survived. Though possible this is not likely, for Dio prided himself on his conduct in opposing Domitian, and would probably have taken care, at least after his exile, to publish his most notable piece of invective. Two considerations may be urged to show that the extant writings do substantiate his claim that he showed a laudable degree of independence. In the first place one must remember the retrospective traditions of the literature of the age. The precept δεῖ ἀρχάιου τινος πράγματος was so firmly established that on one occasion Dio apologizes for talking about Nero and the moderns rather than Cyrus or Alcibiades ; [1] the accepted practice was to represent contemporary persons or events by examples chosen from history. Dio's audience would therefore be much readier than a modern reader to see that Heracles and Eurystheus, or Diogenes and Alexander, stand for Dio and Domitian. Secondly, there is the fate of Maternus [2] to remind us that denunciation of tyrants, even if

---

[1] Or. 21. 10.   [2] See above, p. 140.

couched in general terms, could towards the end of Domitian's reign be perilous to the speaker. Admittedly Maternus delivered his speech at Rome, while Dio was in remote and often semi-barbarous parts of the Empire, but none the less Dio was a marked man through his connexion with Flavius Sabinus. At least it must be said for Dio that if his conduct during the reign of Domitian be compared with that of such upholders of the ancient Roman virtues as Tacitus and Juvenal, it is not the Greek who has the worst of the comparison.

It is evident that towards the end of his exile Dio had acquired a considerable reputation as a philosopher. He himself says that his writings were widely circulated, and we know what enthusiasm was evoked by his appearance at Borysthenes. But the most striking example of his influence and personality (if the story can be believed) is an incident which occurred at the very end of his exile.[1] On his way back from the country of the Getae he was staying incognito in the Roman legionary camp of Viminacium, when the news of Domitian's murder came through. Domitian was popular with the soldiers, and the news of Nerva's succession to the principate aroused the men at Viminacium to the point of revolt. Dio realized the critical nature of the situation, ' flung aside his disguise with the words " Out of the rags stepped forth many-counselling Odysseus " and stood before them, no beggar, but Dio the philosopher '. He delivered a speech in which he denounced the murdered Emperor and praised, from personal experience, his successor ; apparently he was successful in quelling the disturbance. One remembers that Musonius was not so successful in an attempt to soothe infuriated Roman soldiers.[2]

Dio had been ' to the ends of the earth ' in fulfilment of the oracle's advice, and the death of Domitian meant that his exile was at end, for he was immediately recalled by Nerva. He returned to Prusa, to be loaded with honours by his own and neighbouring states. Illness delayed a project of going to Rome on behalf of Prusa, and when it could be realized Nerva was dead and Trajan had succeeded him. The favour he enjoyed from the latter is a tribute both to his own character and to the discernment of the Emperor. Philostratus, in his zeal for glorifying Dio at the expense of Trajan, tells a ludicrous

[1] Philos., *vita Soph.*, *sv.* Dio.   [2] Tac., *Hist.*, iii. 81.

story [1] which gives a completely false picture of their relationship. According to him, Dio is the brilliant sophist, Trajan the simple soldier, admiring but bewildered, ' who would often exclaim " I can't understand a word you say, Dio, but I love you as myself ".' But as von Arnim points out, there were good reasons why an earnest and enlightened ruler like Trajan should have found Dio highly useful. He was a person of much influence in Bithynia, and we know from Pliny that the province was then giving the Emperor considerable anxiety. Again, his fourteen years of wandering and his familiarity with the lives of the common people must have given him a knowledge of conditions in the north-eastern portion of the Roman Empire which few could have equalled. The fact that he had lived for some time among the Getae must also have commended him to Trajan, in view of his plans for taking the offensive against these troublesome enemies. Finally his reputation both as a philosopher and a Hellenist made him an important figure in the Greek-speaking portion of the Roman Empire ; and it was in some sense as a representative of the educated classes of that very important section, that he delivered before Trajan the four speeches περὶ βασιλείας, expressing its hopes and expectations from the new régime. In these speeches one may see the triumph of Stoic-Cynic propaganda, the realization of that conception of the philosopher as the counsellor of kings which the Cynics had depicted in their favourite fiction of Diogenes giving advice to Alexander. But this was no fictitious encounter : the Stoic-Cynic ideas of the βασιλεία were being preached to the ' master of the world . . . the vice-regent of God on earth ', in person.

Oration i, the first to be delivered before Trajan, shows that Dio was well aware of the importance of the occasion. The speech is extremely skilful : the beginning is modest and unassuming : there is a straightforward description ' in plain and simple language ' of the good king according to Homer, ending with the remark, ' If any of these qualities appear to belong to you, happy are you in your noble and gracious character, and happy are we who share in its benefit.' [2] Then a loftier note is struck by the reference to Zeus, ' king of mortals and pattern of kings ', and of the universe, ' the embodiment of bliss and wisdom, sweeping in infinite cycles through infinite

[1] Apparently believed by Dill (op. cit., p. 368).   [2] c. 36.

time, guided by good fortune and the divine power, and by providence (Πρόνοια) and the most righteous and perfect of governing principles'.   But with the remark that these themes are too vast for the time available Dio introduces a ' sacred and edifying parable' (μῦθος) which Trajan is advised to ' reflect upon in private '.   During his exile Dio once lost his way in a remote part of the Peloponnese, and came to a rude shrine, by which dwelt a venerable old woman.   The shrine was that of Heracles, and the woman gifted with the power of divination.   She prophesied that Dio's exile would end before long, as would the ' period of tribulation for mankind ', i.e. the rule of Domitian.   ' Some day ', she told Dio, ' you will meet a mighty man, the ruler of many lands and peoples. Do not hesitate to tell him the following parable, even though many scoff at you.'   The parable is the famous story of the Choice of Heracles, to which we have already referred. Heracles, it will be remembered, makes the choice between Kingship and Tyranny.   Heracles himself is depicted as having several of the traits of Trajan, while the picture of tyranny is unmistakably drawn from Domitian.   At the end of the speech it is said that Heracles would give honour and protection in his life wherever he found a kingdom and a king, ' and this work he continues to this day, for in him you have a helper and protector of your government, so long as you reign like a king ' (ἕως ἂν τυγχάνῃς βασιλεύων).[1]   The other three speeches lack the eloquence of the first, but are equally governed by Stoic-Cynic ideas.   The true king must have καρτερία and undergo πόνος, he is the bringer of ὁμονοία to his people : he is symbolized by the shepherd of the flock, the bull of the herd, the ' king ' of the bees.   The familiar Cynic stock-figure of Sardanapalus as the king led astray by pleasure (φιλήδονος βασιλεύς), of Alexander as the immoderate lover of glory (φιλοδόξος), of Diogenes as the wise adviser, are exhibited, not to a small crowd in some unimportant city of Pontus or Greece, but before the Roman Emperor himself. Despite the evidence of rhetorical ability they display, these speeches were not mere ἐπιδείξεις.   The principles of the

---

[1] The coinage of the second century, particularly that of Antoninus, shows the devotion professed by the Emperors to the cult of Heracles, the guardian deity of the good king.   Rostovtseff, op. cit., sv. Heracles.

βασιλεία they envisaged were actually those that governed the administration of Trajan and his three successors.[1] Admittedly that practical experience of administration which was the legacy of a long line of Roman statesmen had more to do with the establishment of the benevolent government of the age than had the theories of the philosophers. But it is true to say that during this period, the Golden Age of the government in the ancient world, philosophy played well its part of adviser and encourager of men of affairs.

Apart from the orations περὶ βασιλείας there is naturally less trace of Cynic influence in Dio's speeches after his return from exile. The Alexandrine Oration is the speech of an unofficial representative of the Emperor : the numerous speeches delivered in Bithynia and Asia those of a man ' of wide knowledge of men and the world ' giving advice on local politics and government. But his fourteen years' exile had left on Dio an indelible impression, and towards the end of his life we find him coming back to the problem of the poor, and what manner of life they are to lead. His views are set out in the famous seventh oration, which is based upon Stoic and Cynic ethical ideals, though it is the production of a man of wide experience of social conditions in the Roman Empire.[2] It is worth while to give a summary of its main ideas, if only to show how careful one must be not to interpret from modern analogies the description of Cynicism as ' the philosophy of the proletariat '. The discourse was intended to be a serious contribution to a grave social problem rather than a theoretical discussion of poverty, for Dio expresses the hope that it will be found useful both in the government of cities, and for poor people in search of employment.[3] It differs from most schemes of reform offered to the modern proletariat in that economics are throughout subordinated to ethics. The object of man is to live a virtuous life, and of itself poverty is no hindrance to that end. Indeed, says Dio, ' poverty seems to have something holy about it ', and

one must consider whether in word and deed and in their relations with each other the poor are by reason of their poverty at a disadvantage compared with the rich so far as leading a seemly life

---

[1] Cf. Rostovtseff, op. cit., p. 114 ff.
[2] See Note 2 to Chap. VIII. [3] Or. 7, c. 127.

and one according to nature, or whether they do enjoy an advantage in every respect.[1]

The familiar and delightful description of the Euboean peasants proves that in Dio's opinion the latter is the case. Their toil in the fields and their self-sufficiency bring them nearer to the ' life according to Nature ' than it is possible for any one to be in an urban civilization. The occupations of farmer, hunter or shepherd are therefore suitable for the poor : thus employed, they will be able to lead happier and more useful lives than those engaged in the struggle for wealth. Dio then passes to the more difficult problems which confront the poor in a large city. The best solution, he thinks, would be to remove all the ' respectable poor ' (οἱ κομψοὶ πένηται)[2] from the cities and settle them in the country. For urban civilization really demands that all its members should be prosperous, since in a city money is indispensable ; to its poor it can offer little but a choice between degrading employment and idleness. However, failing this solution, even in cities honourable employment can be found for the poor. Unfortunately the discourse as we have it is not complete, and while Dio expressly mentions many occupations that are unsuitable for the poor, we have few indications of those which he felt they could safely follow. The only occupations he expressly commends are those of the hired servant, the attendant, and the school-master ; but since he also approves of the ' artisan ' (χειροτέχνης), it is to be presumed that in the last portion of the discourse the various praiseworthy τέχναι were discussed. None the less, it is apparent that his real desire was to see ' all the respectable poor, by any means possible, become rustics '.[3] There is little need to dwell upon the urgent necessity of some such scheme of ' back to the land ' for large areas of the Roman Empire in Dio's time. In Italy and Greece, in particular, agriculture was at a low ebb, and much land had gone out of cultivation. In the little city to which the Euboean peasants of this oration belong two-thirds of the land without the walls was uncultivated, while much of that within them was sown or pasture-land, and sheep grazed in the market-place. On the other hand the great cities of the Empire, especially Rome and Alexandria, had vast, idle city

---

[1] ib., c. 81.   [2] ib., c. 107.   [3] 108.

mobs who were a standing nuisance to their rulers and for whom no useful occupation was ever found. The difference between Dio's scheme of social reform and the majority of those of modern times is also obvious. There is no attempt to obviate poverty as such : Dio appears to assume that the poor we shall always have with us, and the problem is to provide them with suitable employment. Consequently he can dispense with schemes for redistributing wealth ; once the poor have been found suitable occupations they should be capable of leading happy lives ; if they do not, the cause is not the injustice of social conditions but their own indulgence in the fault of μεμψιμοιρία.

(c) Demonax

The only authority for Demonax is the *Life*[1] that has come down under the name of Lucian. It is obviously conceived as a panegyric, but there is no reason to doubt its evidence on the few details it gives of Demonax' career, nor its general description of his character. Demonax came of a good family

---

[1] The question of its genuineness has long been a vexed one. Those who regard it as spurious mainly rely on two arguments. (*a*) The feebleness of the anecdotes it contains ; Lucian, however prejudiced, is usually amusing. But this is the only work in the Lucianic corpus which belongs to the genre of the ἀπομνημ ὀνεύματα, a genre whose conventions give little scope to the personal merits of the author. (*b*) The remark that the writer has elsewhere written of Demonax' contemporary, Sostratus, who bore the nickname of ' Heracles '. Such a treatise is not to be found in the extant works of Lucian, nor is there any reference to it elsewhere. But this is not a conclusive objection—the work may have been written and never published. At any rate, if published, it seems quickly to have been forgotten, for Philostratus, writing some fifty years after the death of Demonax, takes his account of this ' Heracles ' from a letter of Herodes Atticus. Funk (*Philol.*, Suppl. 10 [1907]) considers the work to be that of Lucian ; he points out that the sceptical, eclectic nature of Demonax is that of Lucian himself, and of his philosophic mouthpiece Menippus. Lucian, he concludes, was greatly influenced by Demonax. One may perhaps quote in this connexion the remark made in the *Fugitivi* that ' there are some few genuine philosophers left in Greece ' (i.e. in Athens). May not this be a reference to Demonax ? On the whole, the case for regarding the work as spurious is not convincing. But, as Zeller says, its value as evidence for Demonax is not affected if we refuse to accept Lucian as the author ; whoever the author was, he was a contemporary of Demonax and had long been familiar with him.

in Cyprus, and received a thorough literary education and rhetorical training. But he was led by an ' inherent love of philosophy ' (ἐμφύτου πρὸς φιλοσοφίαν ἔρωτος) to lead a life which would ' set an example to all who saw him of his intellect and of the sincerity of his philosophy '. His philosophic ' teachers ' were Demetrius, Epictetus and Agathoboulos—two Cynics and a Stoic—his rhetorical training was probably received under the sophist and eclectic philosopher Timocrates of Heraclia. He was himself an eclectic in that ' he would never reveal which form of philosophy he favoured ' ; of the philosophers he ' thought all were admirable, but revered Socrates, wondered at Diogenes, and loved Aristippus '. But in dress he was a Cynic, and what we are told of his work at Athens suggests that he combined the ' philanthropy ' of Crates with the scepticism and nihilism of Menippus.

When he first came to Athens is not known.[1] He was given Athenian citizenship, entered political life, and, possibly because of the reputation he had acquired in Cyprus, quickly attained office. But his outspokenness made him many enemies, and he was prosecuted, like Socrates, on a charge of impiety, for

[1] Few details are certain about his chronology. We know that he lived to be nearly a hundred, but are told nothing of the dates of his birth or death. An anecdote which brings him into contact with Peregrinus Proteus suggests that he must have been teaching in Athens later than A.D. 159, the probable date of Proteus' arrival in Greece ; on the other hand we are told of a remark he made about Apollonius of Tyana when the latter was ' going from Athens to be tutor to the Emperor '. The Emperor in question was Titus (Philost., vi. 30) ; which would mean that Demonax was already in Athens about A.D. 72, and hence can hardly have been born later than A.D. 50. Of the two stories I prefer to reject the second, since all other persons with whom he is said to have been in contact in Athens belong to the second century so far as we know. The later date, too, best fits what is said of his lengthy philosophical training. Epictetus set up his school at Nicopolis in 94 ; Demetrius cannot have ' taught ' in Greece earlier than 75 ; the *floruit* of Agathoboulos was *c.* 120. Moreover, Demonax appears to have taken some part in the politics of Cyprus ; probably he was middle-aged when he came to Athens. For the date of his death, the passage of the *Fugitivi* quoted in the last note is relevant. If the reference is to Demonax, he must have been living after the death of Peregrinus in 167. I therefore suggest that his life may best be dated *c.* A.D. 70–170 ; that he ' studied ', probably in that order, with Demetrius, Epictetus, Timocrates, and Agathoboulos, and that he came to Athens about 120.

he refused to sacrifice to Athena, and was the only citizen of Athens who had not been initiated into the Eleusinian mysteries. The boldness of his defence caused him to be acquitted; thenceforward he acquired an extraordinary influence and prestige at Athens, until at the end of his life he was regarded with universal veneration and affection.

His philosophical activities appear to have been entirely devoted to the παραινετικὸς τοπος.

When any of his friends were apparently prosperous, he would remind them that they were elated over imaginary and ephemeral blessings. Others, who were bewailing poverty, or finding exile hard to bear, or complaining of old age or sickness, he would laughingly console, pointing out that they did not realize how soon their troubles would end, and that they would soon find forgetfulness of their lot, good or bad, and lasting freedom. He also made it his concern to compose the quarrels of brothers, and to negotiate peace between husband and wife. On occasion he spoke words of reason to angry mobs, and usually persuaded them to serve their country in a sensible manner.

These activities, together with what we are told about his kindliness and charm of manner, and his dictum that we should hate sin but love sinners, recall Epictetus' conception of the Ideal Cynic; doubtless Epictetus' views had much influence on his pupil.[1] But Epictetus held that the Cynic should abstain from political affairs, while Demonax ' played a part in society and politics ', and, as we have seen, even held office. It will be remembered that Dio Chrysostom, after his return from exile, was concerned with political issues much more important than the municipal affairs of Athens, and indeed he held that ' the work of the true philosopher is no other than the rule of men '.[2] From Chrysippus onwards the Stoics were divided as to the proper attitude of the σοφός to politics. Those who regarded philosophy, as Epictetus did Cynicism, as a special service for an emergency, would allow nothing to interfere with the primary duties of the philosopher; and of course a ' political career ' with its attendant ambitions would at all times be improper for the σοφός. But where a philosopher possessed influence in the State (whether through family connexions and philosophic reputation combined, as in the case of Dio, or, like Demonax, through mere force of character),

---

[1] See below, p. 190 f.　　　　[2] Or. 49.

then it was proper for him to come forward and give advice on public affairs. For the philosopher's duty is to ally himself with the Law and Order of the Universe, whose earthly manifestation is the Law and Order prevailing in the well-ordered State (cf. once more Dio's conception of the virtues attendant on the Good King, and his duties as the bringer of Peace and ὁμονοία). It was in this spirit that Demonax quelled civic disturbance by his mere appearance in the Assembly,[1] and dissuaded the Athenians from instituting gladiatorial shows in emulation of Corinth.

In sharp contrast with his contemporary, Peregrinus Proteus, he mitigated the austerities of Cynic life; he abandoned its vagrancy and mendicancy ; its traditional squalor and theatricality, in fact, as Praechter [2] says, all that aspect of Cynicism governed by the slogan παραχάραττειν τὸ νόμισμα. Towards the end of his life

he used to eat and sleep uninvited in any house which he happened to be passing, and its occupants regarded it as some divine visitation, and thought that a Good Spirit (ἀγαθὸς δαίμων) had entered their house. The bread-women would try to attract his attention as he passed by, each wanting him to take bread from her, and the one who was successful thought she had brought herself luck. The children, too, would bring him fruit, and call him father. . . . When he died, the Athenians gave him a magnificent public funeral . . . afterwards they would bow down before the stone on which he used to rest when tired ; and hang it with garlands, feeling that the very stone on which he sat was sacred. The whole city attended his funeral, especially the philosophers, who carried his body to the grave.

Unless the panegyric is grossly exaggerated—and there is no reason to believe that it is—Demonax can stand with Crates as an embodiment of the Cynic ideal of φιλανθρωπία—the service of mankind. The scene of his ministry, the Athens of the second century, was of course a place of no great importance ; its greatness had long left it, and it was now little more than a University town in a declining province. But it would have been well for the Roman Empire if men like Demonax had been found in its municipalities in the next two centuries.

---

[1] Cf. the stories of attempts by Musonius and Dio to quell riots, p. 153.
[2] In Ueberweg, Gesch. d. Phil., Vol. i, p. 511.

For the alienation of so many of the better elements from any interest in public life or the conduct of political affairs was one of the most potent causes of the decline and fall of the Empire.

(d) Oenomaus of Gadara

Authorities for the date of Oenomaus disagree, though it is highly probable that his *floruit* was in the reign of Hadrian.[1] There is no evidence for the dates of his birth and death, nor for his family. His native city was Gadara in Peraea, one of those Greek cities in Syria whose ruins testify to the high degree of material prosperity they enjoyed in the second century A.D. It was perhaps in revolt against the luxury of his day that Oenomaus turned his thoughts to philosophy, and came to Colophon to ask Clarius Apollo for guidance and advice. How he was disappointed will be seen; at present it is to be remarked that he does not say that his search for a master was successful, and he may well have been, like Dio Chrysostom, αυτοδίδακτος πρὸς ἀρετήν. We do not know whether he followed the vagrant Cynic life; Demonax was his contemporary, but there are no stories of contact between them. Indeed, all that we hear of his relations with contemporaries is the interesting evidence, collected by Vallette,[2] which suggests that he may be identical with that pagan philosopher 'Abnimos Hagardi', who appears in Hebrew tradition as the friend of the second-century Rabbi Meir. The identification, however, is far from certain, for according to Hebrew scholars the Hebraic equivalent of Abnimos can with difficulty stand for the Greek Oenomaus; and the anecdotes themselves are devoid of any individual characterization which might offer a pointer. Probably little more can be said than that there is nothing inherently unlikely in a story of contact between a Cynic and a Jewish rabbi in Syria in the second century A.D.

Unlike Demonax and Demetrius, then, Oenomaus is known to us only through his writings. To judge from their titles, these appear to have followed the old Cynic models. The list of Suidas mentions the following: Περὶ Κυνισμοῦ, Πολιτεία, περὶ τῆς καθ' 'Ομηρον φιλοσοφίας, περὶ Κράτητος καὶ Διογένους κτλ. Julian speaks of an αὐτοφωνία τοῦ κυνός, a κατὰ τῶν

---

[1] See Note 3 to Chap. VIII.　　[2] De Oenomao Cynico, p. 6 ff.

χρηστηρίων and of tragedies.[1] Vallette conjectures that ' αὐτοφωνία τοῦ Κυνός ' is an alternative title for the book περὶ
Κυνισμοῦ ; Julian says that ' according to Oenomaus,
Cynicism is neither Antisthenism nor Diogenism ',[2] no doubt
in reference to the famous claim that Heracles is the real prototype of the Cynic life. χρησμοὶ αὐτοφώνοι are oracles
delivered directly by the god, without the agency of priest
or omen. The ingenious χρησμοὶ αὐτοφώνοι of Alexander of
Abonuteichos were one of his most effective pieces of publicity,
as we know from Lucian. In the αὐτοφωνία τοῦ Κυνός then,
Oenomaus may well have given the precepts of the ' philosophy '
itself, as Crusius says, it represented Des Kyon leibhafte Stimme,[3]
heard directly and not through its prophet Diogenes. One
may further suggest that these precepts were in verse, and
were parodies of oracles like those found in the γόητων φώρα.
This would be in the vein of Crates ; in the Politeia and the
Tragedies Oenomaus was following the model of Diogenes.
These last seem to have maintained the traditional Cynic
ἀναίδεια, to judge from the horrified comments of Julian.
Of the book On the Philosophy according to Homer nothing
more than the title is known ; Vallette conjectures that it
burlesqued the stories of gods and heroes. Our judgement of
Oenomaus must be based on the surviving passages of the
γοήτων φώρα—The Charlatans Exposed, which Valette identifies
with the book Against the Oracles mentioned by Julian.[4]

The γοήτων φώρα.—The book is known to us through passages
quoted by Eusebius in the Praeparatio Evangelica to support
his attack on divination ; some of his quotations were used
again by Theodoretus. It does not seem likely that the
passages as quoted by Eusebius preserve the order of Oenomaus,
but as we have them, they fall into three divisions : (1) an
analysis of famous oracles, revealing their worthlessness, (2)
the story of Oenomaus' own experiences at the shrine of
Clarius Apollo, (3) a general refutation, on quasi-philosophical
grounds, of the possibility of prophecy. The oracles quoted
are all taken from classical Greek history or mythology ; the
reason being obvious in the light of Plutarch's statement [5] that,
owing to the decay of the Greek cities and their loss of

[1] Or. vii. 209.   [2] Or. vi., 187 B.C.
[3] Crusius, xliv. (1889), p. 309 ff.
[4] Cf. Vallette, op. cit., p. 54, &c.   [5] Plut., de Pyth. Or., 28.

independence, no important public oracles had been given
for several generations. The Delphic god himself is the
' imaginary adversary ' of the Cynic's diatribe ; his oracles
are analysed, shown to be absurd or worthless, and in most
cases the unfortunate deity is then roundly abused. Two
kinds of oracle are dealt with, (1) those which claim to be
prophecies of the future, e.g. the famous reply to Croesus, or
the oracles given to the Athenians and Spartans in the Persian
War, (2) those which give advice, as the oracle to Lycurgus.
Of the first class, it is observed that they evince no real knowledge of the future, but only shrewdness in realizing the possible
issues of the event, and ingenuity in composing a response
which would be equally applicable to any one of them. One
example will suffice to show Oenomaus' method—his treatment of the oracle given to the Athenians at the beginning of
the invasion of Xerxes. The oracle says that the wooden
walls will alone be invincible, ' let them not withstand the foe
with horse and foot, but turn their backs : elsewhere shall the
foe front them. O divine Salamis, thou shalt destroy the sons
of women, either when Demeter scatters or when she is
gathering the corn.'[1] It did not need a god, is Oenomaus'
comment, to forecast that the Athenians, weak in infantry and
cavalry, would find their best refuge in the ' wooden walls ' of
their fleet. And as for the couplet about Salamis, the god
has not predicted what the result of the battle will be ; as
for its season, he knew that naval battles are not fought in
winter, and the phrase ' either when Demeter scatters or when
she gathers the corn ' pretty well covers the rest of the year.
(It may be urged that Apollo did get the place of the battle
right, but Oenomaus characteristically refuses to give him
any credit for it.) When the god has been exposed as a prophet,
he is then arraigned as a giver of advice. The divine advice,
as revealed in oracles, is ' either commonplace or harmful.
Consider the precepts of good government given to Lycurgus.[2]

So long as ye keep your promises and oaths to the oracles, and
preserve justice in relations with each other and with strangers and
with piety and reverence honour old age, and honour too the Tyn-
daridae and Menelaus and the other deathless heroes whom divine
Lacedaemon contains, even so long shall Zeus spare you.

---

[1] Vall., op. cit., p. 39 ff. [2] id., ib., p. 50.

Commonplace stuff, says Oenomaus—is that the sort of thing people come from the land of the Hyperboreans to hear? Any nurse could have done better. Again, oracles giving advice on marriage, on the begetting of children, and on exile are unfavourably compared with the teachings of Socrates on the same subjects. Sometimes Oenomaus, in the manner of Crates, emends the response of the oracle, so that they convey the true precepts of philosophy. When not platitudinous, he says, the oracles are harmful, as when they promise immortality to stupid athletes like Theagenes or indecent poets such as Archilochus, or befriend tyrants, as in the case of Cypselus.

The whole tone of the attack is rhetorical, with small regard for either logic or consistency ; any stick will serve to beat Apollo. For while dislike of athletes comes well enough from a Cynic, the criticism of Archilochus for obscenity ill befits Oenomaus, whose own writings were so indecent that Julian cannot find a fit comparison for them. The oracle is reproved for not encouraging the Athenians and Spartans in their patriotic duties in the Persian War ; it is also reproved for answering Homer's question about the city of his birth—as well, says Oenomaus, might the god tell a dung-beetle about its native dung-heap. Again, Apollo is blamed for his treachery to his devout worshipper, Croesus of Lydia ; but for his support of Cypselus of Corinth he is stigmatized as the ' friend of tyrants '. In other words, Oenomaus is perfectly willing to drop the mask of the Cynic whenever it suits him to do so, just as the arch-sceptic Lucian poses on occasion as a pious believer in the Olympian gods.[1] But nowhere is his unfairness more obvious than in his treatment of the oracle given to Laius.[2] We have seen how Oenomaus has satirized oracles worded so ambiguously that they would fit any event ; in this case, Apollo was quite definite, Laius was to be slain by his son. Such a prediction, say Oenomaus, is impossible, it involves too many unknowns, for Laius might refuse to beget children, or Oedipus, if born at all, might refuse to be tyrant of Thebes, and so on. Apollo is therefore pretending a knowledge he cannot have possessed. But, says the god, it turned out as I foretold. ' Pure luck ', is the reply.

[1] *De mort. Per.*, c. 13 and 21 ; cf. Bernays, *Lukian und die Kyniker*, p. 56.
[2] Vall., op. cit., pp. 74 ff.

To the modern reader, however, the most interesting passage is that in which Oenomaus describes his own experiences with the oracle of Clarius Apollo at Colophon.[1] The shrine was one which enjoyed great celebrity at the time, perhaps due to the manner in which its responses were given. For, according to Tacitus,[2]

. . . the priest merely ascertains the number and the names of the consultants ; then he goes into a cave, drinks water from a hidden spring, and, though as a rule he knows nothing of poetry or letters, he delivers oracular replies in verse on the subjects which each man has in mind.

An apt response would thus be an impressive achievement on the part of the god, and on one occasion a sceptical Roman proconsul was notably disconcerted.[3] Oenomaus does not tell us the precise form of the question he put to the god ; he calls it ' a philosophical transaction ' (ἐμπορία περὶ σοφίας), and it is clear that it had to do with the acquisition of σοφία or ἀρετή. The oracle replied :

There in the land of Trachis the garden of Heracles bloometh,
Bearing all manner of fruits, which all men daily do gather,
Naught shall be lacking there, 'tis dowered with waters unfailing.

' Fool that I was,' says Oenomaus, ' I was elated when I heard of Heracles and his garden,[4] and the mention of Trachis made me think of the sweat of Hesiod, and then again I thought I should have an easy life through the flowering garden.' His train of thought is elucidated by Vallette. Τρῆχινος ἄιη made

---

[1] id., ib., pp. 34–8. [2] *Annals*, ii. 54.
[3] Plut., *de Def. Or.*, c. 45.
[4] εἶτ' ἐγὼ ἀκόυσας ὁ βάκηλος καὶ αὐτὸς ὑπὸ τοῦ ῾Ηρακλέους ἐφυσήθην καὶ τοῦ ῾Ηρακλήιου κήπου θάλλοντος . Of the last four words Vallette says ' haec verba quid sententiae addant equidem non perspicio '. He is attracted by the emendation of Guenther (*Genethl. Gotting.*, p. 19), who transposes the text to read, εἶτ' ἐγὼ ἀκόυσας ὁ βάκηλος τοῦ ῾Ηρακλήιου κήπου θάλλοντος, καὶ αὐτὸς ὑπὸ τοῦ ῾Ηρακλέους ἐφυσήθην. But it may be suggested that the text makes sense as it stands. May not the ' garden of Heracles ' have reminded Oenomaus of the other Cynic paradise, ' the isle of Pera ' described by Crates ? (see above, p. 44). Heracles was the great example of the life of πόνος and also the patron saint of the Cynics : Oenomaus may well have taken the oracle as a command to lead the Cynic life. Of course, according to the Cynic paradox the κυνικὸς βίος was the easiest open to mankind.

him think of the τρηχὺν οἶμον of the famous lines of Hesiod, which were so constantly quoted as a maxim of philosophy.

τῆς δ᾽ ἀρετῆς προπαρόιθεν θέοι ἱδρῶτα ἔθηκαν
ἀθανατόι. μακρὸς δὲ καὶ ὄρθιος οἶμος ἐς αὐτὴν
καὶ τρηχὺς τὸ πρῶτον. ἐπὴν δ᾽ ἐς ἄκρον ἵκηται
ῥηιδίη δὴ ἔπειτα πέλει, χαλεπὴ πὲρ ἐοῦσα

That πόνος must precede ἀρετή was of course axiomatic ; Oenomaus therefore took the oracle as meaning that if he would undertake the rigours demanded by Philosophy he should thereafter have a happy life. But as he was putting the question as to whether the gods would help him in his project, one of the bystanders said that he had heard precisely the same reply given to one Callistratus, a business man from Pontus. Oenomaus, not unnaturally, was indignant that the god should make no difference between questions relating to philosophy and mundane business affairs—' I felt as though Callistratus had robbed me of my ἀρετή,' he says. Nevertheless, he asked Callistratus whether he too had been cheered by the mention of Heracles. Callistratus, it seemed, had also interpreted the oracle according to his lights, ' he expected that he would have to work hard, then he could expect a profit, and after that he would be able to have a good time '.

When I realized [says Oenomaus] what his labours were like, and also the orgies he had in mind, I refused the comparison and the oracle alike. . . . For after all, robber, soldier, lover, flatterer, rhetorician, and sycophant, might all claim that oracle, for each one of them might expect toil, to be followed by pleasure.

But apparently Oenomaus had not yet lost faith in oracles. For ' when he was making some progress, and needed a guide to philosophy, but such a man was hard to find ', he came again to Colophon to ask Apollo's guidance. ' Thy business shall be done 'midst easy men, and Greeks,' came the reply. Too vague, is Oenomaus' complaint—after all, if a man were seeking a master in painting or sculpture he would hardly be satisfied with the reply, ' Thy business shall be done 'midst easy men, and Greeks.' In order to get more explicit information, he asked, ' Where had I best go from Colophon ? ' But either the oracle was by now getting tired of Oenomaus, or else it decided that his wish for a personal response should be at last gratified. At all events, he was answered with this effusion :

Far, far off from hence stands a man who whirleth a slingbow,
Countless the geese he slays with stones, as they browse upon herbage.

This was the last straw for Oenomaus. Who could find a meaning for the countless geese ? he asks. Away with you, Apollo, innumerable geese, incomprehensible oracle, and all !

In the final portion [1] of the passages quoted Oenomaus passes from the particular to the general, and demonstrates the uselessness of divination on the theory of predestination, and its impossibility on that of free-will. As representatives of the former theory he names Democritus, whose mechanical chain of cause and effect leads mankind into slavery, and Chrysippus, whose doctrine of ' principal and secondary causes ' involves a ' modified slavery ' ($\dot{\eta}\mu\iota\delta\upsilon\lambda\epsilon\dot{\iota}\alpha\nu$), which is the most ridiculous theory of all. For, if everything is predestined, what is the use of such oracles as that given to Carystus ? ' Carystus, dear son of famed Cheiron, leave Pelion and seek the heights of Euboea, where it is decreed that thou must found a sacred shrine. Go, and delay not.' ' But is anything in the power of man ? ' Carystus might say ; ' is it in my power to wish to leave Pelion ? I have heard wise men, many of them, say that if it is determined that I shall ascend the heights of Euboea and found a sacred shrine, I shall ascend them and found it, whether you bid me or no, whether I am willing or not.' Again, on the theory of predestination, how can one find fault with the bad ? One can praise virtue, but not the virtuous, like Chrysippus or Cleanthes, for they are so through no merit of their own. And what right have they to abuse Epicurus ? On this theory, then, oracles will be useless, since no warning can avail to divert destiny from its course.

But, according to Oenomaus, the theory of predestination is wrong. For the only basis of knowledge is the evidence of our senses, and our perception of ourselves ($\dot{\eta}$ $\sigma\upsilon\nu\alpha\dot{\iota}\sigma\theta\eta\sigma\dot{\iota}\varsigma$ $\tau\epsilon$ $\varkappa\alpha\dot{\iota}$ $\dot{\alpha}\nu\tau\iota\lambda\dot{\eta}\psi\iota\varsigma$ $\dot{\eta}\mu\tilde{\omega}\nu$ $\alpha\dot{\upsilon}\tau\tilde{\omega}\nu$). By this faculty we may discern the motions and impulses that lie within our own choice ($\tau\tilde{\omega}\nu$ $\dot{\epsilon}\nu$ $\dot{\eta}\mu\tilde{\iota}\nu$ $\alpha\dot{\upsilon}\theta\alpha\iota\varrho\dot{\epsilon}\tau\omega\nu$ $\varkappa\alpha\dot{\iota}$ $\beta\iota\alpha\dot{\iota}\omega\nu$). Hence we know the difference between walking and being led, between choosing

[1] Vall., op. cit., pp. 68-80.

and being forced. Our own will is therefore itself the ' first cause ' (ἀρχή) of many matters. Consider, in the light of this, the oracle given to Laius, that he should be killed by his own son ; the oracle which Chrysippus chose to demonstrate his own compromise between free-will and predestination. According to Chrysippus, it was within the power of Laius to refuse to beget children, but the god could foresee that if he did beget them, he would be slain by his son. But the son, too, is master of his will; it is within his choice whether or not he will slay his father. Similarly, the oracle ' that the whole of his house shall be drowned in blood '—the event depends on too many unknowns to make prediction possible. For,

on either argument [i.e. ' complete free-will, or the modified free-will of Chrysippus '], living things give rise within themselves either to few or to many First Causes. Now each First Cause cuts out what has gone before it and introduces other events (αἱ δὲ ἀρχαὶ ἀεὶ τὰ μέχρις αὐτῶν διακόψασαι αὐταὶ ἄλλα προάγουσι πράγματα). These in their turn can progress only so long as no other First Cause appears to prevent what comes after it from following on what went before it, and to force succeeding events to be dependent on itself. An ass or a dog or a flea can be a First Cause : let none deprive even a flea of its functions. For your flea is a being moved by an impulse (ὁρμή) of its own, which may sometimes become involved in human affairs, and constitute itself the First Cause of some chain of events.

In the section under consideration Oenomaus shows a knowledge of philosophy unusual in a Cynic, but of course he is not the originator of the arguments employed. The Stoic theory of εἱμαρμένη (fatum) is refuted by arguments which, as Vallette [1] shows, are used by Cicero in the De Fato and the De Divinatione. Cicero himself, as is well known, employed the weapons of the New Academy, and particularly of Carneades. The theory of sense-perception is not Academic. Vallette thinks it may be that of the Epicureans, although it does not reproduce accurately their terminology. Oenomaus thus borrows familiar arguments to prove his point, in exactly the same manner as Eusebius was later to borrow from him.

The conclusion to be drawn from the whole treatise is that, since knowledge of the future is impossible, oracles do not proceed from the gods, but are impudent frauds perpetrated

[1] op. cit., pp. 116, 117.

by the human custodians of the temples. It will at once be seen how Oenomaus differed from Epictetus, whose idealized Cynic enjoyed the privilege of ' dreams and omens, and converse with the gods ' ; also from Demetrius, who appears, from his profession of resignation to the will of Heaven, to have believed in the Stoic theory of εἱρμαρμένη. It does not follow from Oenomaus' arguments that the gods do not exist, for it is open to him to agree with the Epicureans that they do exist, but take no ' interest in human affairs '. But it is easy to see why Julian calls him ' a scorner of everything human and divine ', whose object was ' to do away with all reverence for the gods and to dishonour human wisdom ' (he means, of course, the wisdom of the Stoics). For according to Julian, the gods manifest their providence (πρόνοια) for the human race through the medium of oracles ; but the arguments of Oenomaus about the impossibility of knowledge of the future sweep away providence and oracles alike. If his views of the freedom of choice possessed by the human will were accepted, there would be an end of the reign of the gods, whose statues he calls ' the wooden and stone masters of man '. But those who do not share the scruples of the pious Emperor must admit that the book is perhaps the most interesting piece of Cynic literature we possess.[1] Despite its rhetorical tone, lack of original thought, and deficiencies in logic, it is good popular polemic, on much the same intellectual level as popular contributions to the Darwinian controversy in the last century. And it is yet another example of that vein of mocking scepticism which, remembering Menippus and Lucian, we may call the peculiar contribution of Syria to Greek literature.

(e) Peregrinus

Unfortunately, authorities for Peregrinus are not satisfactory. The brief references in Tatian, Athenagoras, Aulus Gellius, Philostratus, and Ammianus Marcellinus are of minor importance compared with Lucian's work On the Death of Peregrinus, but the use of this last is beset with obvious difficulties. It is throughout a polemic, for Lucian had an intense dislike of Peregrinus on both general and personal grounds. No eighteenth-century divine had a more rooted objection to

---

[1] Bernays (op. cit., p. 35) calls it ' einer Schrift, die zu den lebendigst geschrieben Prosawerken des zweiten Jahrhunderts gehört '.

' enthusiasm ' than had Lucian ¹—and indeed it cannot be denied that scepticism such as his was a healthy antidote to the generally superstitious atmosphere of his age—but as a result he is always open to suspicion when he is dealing with persons of a mystic or religious temperament. Moreover, Lucian's information about Peregrinus' private life is derived from his fellow-citizens, and we know that as a result of lawsuits there was much ill-feeling towards him in Parium. The story of his career is told in a speech by an unnamed person at the Olympic festival, in opposition to the encomium of his follower Theagenes : it is really, as Bernays ² conjectures, an invective by Lucian. Ancient invective never dealt in halftones, its villains were always coloured in the deepest dye. The danger of any attempt at revaluation is of going too far, and achieving a ' whitewashing ' equally far from the truth. But in the few cases where we can check the account of Lucian, it is obvious how distorted a picture he presents. For example, Lucian insinuates that Theagenes, despite his profession of poverty, has a hoard of 15 talents hidden away at Patrae ; but the unimpeachable authority of Galen ³ shows him at the end of his life living in the most stringent austerity, ' in a wretched hut . . . without wife or child or attendant '. Again, Lucian tells us nothing of Peregrinus' teaching, but infers that it was a mere empty display of gross ἀναίδεια. Aulus Gellius, who was for a time a pupil of his, speaks of him as ' virum graven atque constantem ', and testifies to the value of his teachings. But though one must always suspect Lucian's imputation of

---

¹ The example usually quoted, that of Lucian's treatment of Alexander of Abonuteichos, is not very striking ; for when all allowances are made, it is doubtful whether any apologetic can make a case for Alexander as an apostle of the Higher Thought. Far more significant is what Lucian, in this same work, has to say about the Christians. ' They still worship the man who was crucified in Palestine, on the grounds that he introduced a new mystic religion (τελετή) into life. . . . The poor wretches have persuaded themselves that they are immortal and will live for ever, which is why they despise death, and in some cases willingly yield themselves up. Their founder has also persuaded them they are brethren of one another. . . . So that if any charlatan comes among them, some clever man who knows the way of the world, he can soon make money and laugh at the poor fools ' (§§ 12, 13).
² *Lucian, und die Kyniker.*
³ Method. med. 13, 15 ; cf. Bernays, op. cit., p. 14 ff.

motives, somewhat more reliance can be placed in his mere statement of facts. After all, the story of Peregrinus' self-immolation at Olympia would be almost incredible but for the evidence of Lucian, who himself witnessed it. Since Lucian says that it was then the fourth Olympic festival he had attended, he may well have been present at the two previous festivals at which Peregrinus achieved notoriety. It is therefore a fair assumption that the main outlines of Peregrinus' career as given by Lucian are trustworthy.

Life.—Since Peregrinus committed suicide at the Olympic festival of 167 [1], and was then an old man, he must have been born in the closing years of the first century. His native city was Parium on the Propontis, and his father was evidently one of the more prosperous members of that not very flourishing community.[2] His father was esteemed by the city, and Peregrinus was under suspicion of having killed him because he was an intolerable nuisance in his old age. This charge is mentioned as one that would be familiar to those listening to the invective against Peregrinus ; whatever its truth, Peregrinus went into voluntary exile. During his wanderings he came into contact with the Christian community in Palestine, amongst whom he quickly rose to a position of authority.[3]

Connexion with the Christians.—' Some of their books he expounded and interpreted ; many others he wrote himself, so that they honoured him as a god, used him as a lawgiver, and enrolled him as a patron.'[4] His works as a Christian apologist are cited in a third-century catalogue from Memphis ; Völke's theory, that he was responsible for the six Epistles from Asia, ascribed to Ignatius, has not commanded general acceptance.[5] His position as leader of the Christian community brought him into contact with the Roman authority,[6] and he

---

[1] Nissen, *Rh. M.*, 1888.

[2] He is said to have left a fortune of 30 talents. According to Lucian, the total wealth of Parium together with five neighbouring cities would not have amounted to 5,000 talents.

[3] According to Lucian, he became προφήτης καὶ θιασάρχης καὶ ξυναγωγεὺς καὶ παντὰ μόνος αὐτὸς ὤν.

[4] § 11.

[5] *Die Apost. Vat. neu. untersuch*, Vol. 2, 10. 2.

[6] Ueberweg (*Gesch. der. Phil.*, Vol. 1, p. 512) conjectures that this must have been ' infolge eines besonders herausfordernden Verhaltens (eine allgemeine Christen Verfolgung kommt bei der freien Bewegung

suffered a term of imprisonment. During his imprisonment the Christians lavished such attention on him that Lucian's ridicule is aroused.

Old women and orphans would hang about the prison all day long ; the leaders of the community bribed the gaolers to let them in to sleep with him. Elegant meals were carried in, the sacred writings were read, and the good Peregrinus—for such was the title he still bore—was proclaimed as the new Socrates. . . . It really is extraordinary to what trouble this sect will go about any matter that affects their common interests.

The importance of Peregrinus is proved by the fact that the Christian communities in Asia sent deputations and loyal advice. He expected and perhaps desired martyrdom, but the governor of Palestine, ' a man given to philosophy ', released him from prison.

After his release Peregrinus adopted the Cynic garb, and, thus attired, returned to his native city. He gave the residue of his father's property to the state ; an action which Lucian represents as a clever move to quash proceedings being taken against him for his father's murder. But of course renunciation of property was the approved Cynic practice, and had the authority of Crates. That Peregrinus claimed to be following his example is to be inferred from the fact that he was hailed by his fellow-citizens as ' the true disciple of Diogenes and Crates '. Once more he resumed his wanderings—and Lucian suggests that he did not follow the Cynic poverty, for he was supplied lavishly with all necessities by the Christians. His connexion with the Christian community lasted for some time longer, and it is interesting to find Peregrinus in the garb of a Cynic professing the Christian faith.[1] But eventually Peregrinus offended the Christians in some way, and was expelled from their community.

Cynics and Christians.—This episode in Peregrinus' life is

der übrigen Gemeindeglieder nicht in Frage) '. Lucian definitely says that he was imprisoned because of his profession of Christianity (ἐπὶ τούτῳ συλλήφθεις). It was a frequent practice of the authorities to arrest the leaders of Christian communities, probably as sureties.

[1] At about the same time Justin was teaching Christianity ' in the garb of a philosopher ' ; a further proof of Augustine's statement that the Church forced men to change their beliefs, but not their dress.

of especial interest as being the earliest and best authenticated example of connexion between the Cynics and the Christians. *A priori* there are obvious grounds of sympathy between the movements ; the Jews, the Cynics, and the Christians were alike hostile to the general standards of Graeco-Roman civilization. The sympathy of outlook is commented upon by Aelius Aristides, who says that the Cynics

resemble the impious sect in Palestine in their customs. For with the latter a mark of their impiety is that they do not reverence the gods ; and so do these philosophers in like manner cut themselves off from the Greeks, and, indeed, from all divine authority.[1]

Aristides, it is to be noticed, speaks of a resemblance and not of a connexion, but the career of Peregrinus is not the only evidence of the relations between the two movements. The ascetic sect of the ' Encratites ' were undoubtedly influenced by the Cynics, as their name suggests ; and Hippolytus calls them ' more Cynic than Christian '. Their leader Tatian was a contemporary of Peregrinus and quotes his writings, and the Cynic philosopher Crescens, though responsible for the martyrdom of Tatian's disciple Justin, was evidently in close touch with the Christians, for Justin says of him that he found it necessary to ' avoid the suspicion of being himself a Christian '.[2] It is also noteworthy that Theagenes, reviewing the claims of Peregrinus to fame,[3] mentions his imprisonment in Syria, which implies that the Christian connexion was not deprecated by the Cynics themselves. Later, of course, the connexion was to become still closer, and we get such phenomena as the Cynic Maximus being Christian Bishop of Constantinople. The influence of the Cynics on the monastic orders and on the Egyptian eremites was probably considerable, though it is hard to trace ; and the Church's toleration of Cynicism is seen not only from Augustine but from the fact that there were Cynics in Byzantium.

After his expulsion from the Christian community Peregrinus returned to Parium, and tried to get an Imperial order to recover the legacy he had given to the city. His enemies naturally said that he wished to recover the money for his own use ; Bernays suggests that he might have found that it was

---

[1] Vol. 2, p. 402, Dindorf cf. Bernays, op. cit., p. 100 f.
[2] Apol., 2.   [3] *De mort. Per.*, § 4.

being spent in a way of which he disapproved. Whatever the truth of the matter may have been, his appeal was rejected on the grounds that the gift had been entirely voluntary. On two occasions, then, Peregrinus had come in contact with the imperial authority to his own disadvantage, and a sense of personal grievance may well have been a contributary cause of the anti-Roman feeling which he showed at a later stage of his career. But one may suspect that an even more important influence in this direction was that under which he next came. ' In his third wandering abroad ', says Lucian, ' he came to Egypt to study with Agathoboulos, whence he derived that wonderful rationale of his.'

Agathoboulos is to us little more than a name, but there is evidence that he was a person of importance in his own day. Eusebius names him with Plutarch, Sextus, and Oenomaus as the most notable philosophers flourishing about A.D. 120 ; [1] and that he was one of the most prominent Cynics is to be inferred from the fact that he ' taught ' both Demonax [2] and Peregrinus. Nothing more can be said about his life except that it extended beyond A.D. 155, the date of Peregrinus' visit.[3] He practised Cynicism in its most ascetic form, laying particular stress on its squalor,[4] on the public exhibition of

---

[1] *Vide* p. 184, n. 3.   [2] *Vide* Dem., 1.

[3] Perhaps he came from Rhodes, and was the ' famous Rhodian ' from whom Demetrius of Sunium learned the Cynic philosophy (see Lucian, *Toxaris*). I agree with Zeller that Demetrius of Sunium can hardly be identical with the famous Cynic of the first century A.D. Zeller's reason for doubt on this point is the uncertainty of the *Toxaris* belonging to the Lucianic corpus. More recently the editors of Lucian have been inclined to regard it as genuine, but there are other reasons for doubt about Demetrius of Sunium. The name Demetrius is a particularly common one, nearly one hundred persons of that name are listed in *Pauly-Wissowa*. Moreover, we nowhere hear of the first-century Demetrius as going to Egypt, still less to India, as Demetrius of Sunium is said to have done. Connexion with the Brachmani of India was a feature of the Cynicism of Peregrinus and Theagenes ; if Demetrius of Sunium was a pupil of Agathoboulos, he may well have been their link with the Eastern sages. We know of no ' famous ' Cynic, Rhodian or otherwise, from whom the first-century Demetrius could have learned the philosophy. The most satisfactory inference is that Demetrius of Sunium is not the same person as the friend of Seneca, but lived considerably later and was the pupil of Agathoboulos.

[4] χϱιομένος δὲ πηλῷ τὸ πϱοσώπον, Luc., *vit. Per.*, 17.

ἀναίδεια and of the endurance of pain.[1] These austerities, however, were not the sole activity of the Cynics of Alexandria. In the *Oration to the Alexandrians* Dio Chrysostom [2] speaks of them as being a bad influence on the populace, and suggests that their speeches inflamed the excitable temper of the city mob and so helped to cause the frequent riots which broke out in Alexandria, a notable example of which had occurred just before his visit in A.D. 105. Rostovtseff [3] gives the best explanation of the peculiar turbulence of Alexandrian politics throughout the early Empire ; according to him, the usual social struggle between rich and poor was complicated by an anti-Roman feeling, and since the Roman government supported the richer classes, the outbreaks of the city mob, though they might take the form of Jewish pogroms, were really demonstrations against the Roman authority. Nor is documentary evidence lacking to show that the Cynics encouraged the anti-Roman feeling of the Alexandrian lower classes. That curious document known as the ' Acts of the Heathen Martyrs ', though a compilation of the age of Commodus, contains, according to Rostovtseff, much material of an earlier date. He points out how its whole tone is anti-Roman, and also how Cynic influence is to be seen in the denunciation of tyrants. Now immediately after his stay with Agathoboulos Peregrinus went to Rome and began to abuse the Emperor, and afterwards stirred up anti-Roman feeling to the point of armed rebellion in Achaea. All indications point in the same direction—that Agathoboulos was the most prominent of these Alexandrian Cynics who throughout the second century were notorious for their anti-Roman attitude and for their influence on the city mob.[4]

After his stay in Egypt Peregrinus sailed for Italy. ' Straight off the boat ', says Lucian,[5] ' he began a campaign of invective, especially against the Emperor, whom he knew to be most mild and forbearing.' This hostile voice in the reign of the almost universally beloved Antoninus must have

[1] For τὸ ἀνεκτικόν as a Cynic duty, cf. Epict., iii. 22. 100.

[2] D.C., Or. 33 (657 R).

[3] *Social and Economic History of the Roman Empire*, s.v. Alexandria.

[4] A revolt broke out in Egypt shortly before the visit of Peregrinus, probably in 153. But since it was in Upper Egypt it is hardly likely that the Cynics of Alexandria can have been directly involved.

[5] § 18.

attracted attention, but there were no great nobles of Republican leanings to make Peregrinus their philosophic model, and the policy of the Emperor was not to punish any one who wore the garb of a philosopher. According to Lucian, Peregrinus gained a following ἐν τοῖς ἰδιώταις, by which he must mean the lower classes. And it was probably while in Rome that he came in contact with Theagenes, who appears as his chief disciple at the final immolation. Eventually his abuse became too excessive to be tolerated, and he was expelled by the City Prefect on the grounds that ' Rome did not need a philosopher of that kind '. His followers immediately compared him with Musonius, Dio and Epictetus, philosophers who had also paid the penalty of freedom of speech. In the speech of Theagenes the expulsion from Rome is mentioned together with the imprisonment in Syria as the most notable persecutions Peregrinus had endured in the name of philosophy ; and it was clearly in something of an atmosphere of martyrdom that he left Italy for Greece.

Since one of his first activities in Greece was to ' abuse the Elians ', it is to be conjectured that he went there to attend the Olympic games of 159 B.C. Probably the Elians were abused as harbouring the games, an attitude which would be consistent with the Cynic hostility to athletes. But of course the great festivals themselves were useful for the Cynics in that they provided the greatest publicity attainable in the Greek world, as we see from the stories of Diogenes at the Isthmian games, in Dio Chrysostom's eighth and ninth orations. Whether the ' armed insurrection against the Romans ' which Peregrinus provoked was before or after the Olympic festival cannot be determined; the *Vita Antonini Pii* [1] alludes to ' rebelliones in Achaia atque Aegypto ', without indicating any dates. The reference to Peregrinus is therefore our only authority for supposing that the rebellion in Greece took place later than that in Egypt. At the Olympic games Peregrinus abused the millionaire and philanthropist Herodes Atticus for his benefactions to Greece, and especially for bringing water to Olympia : ' He was turning the Greeks into women,' was the Cynic's comment. The infuriated crowd attacked and stoned Peregrinus, so that he was forced to take refuge at the altar of Zeus.

[1] c. 5.

His teaching.—The last eight years of his life Peregrinus
probably spent in Greece ; he seems to have attracted numerous
disciples. Aulus Gellius [1] tells how he frequently visited him
in a hut outside Athens, and ' heard him say many useful and
noble things '. He was, Gellius says, a dignified and earnest
man [*virum gravem atque constantem*] ; but he tells us little
of his teaching beyond the insistence, made in the spirit of
Socrates, that the good man will not sin even if he can be
sure of escaping the observation of gods and men. From
Tatian we know how he said that not even the αὐταρκεία of
the Cynic could be absolute, ' for he has need of services of
the leather-cutter for his wallet, the woodcutter for his staff,
and the weaver for his cloak '. Scanty as these indications are,
Bernays is right in emphasizing them as a contrast to the
evidence of Lucian, from whose pages it is hard to view Peregrinus as anything but a charlatan. He seems to have maintained the asceticism of Agathoboulos, to judge from the story
of an attempt to rebuke the less austere Demonax. ' Demonax,'
said he, ' you do not play the part of a Cynic.' ' Peregrinus,'
came the retort, ' you do not play the part of a human being.' [2]
But the difference between Peregrinus and Demonax was more
than one of different levels of asceticism. Demonax and
Oenomaus represent in the second century the sceptical,
nihilistic side of Cynicism : while it is obvious that mysticism
played an important part on the system of Peregrinus. Unfortunately, the references of Lucian are not sufficiently detailed
to afford a coherent picture of this side of his teaching, but
indications point to such a blend of Hellenic religion, Oriental
mysticism, and neo-Pythagoreanism as we find in Apollonius
of Tyana.[3] Peregrinus claims to hear the commands of Zeus
in dreams : he is careful to avoid polluting the sacred pre-
cincts : after his death he is to be worshipped as a hero together
with Heracles and Hephaestus. His suicide by fire was to
be an example of endurance like that of the Brachmami.[4]
One recalls the sympathy of the Cynics for the ' Gymnoso-

---

[1] *Noct. Att.*, 8. 3.　　　[2] *Vit. Dem.*, 21.
[3] See Note 4 to Chap. VIII.
[4] Bernays observes that such a manner of death was rare among
the ancients, despite the frequency with which they committed
suicide. Its rarity is the only excuse that can be found for Lucian's
remark that it is practically painless.

phists ' of India, already seen in Onesicratus and in the Berlin Pap., No. 13044 ; one of these sages had actually appeared at Athens during the reign of Augustus, where he publicly burned himself to death ' in accordance with ancestral custom '. During the time of the Roman Empire, as to-day, the ' wise men of the East ' exercised that curious fascination they have always had over a certain type of Western mind ; the picture they present in Philostratus is very like many a modern attempt to portray them as the guardians of esoteric wisdom. The influence of neo-Pythagoreanism on Peregrinus can be seen in certain ritualistic details of his suicide [1] ; a blending of Cynic and neo-Pythagorean ideas is to be seen in the Pinax of Cebes.

At the Olympic games of 163 Peregrinus delivered a speech (which Lucian maliciously says had taken him four years to compose) apologizing for his attack on Herodes Atticus, and ' explaining ' his flight to the temple of Zeus. The explanation he may have felt to be necessary because a Cynic was supposed to endure stoning and flogging : perhaps Peregrinus justified himself on the plea that it was in the interests of mankind that he should meet death in another fashion. At all events, shortly after this festival was over he issued his famous proclamation announcing his intention of publicly burning himself to death at the next. Now it is clear that Peregrinus had a great following among the Cynics, and was probably regarded by them as in some sense the leader of the sect. The oracles circulated just before his death call him ' the best of all the Cynics ' [2] ; and we are told that Theagenes did not think Diogenes fit to compare with Peregrinus. In view of the great reverence usually expressed for the founder of the sect, this is of some significance. There was, of course, always a tendency to find the ideal σοφός incarnate in the person of a contemporary, as was done by admirers of Demetrius and Demonax. But the case of Peregrinus seems an attempt to increase the influence of Cynicism by providing it with a cult ; the Cynic φιλανθρωπία is to be exercised by Peregrinus even after death, and he will

[1] The ceremony took place at moonrise : Peregrinus was clad in a white linen robe ; he turned to the south before leaping into the flames, &c.
[2] § 29.

become ' a guardian spirit of the night ', the associate of the great benefactors of mankind, Hephaestus and Heracles.   The foundation of a cult was of course not without precedent in the second century, as we know from the popularity of the worship of Antinous.   Sceptics like Lucian professed to find no other motive for Peregrinus' action than vainglory ; he compares Peregrinus with an obscure individual from Ephesus, who could find no other road to fame than burning down the temple of Diana.   The comparison is obviously unjust, and in point of fact Lucian does allow Peregrinus' own version of his motives to appear.   ' During the last portion of his life ', we are told, ' Peregrinus wished to be called Phoenix, after the Indian bird which burns itself to death in advanced old age.'   To commit suicide in old age was of course the accepted Cynic practice; the peculiarity of Peregrinus' death was the form it took, which is explained by the few words Lucian allows to him to say for himself.

He said that he wished to put a golden finial to a golden life. For he, who had lived like Heracles, must die like Heracles, and commingle with the aether.   And I wish, said he, to help mankind by showing them how to despise death.   For all men must be the Philoctetes to my Heracles.[1]

The passage is a good example of the blend of Cynicism and neo-Pythagoreanism characteristic of Peregrinus.   To live like Heracles was the aim of every Cynic.   Why should not emulation be extended to the manner of his death ?   The Cynic's duty was to set mankind an example in enduring pain and despising death ; this end also would be served by the proposed self-immolation.   Moreover, according to neo-Pythagorean belief, the burning by fire would purify the soul till it commingled with the aether, a condition necessary for immortality.[2]   Perhaps, as has been recently suggested,[3] a further consideration which led Peregrinus to adopt this form of suicide may have been a desire to emulate the Christian martyrs—particularly Polycarp—whose fortitude in meeting death had been attracting much attention.

The four years' interval between the Olympic festivals had enabled news of Peregrinus' intention to be circulated through-

[1] 27, 28.   [2] See Note 4 to Chap. VIII.
          [3] See Note 4 to Chap. VIII.

out the Graeco-Roman world. How much interest he had attracted can be read through Lucian's description. He was followed by great crowds, not only of Cynics but of the general public ; the crowd greeted him with shouts of σῶζου "Ελλησιν, ' Save yourself for the Greeks ! ' ; an expression of scepticism was apt to provoke a brawl. The immolation took place on the last night of the festival, at Harpina, some 20 stades distant from Olympia, in order to avoid pollution of the holy place. The final scene is best read in the pages of Lucian, together with the latter's demonstration of how easily a legend may be started.

But perhaps the most interesting feature of this extraordinary story is its sequel.

To almost all the principal cities [says Lucian] [1] Peregrinus had despatched letters in the form of testaments (διαθήκας), exhortations, and codes (νόμους). Several of his companions he chose as ambassadors for this purpose, with the titles of Messengers and Couriers of the Dead.

This was of course in keeping with the Cynic's profession to be the messenger of God and the schoolmaster of mankind. What of the cult ? Lucian's remark that ' there is nothing odd if some of the many fools abroad should claim to have been relieved of quartan fevers through his agency ' is recognized by Bernays as a ' prophecy after the event ' ; and we know from Athenagoras [2] that at some date earlier than 180 there was a statue of Peregrinus in the agora of his native city Parium, which was credited with prophetic powers. If we interpret other and similar remarks of Lucian in the same way, it seems that statues were also set up at Elis and elsewhere, and that on the site of the pyre near Olympia there was a regular oracular shrine, with all the machinery of priests, mystic rites, and inmost sanctuary. Lucian expects that his friend Cronius will meet many who regard Peregrinus with awe : and apparently some one, whether devotee or collector, was found to pay a talent for the staff which he was holding before he sprang into the flames. [3] There, so far as antiquity goes, the curious story ends—for we do not know how long the cult of Peregrinus lasted. There is one later incident which may be mentioned, since it is oddly in keeping with

[1] § 41.   [2] *Supp. pro Christ.*, 26.   [3] Lucian, *adv. ind.*, 14.

the rest—that in the seventeenth century Lucian's book *On the Death of Peregrinus* was placed on the *Index Librorum prohibitorum*.[1]

(*f*) *Sostratus*.—Sostratus, the paragon of physical prowess, mentioned at the beginning of the *Life of Demonax*, is probably to be numbered among the Cynics of the time.[2] His nickname of ' Heracles ', perhaps originally given to him on account of his physique, he proceeded to justify by emulating the hero and Cynic patron saint in his ' labours on behalf of mankind '. Sostratus seems to have been a ' strong man ' of the type that from time to time becomes the wonder of a countryside. He was about eight feet high, was well made, and had an appetite proportionate to his size, though his diet was restricted to barley and milk. He was born in Boeotia, and spent his life in the country districts of Boeotia and Attica, sometimes living on Mount Parnes, at others wandering about, maintained by the farmers, who called him ' Goodfellow ' and thought he brought them luck. It was natural that a certain amount of superstition should spring up around him : according to Lucian, some of the Greeks actually thought that he was a reincarnation of Heracles, while Philostratus says that he himself claimed to be the son of the rustic hero Marathon. He used to wear the skins of wolves[3] and after the pattern of Heracles ' slew wild beasts and robbers, made highways in deserted country, and built bridges over impassable places '. These exploits doubtless increased the regard which was felt for him by the country people ; and archaic though they sound, were probably by no means superfluous in the Greece of the second century A.D.   The fall in the population and the decay of agriculture which characterized the period in Greece must have led to many roads and bridges falling into disuse and disrepair : there would also be an increase in the number of wild animals : as for brigands, Dio Chrysostom mentions them as one of the dangers to be feared by the little city in Euboea, not very far from the district of Sostratus. There is therefore nothing impossible about the exploits of Sostratus ; indeed, it could be claimed for him that here was a man who led the ' Life of Heracles ' in simple fact and not in allegory.

---

[1] Bernays, op. cit., p. 87 f.   [2] See Note 5 to Chap. VIII.
[3] Cf. the Cynic Honoratus, whose garb was a bear-skin. Lucian, *Demon.*, c. 19.

But the probability that this rustic prodigy is to be numbered among the Cynics of the second century is but another indication of how little Cynicism at that period necessarily had to do with anything that we should recognize as philosophy.

Theagenes.—Lucian only mentions by name one of the numerous followers of Peregrinus—Theagenes, whom he casts as δευτεραγωνιστής in the farce of Peregrinus' death. Theagenes is also the only one of whom we hear anything further and that because he figured in Galen's case-book (Galen, *de method med.*, 10). After the death of Peregrinus, Theagenes went to Rome, where he taught daily in the Forum of Trajan, and became a familiar figure in the city. He was celibate, and lived in the utmost frugality, without any attendant, and in a humble house. Finally he contracted fever, and succumbed as a victim to medical experiment. His doctor was Attalus the ' Thessalian ', Galen's opponent, and Galen describes with true medical gusto how the patient died under his rival's treatment. With the death of Theagenes our knowledge of an epoch of Cynicism comes to an end. The sect itself undoubtedly continued, but apart from a single reference to Antiochus, who lived in the reign of Septimus Severus, nothing more is known of the Cynics till the reign of Julian.[1]

NOTES TO CHAPTER VIII

1. Von Arnim [2] shows the use made of Cynic material in the sixth oration, which he believes to have been compiled from four different sources, (a) a description of the way of life of Diogenes, (b) a collection

---

[1] The other Cynics named in the literature of the period demand only brief notice. With the Didymus Planetiades of Plutarch, as with the Alcidamas of Lucian's ' Banquet ', it is uncertain whether one is dealing with a real person or a fictitious character. Athenaeus (*Deipnos*, 155e) mentions a Cynics' *Symposium* written by one Parmeniscus, which appears to have resembled Meleager's ' Contest of Thick and Clear soup '. Lentil soup followed lentil soup throughout the courses, and the Cynics present discussed with a gourmet's appreciation the flavour of water in various localities. One of the characters was a ' Carneius of Megara, ' who may be the same as the ' Carneades ' mentioned by Eunapius (454) as a ' famous Cynic '. If so, then Carneius, Cebes of Cyzicus and the rest, must have belonged to the first century A.D., for Eunapius speaks of Carneades as the contemporary of Demetrius and Musonius. Athenaeus also mentions an *Art of Love* written by a Cynic called Sphodrias (*Deipnos*, 162b).

[2] op. cit., p. 263.

of χρεῖαι and ἀποφθέγματα attributed to Diogenes, (c) a Cynic diatribe on the animals as examples of the ' natural ' life, (d) another,
later diatribe on the miseries of tyrants.

2. Though the Cynic stress on αὐτάρκεια is apparent throughout
the passage, there is no trace of their traditional ἀναίδεια and the description of the family lives of the shepherds is rather in the spirit
of Musonius. Musonius, too, was an advocate of the farmer's life
as suitable for the σοφός.

3. Suidas [1] says that he was not much older than Porphyry, which
would give a floruit in the first half of the third century A.D. Hieronymus,[2] however, says that in the year 120 ' Plutarch of Chaeronea,
Sextus, Agathoboulos, and Oenomaus were well-known philosophers '.
Rohde [3] prefers to rely on Suidas, finding support from Eusebius'
reference to Oenomaus as ' a recent author ' (τις τῶν νεών). But
Vallette [4] shows that Eusebius' statement is too vague to be admitted
as evidence, also that Eusebius himself elsewhere says that Oenomaus,
Sextus and Agathoboulos flourished ' in the year when Plutarch was
procurator in Achaea ', i.e. A.D. 120. Vallette thinks that Oenomaus
is placed ' a little before Porphyry ' by Suidas because Porphyry
resisted his attacks on religion. But, he says, this could easily happen
if Oenomaus lived a century or more earlier than Porphyry ; indeed,
we know from Julian that as late as the fourth century Oenomaus
was considered one of the most notorious opponents of Greek religion.
The authority of Hieronymus is therefore to be preferred, and one
may with some confidence place the floruit of Oenomaus in the reign
of Hadrian. Moreover, such a date best fits the famous attack on
oracles contained in the γοήτων φώρα. As is well known, shortly
after Plutarch wrote On the Cessation of Oracles a revival of oracles
occurred, and the shrines of Colophon, Branchidae, and Amphilochus
in particular enjoyed great prestige. Amphilochus and Colophon
are both mentioned by Oenomaus ; and his book falls naturally into
place as a contribution to a discussion of the value of oracles, together
with the Alexander and Zeus Elenchomenos of Lucian, the De super-
stitione of Plutarch and the XIXth Dissertation of Maximus of Tyre.

4. H. M. Hornsby's article on ' The Cynicism of Peregrinus Proteus '
(Hermathena, 1934) examines three theories that would account for
the strain of mysticism found in Peregrinus and his followers, (a)
that such a strain was present in Cynicism from the beginning, and
could be traced to the influence of Antisthenes, (b) that the Cynicism
of Peregrinus was tinged with Neo-Pythagoreanism, (c) that by the
middle of the second century Cynicism had come to terms with the
general superstition of the age. (c) is regarded as the true explanation ; and I agree that such terms were made by Peregrinus and his

---

[1] Vide sub 'Οινομάος.   [2] d. 2135.   [3] Rh. M., xxxiii., p. 165.
[4] De Oenomao Cynico (Paris Thèse, 1908) ; much the best thing
on Oenomaus, which supersedes earlier dissertations.

followers. But the sceptical strain represented by Demonax and Oenomaus must not be forgotten, and indeed she admits that there was considerable divergence of belief amongst the Cynics of the period. There seems no reason why theories (b) and (c) should be mutually exclusive ; the rejection of any connexion between the Cynics and Pythagoreans fails to take any account of the *Pinax* of Cebes.

5. Funk [1] was the first to point out that the ' Sostratus-Heracles ' of Lucian was the same person as the ' Agathion-Heracles ' of Philostratus.[2] The identification is incontestable : date, place, and description agree : and the objection that Philostratus calls him ' Agathion ' instead of Sostratus is removed by the consideration that ' Agathion ' appears to have been simply another nickname, given to him by the farmers of Boeotia and Attica. The description of Philostratus is quoted from a letter of Herodes Atticus, who had some association, apparently a brief one, with Sostratus himself.

---

[1] *Phil. Suppl.*, 10, 1907.   [2] *Vit. Soph.*, 47.

CHAPTER IX

CYNICISM AND THE PHILOSOPHIC SCHOOLS IN THE FIRST AND SECOND CENTURIES A.D.

(*a*) DURING the second and first centuries B.C., as we have seen, Cynicism was of little importance ; both Epicureanism and the Middle Stoa, the dominant systems of the period, were hostile, while with the New Academy, preoccupied with dialectic, it had no point of contact. But about the time of the Cynic revival, early in the first century A.D., Cynicism once more influenced a philosophical system of some importance. The system in question was that of Philo, whose blending of Greek, Jewish, and Oriental thought was so characteristic a product of the intellectual atmosphere of his native Alexandria. Wendland [1] was the first to point out the parallels between numerous passages in Philo and Musonius, and to argue that they must have had a common origin in Cynic-Stoic diatribe. Philosophy for Philo meant primarily Stoicism, and the Cynic ingredients of the older Stoicism reappear in his ethics, as do the standard themes and figures of the popular preaching which was common to Stoic and Cynic alike. But so far as is known, the influence of Cynicism on Philo was purely historical and literary ; he seems to have had no personal relations with contemporary Cynics, of whom he speaks with contempt and disgust. Bréhier [2] has shown the part played by Cynic ideas in Philo's moral system and in his views of ἄσκησις. Virtue is the supreme Good for man ; ἡδονή the great enemy which hinders him in attaining it. Unremitting πόνος is essential if Virtue is to be attained ; [3] to God alone belongs the faculty of possessing the Good without πόνος. The ability of the soul to endure and even welcome the hardships inseparable from πόνος are due to the mystic love of the soul for God. Philo's view of ἄσκησις,

---

[1] *Philo und die Kynische-Stoische diatribe.*
[2] *Les idées morale et religieuse de Philon.*   [3] *De fug. et. invid.*

which must exercise every part of the body and mind to aid in the struggle for Virtue, recalls the educational theory which we have seen reason to attribute to Diogenes. The Cynic origin of these ideas is obvious, as are the additions made by Philo himself. As Bréhier says, a sharp distinction must be drawn between the ideas proper to Cynicism and the mysticism which Philo imposed upon them. He was using borrowed material for purposes of his own as openly as when he took the old allegory of ' The Choice of Heracles ' and adapted it to the story of Cain and Abel.

The influence of Cynicism on Philo is an isolated phenomenon ; there was no sequel or reaction, and to an essay dealing with the history of Cynicism Philo is a cul-de-sac. None the less the digression is worth making because it shows the ideas of Cynicism incorporated in a fully developed system of philosophy—an achievement already noted in the case of Zeno, but one beyond either the interest or the intellect of the Cynics themselves.

(b) *Stoicism*.—It has already been shown that the evidence for the independent survival of Cynicism discredits the view that the Cynic revival of the first century A.D. was a rebirth of Cynicism out of Stoicism. But the attention paid to Cynics by the literature of the period, as compared with their obscurity in that of the previous century, was largely due to the renewed interest of Stoicism in its poor relation. The development of Roman Stoicism from its Republican representatives to those of the age of Nero is a subject which lies beyond the scope of this essay. In any case, the facts are familiar, and may be thus briefly summarized. Stoicism rapidly advanced in popularity at the expense of its rivals, until it almost monopolized what attention was devoted to philosophy at Rome. The qualification is necessary, for the commercial classes, and people in country districts—a large section of Rome and Italy —remained untouched by philosophy.[1] But the street preachers whom we meet in the pages of Horace [2] carried on their propaganda amongst the poor of the cities in increasing numbers ; while what may be called ' official Stoicism ', represented by such men as Attalus, Musonius Rufus, and Epictetus drew most of its adherents, as formerly, from the Roman

[1] Trimalchio in this respect stands for his class.
[2] See above, p. 120.

aristocracy. The matter of the street preachers' diatribes, composed of a few familiar precepts and standardized anecdotes, varied little with the new age, but official Stoicism altered to meet the new demands of its patrons. The Stoicism which first took root in Rome was that of Panaetius and Posidonius ; a liberal, relatively speculative creed well suited to the tastes of the great nobles of the Scipionic circle, devotees of the new Greek learning and as yet political masters of the Roman world. But for Cato and his friends Stoicism played that rôle of consoler to a losing cause with which it became so familiar in the next century. Under the Empire the Roman nobility's long misgovernment of the world came to an end ; the policy of the Emperors to the aristocracy as a class was to conciliate it, so long as it combined dignity with impotence, but above all to keep it firmly in check. At best, then, the Roman noble who remembered the ruling traditions of his class had to practise resignation; at worst, he must face sudden changes of fortune, exile, possibly death.[1] On their behalf, Philosophy was recalled from even that mild indulgence in speculation which had been hers for the last two centuries, and reminded of her duties in regulating the lives of men, and enabling them to take arms against a sea of troubles. All the Stoic authors of the first century A.D. stress the practical aspect of philosophy : ' facere docet philosophia, non dicere ' is the slogan.

The phenomenon is one which, as they might have said themselves, ' does not need numerous proofs '. [2] Seneca quotes with approval the dictum of Demetrius that it is much better to know a few of the precepts of philosophy, providing they are kept ready at hand and in constant use, than to have a scholarly knowledge of many which are yet not readily available, and quotes his illustration from the wrestling ring.

As the good wrestler is not the man who knows every kind of grip and hold, such as are seldom of use against an opponent, but rather he who has patiently practised one or two holds and is ever on the

---

[1] A long list of Roman Stoics were put to death or committed suicide in the first century. Those under Nero and Domitian we have already mentioned : to them may be added, under Tiberius, Cremutius Cordus, under Gaius, Canus and Rectus, under Claudius, Caecina Paetus, under Vespasian, Helvidius Priscus.

[2] Cf. M.R., ὅτι οὐ δεῖ πολλαῖς ἐπιδειξέσιν.

look-out for an opportunity to use them (for it does not matter how much he knows, provided he knows enough to win) ; so in the contests of philosophy, there are many things that bring delight, but few that bring victory.[1]

So Musonius [2] insists that virtue is not merely a theoretical science, but a practical one, on a par with medicine and music. Just as doctor or musician do not merely learn the theory of their science, but train themselves in action according to that theory, so must the man who is to be virtuous not merely learn what studies are conducive to virtue, but must also drill himself therein faithfully and assiduously. How can a man straightway become temperate, if he only knows that it is wrong to be mastered by pleasure, but is not himself schooled to withstand it ?   Or how just, knowing that one must love fairness, but not being accustomed to avoid selfishness ? ($\pi\lambda\varepsilon o\nu\varepsilon\xi la$). Cynicism in the past had been called a ' short cut to virtue ' ; its merit lay in that it offered the spectacle of the Wise Man in action which above all others commended itself to the Stoicism of the Empire. The true Wise Man, says Seneca, appears on earth as seldom as the phoenix, yet such was Demetrius ' an outstanding figure, even if compared with the greatest ', and worthy to rank with Socrates, Diogenes, and Cato. He was sent to earth by Providence, ' that our own age might not lack both example and testimony '.[3]   The same claim is advanced for Demonax in the Life which goes under the name of Lucian,[4] and as we shall see, the conception of the Cynic as the ' messenger of God ' is most fully developed in Epictetus.

The stress laid by the new Stoicism on $\mu\varepsilon\lambda\varepsilon\tau\eta$ and $\check{a}\sigma\varkappa\eta\sigma\iota\varsigma$ meant that their regimen approached the Cynic austerity.   In Seneca, the multi-millionaire and Imperial minister, this is naturally not the case ; he is careful to tell us of his frugal diet, but for the rest he ' does not mind seeming too rich in the eyes of those to whom Demetrius seems too poor '.   But the teachings of Musonius on diet and dress have the Cynic ring.   Diet should be vegetarian as far as possible, though we cannot rival the frugality of the gods, who live on exhalations.   Water is sufficient drink ; and above all, gluttony ($\gamma a\sigma\tau\varrho\iota\mu a\varrho\gamma la$) must be avoided because, unlike other pleas-

---

[1] De Ben., vii. 1. 3.   [2] M.R., p. 22. 5 (Hense).
[3] Sen., De Ben., vii. 8.   [4] Luc., Dem., i.

ures, it may be indulged twice or more every day. We should go barefoot, and be accustomed to withstand heat and cold in moderation—which implies that Musonius did not approve of the extreme forms of hardihood attributed to Diogenes. As for dress, ' one cloak is better than two, and no cloak, but a single garment (ἱμάτιον) better than one '. A natural cave which gave adequate shelter would really be the best type of house ; but since these are scarce, we must look for the simplest available house, and furnish it as sparsely as possible. Since πόνος is essential to the philosopher, the life best fitted for him is that on the land, whether as farmer or labourer.[1] Parallels between these passages and the pseudo-Lucianic dialogue, *The Cynic*, are quoted in Hense's edition of Musonius. It is interesting to notice in these passages how Musonius speaks of two levels of asceticism, of which the more extreme is commendable, but is not for every one to follow. The disciples of philosophy, he suggests elsewhere, need not ' exceed normal limitations ' (ἐκβαίνειν τὸ κοινὸν τῶν πολλῶν).[2]

Sympathy for Cynicism is even more marked in Musonius' pupil, Epictetus. This was only natural, for while Musonius was of the equestrian order, a descendant of an old Etruscan family with a long Roman tradition behind him, Epictetus was of Asiatic birth, the slave of Nero's freedman Epaphroditus. His sympathies, however, were not for the Cynics of his own day, but for an ideal standard of which they fell far short. Fortunately, there is no need to reconstruct this ideal from scattered references, it is the subject of one of the best known and most eloquent of the *Discourses*—that entitled ' *On the calling of a Cynic* '.[3] The essay is so familiar that a translation would be superfluous, and I will therefore confine myself to an analysis of the ideas it contains.

The discussion arose out of the desire of a young man, presumably one of Epictetus' pupils,[4] to embrace the Cynic profession, and his inquiry, put to the Master, as to what

---

[1] These details are from *M.R.*, fr. xviiiA and xviiiB, xix, and xx (Hense). For a fuller treatment of Musonius, cf. M. P. Charlesworth, ' *Five Men* '.

[2] *M.R.*, p. 88. 9 (Hense).   [3] Epict., iii. 22.

[4] He is said to be τῶν γνωρίμων τις, but the description of the austerities to which he was already accustomed make it almost certain that he was a pupil of Epictetus (§§ 9-11).

sort of man the true Cynic should be. In reply, Epictetus' first care is to warn the young man that he is entertaining a project of the utmost seriousness, which cannot be embarked upon without the help of God, since failure means public disgrace. He then employs the familiar Stoic-Cynic figure of the Household of the World : can we be sure that the Lord of the Mansion has allotted to the young man the task of a Cynic ? Let us look more closely and see what that task really involves. The popular conception is utterly inadequate—a man is a Cynic if he has a wallet and a staff and big jaws, with which he gobbles up everything given to him, or reviles tactlessly any one he meets. Such an impression is certainly fostered by the present-day representatives of the profession, ' dogs of the table, guardians of the gate ', followers of Diogenes in shamelessness alone.[1] Possibly the young man thinks he will have to do little more than to maintain his present asceticism, and to take up the Cynic insignia and lead the vagabond, begging life, rebuking the more obvious forms of luxury, such as the use of depilatories, or the wearing of gaudy clothes. If he conceives the matter in some such way as that, he should give it a wide berth, it is not for him. But if he has some impression of its true magnitude, and confidence in himself, let him take a mirror, and look at his loins, for he is entering for an Olympic contest. Like the athletes, he will be called upon to enter on a long and arduous period of training : only in his case the aim to be achieved is the complete eradication of sensual desire, ambition, and emotion. By these means alone can he acquire that sine qua non of his calling—a Guiding Principle that is absolutely pure. τὸ ἡγεμονικὸν δεῖ καθαρὸν ποιῆσαι—Epictetus twice repeats the phrase. His plan of life must be the following.

From now on my mind is to be my material, like timber to a carpenter, or leather to a shoemaker ; and my work is to make the right use of my impressions (ὀρθὴ χρῆσις τῶν φαντασίων). My paltry body and its parts are nothing to me, as for Death let it come when it will. . . . Exile ? Whither can I be thrust out, since I cannot be thrust out of the Universe, and wherever I go there are the sun, moon and stars, dreams and omens, and my converse with the gods.

---

[1] § 80.

Perfected in this training, he will be able to understand the true nature, and undertake the duties, of his profession.

He is sent as a messenger of God to mankind, to show them how they have gone astray in questions of good and evil, and are seeking the nature of the good where it is not, and know not where it is ; he is furthermore a scout, sent like Diogenes to Philip after the battle of Chaeronea.[1]

These conceptions represent two complementary aspects of the Cynic's mission ; in the first rôle he reports to mankind, on the authority of God, that they are ignorant of the true way of life; in the second, he must himself penetrate more deeply than other men into the realm of human experience, as does a scout into enemy country, and bring back to his fellows a true report of what lies ahead of them. There is nothing new in these conceptions, and the religious tone is characteristic of the age, though perhaps its fervour is Epictetus' own. We then have a specimen of Cynic diatribe, using Agamemnon as imaginary adversary to show the folly of popular conceptions of the good. ' Tell us, sir messenger and scout, where lies the good, if not in these things ? ' is humanity's natural demand. Now comes the central doctrine of the Cynic evangelism—that happiness, serenity, freedom from restraint, can only be found within, since our will alone is completely our own. ' My mind to me a kingdom is ' is the burthen of his teaching—a kingdom that bears sway over desire and revulsion, choice and refusal. Everything external must be renounced ; but again comes the question : ' How is serenity possible for the man who has nothing, who is naked, without home or hearth, living in squalor, without a slave or a city, to live in serenity ? ' The Cynic ' non praeceptor veri sed testis ' must be able to supply the answer by practical example, to show that he fulfils all these qualifications. ' Yet he is free from pain and fear, gets what he desires, avoids what he does not, blames neither God nor man. . . . Such are the words that befit a Cynic, such his character and way of life.' Epictetus also uses the familiar figures of the Cynic as Schoolmaster, the κοινὸς παιδευτής of the world, and as King, whose staff is his sceptre, and whose kingly appearance forces all to acknowledge his mastery.

[1] §§ 23–5.

Cynicism is therefore a special service for an emergency, the emergency being constituted by the present chaotic state of human life. Epictetus expressly says that in a city of σοφοί no one would lightly embrace the Cynic profession, for whose interests could he serve by so doing? If he did become a Cynic, he would form human relationships just as do other men, for then his wife would be a philosopher, likewise, and his children. But the present state of affairs is like a battle-field, hence the Cynic should avoid incurring any commitments which will interfere with his service of God. Since marriage is of all human relationships the most binding, the Cynic will refrain from marrying, ' lest he lose his kingdom '.[1] At first sight this doctrine might appear to contradict the contention of Musonius [2] that marriage is no hindrance to the philosopher, more especially as Musonius cites Crates to prove his point, while Epictetus, as we have already seen, is at pains to point out that the marriage of Crates was a very special instance, fulfilling conditions that normally could only be looked for in the ' city of σοφοί '. But the contradiction is more apparent than real. Epictetus recognizes that the duties of marriage and family life, to which Musonius attaches so much importance, are part of the rôle of ' the good and worthy man ' (τὸ τοῦ καλοῦ κ' ἀγαθοῦ προσώπον) ; only to the Cynic, conscious of his special mission, would they be an impediment. The married Cynic would find himself in a dilemma, for if he neglected his family duties he could no longer be a good man, while if he carried them out conscientiously he would have no time left for his duties as the messenger and scout that he is. It is therefore best for him to abjure a tie that makes so many demands, and to reflect that he has ' taken all mankind for his children : the women he has for daughters, the men for sons : in that spirit he approaches and cares for them all. . . . He reproves them as a father, as a brother, as a servant of God, who is the Father of us all.' [3]

And as his family life is concerned with the Family of Mankind, so will his political cares be for the city of Zeus rather than for the city of Cecrops. What nobler politics could be found than those in which he is engaged? Is he to come forward in Athens and talk about incomes and revenues, when he ought to be addressing all men about happiness and un-

---

[1] §§ 68, 69.   [2] M.R., p. 70. 1. 14 (Hense).   [3] § 82.

happiness, slavery and freedom, failure and success ? [1] Nor will he hold office, for no office is nobler than that he now has. And if any one tries to scare him by mentioning those who bear rule and are held in honour, he bids them go look for children, since he does not fear a painted devil. Nor will ill-treatment at the hands of the populace deter him from his mission. He must be prepared to find ' that there is this very pleasant strand woven into the Cynic's life, that he must needs be flogged like an ass, and while he is being flogged, he must love the men who flog him, as though he were the father and brother of them all '.[2] In no point is the resemblance between the Cynics and the Franciscans, so often commented on, more striking, though even here the analogy must not be pressed too far. The Franciscans courted flogging as a healthy moral tonic : the Cynic, through his spirit of endurance (τὸ ἀνεκτικὸν), supports any ill-treatment that may come his way. For in all things he is utterly submissive to the will of Heaven, having always on his lips the words

> Lead thou me on, O Zeus and Destiny,
> Wherever is ordained by your decree.[3]

Epictetus also idealizes the Cynic dress and rationale, its frugality he leaves unaltered, but refuses to tolerate its customary squalor. The Cynic's body must be strong and healthy, an advertisement of the merits of his simple open-air life. If he can achieve the radiant complexion traditionally associated with Diogenes, his testimony will carry the more weight. He should not excite pity, for then people will regard him as a

---

[1] Possibly a reference to Demonax, who held office in Athens, is intended.

[2] The only actual mention we have of a Cynic being flogged is that already mentioned of the Diogenes who spoke against the marriage of Titus and Berenice. But it is clear that Epictetus is not speaking of flogging as a punishment for political agitation. The situation he envisages is one in which the ordinary man would immediately appeal to the Proconsul, obviously a case of assault at the hands of private individuals. The Cynics were exposed to such ill-treatment ; they were often considered as popular butts, and the stories of assaults on Diogenes, historically doubtless apocryphal, show the kind of thing a Cynic might have to endure (D.L., vi. 41, 42, 66, &c.). This is confirmed by what Dio Chrysostom says about popular opposition to Cynics in Or. 72.

[3] § 96.

beggar and turn away from him. Presumably Epictetus does
not mean to discourage the Cynic from begging for his livelihood, for it is hard to see how else he is to obtain it ; unlike
Musonius, Epictetus does not mention farming as the philosopher's most suitable avocation. The point is that the Cynic
must differ from the beggar in outward appearance, so that
men will pay attention to his teachings ; a requirement which
Dio Chrysostom during his Cynic period apparently failed to
satisfy.[1] Even in the squalor of the Cynic, says Epictetus,
there must be something cleanly and attractive. Nor is
παρρησία sufficient by itself, for unless united with great
natural charm and wit, his talk becomes mere snivel (μύξα
γίνεται καὶ οὐδὲν ἄλλο). Here again Diogenes is held up as
the ideal, but in another respect, to which Epictetus attaches
the greatest importance, even he is found seriously deficient.
Nothing was more characteristic of the old Cynicism than its
ideals of ἀναίδεια and ἀναισχυντία. Epictetus on the contrary
postulates αἰδώς as indispensable, for it must serve the Cynic
as his house, his gates, his guards at the bedroom door, his
concealing darkness; if once it breaks down, he is caught in
broad daylight and disgraced, and cannot continue to supervise
other men.[2] In this respect it seems possible to detect a wide
divergence in practice between the two groups previously
mentioned as characteristic of Stoicism in the first century.
On the one hand, the street preachers, Stoic and Cynic alike,
seem to have been zealous in maintaining that ἀναίδεια insisted
on by Diogenes, Zeno, and the early Stoics. But the ' official '
representatives of Stoicism, Seneca, Musonius Rufus and
Epictetus, appear to have been as deeply opposed to this aspect
of the older teachings as we have seen was the case with Posidonius and Panaetius. The bowdlerization accomplished by
the Middle Stoa was approved by the great Stoics of the
Empire and again one suspects that the tastes catered for are
those which paid tribute to the old Roman ideal of ' gravitas '.
The difference is particularly noticeable when we compare
the views of Diogenes or Zeno on the sexual appetites with
those of the Stoics of our present period. Diogenes had
advocated the casual gratification of natural desires, ' Let the
man who persuades lie with the woman who is persuaded' ;
Zeno had been notorious for his practice of homosexuality.

[1] Dio Chrys., xiii. 1, &c.   [2] § 15.

Epictetus insists that the Cynic must abjure all desire for
' wench or boy-favourite ' ; Dio Chrysostom regards brothels
as indefensible, and castigates with great severity the arguments sometimes advanced on their behalf. As for Musonius
Rufus, the whole range of classical literature contains nothing
which more closely approaches the Puritan spirit. Sexual
intercourse is absolutely prohibited except to the legally
married, and they should regard it as ordained for the pro-
creation of children and not for the purposes of pleasure.[1]

Such were Epictetus' conception of Cynicism : a profession
the aspirant to which must ' think the matter over carefully,
know himself, ask of God, and do nothing without His consent '.[2] It is an idealization of that philanthropy we have
found best exemplified by Crates, expounded at times in
Epictetus' own psychological terminology, and infused with
that religious feeling which marks him out even in a religious
age. The Diogenes of history fell far short of such an ideal ;
and even the Diogenes of literary tradition was undeniably
lacking in the essential quality of αἰδώς.[3] Epictetus does not

---

[1] *M.R.*, τὶ κεφαλαῖον γάμου, fr. xiiA and B. Here again, as
indeed in Musonius' whole attitude to women, their capabilities and
the respect due to them, the dominant influence appears to be the
old Roman tradition. Admittedly philosophy, as early as the time
of Plato, had protested against the low status of women in Greece,
but the difference between Greek and Roman views is apparent if
we contrast the *Conjugalia Praecepta* of Plutarch with the teachings
of Musonius on marriage. Plutarch's attitude is merely a more
enlightened expression, not essentially different in kind, of the view
of women found in Xenophon's *Oeconomicus*. But one feels that
behind Musonius stand the dignified and accomplished figures of the
great Roman matrons, an Arria or a Calpurnia, and the capabilities,
if not the virtues, of such women as the Empress Livia.

[2] § 53.

[3] That Epictetus derived his knowledge of Diogenes from the
literary tradition and not from Diogenes' own writings is clear from
the references themselves. In i. 24. 3 he quotes a story about Diogenes which Diogenes Laertius gives ' on the authority of Dionysius
the Stoic ' (vi. 43). The reference about Diogenes having the duty
of rebuking men in a kingly manner refers to the numerous stories
of his retorts to Plato, Demosthenes, Phryne, Perdiccas, Alexander,
&c., in fact to nearly all the prominent figures of the fourth century.
Epictetus also shows Diogenes as having conversations with the King
of the Persians and with Archidamus, King of Sparta (iv. 1. 155) ;
also as writing a letter to the Persian King. He also believes in
the story of Diogenes' capture by pirates (iii. xxiv. 59–66, iv. 1.

tell us of any Cynic of his time who approached this level, and this raises an interesting point.   For Demetrius, as we find him portrayed by Seneca, might seem to fulfil many of its requirements; he had achieved complete suppression of desire, his austerity was of unexampled rigour, he professed complete submission to the will of God.   Now Epictetus must have known Demetrius, for he was a pupil of Musonius in Rome during Nero's reign.   Since he only once mentions Demetrius, and since his general references to contemporary Cynicism are contemptuous in tone, it is clear that he did not regard Demetrius, as did Seneca, as the example of the ideal Wise Man.   Precisely why not we cannot say, though reasons may be suggested.   Demetrius was apparently married; furthermore, he was guilty of political agitation, at least during the reign of Vespasian : both forms of activity which Epictetus declared inappropriate for the Cynic.   But an action even more likely to awaken Epictetus' dislike was his opposition to Epictetus' master Musonius in the prosecution of Egnatius Celer.   It is clear from Tacitus how much odium Demetrius thus incurred, an odium which must have been particularly deeply felt in Stoic circles where Celer was regarded as an arch-traitor.   Besides his personal ties with Musonius, Epictetus admired the great Roman Stoics, such as Helvidius and Paconius Agrippinus, and we know that he shared the resentment felt for Celer's betrayal of his pupil.[1]   Small wonder, then, if he had no great admiration for the philosopher who took Celer's side.[2]   None of his contemporaries, then, seemed to Epictetus to personify the ideal of the true Cynic ; it had been most nearly, though even so not wholly, attained by his favourite exemplar, the Diogenes of literary tradition.   In

---

155, &c.), which we have seen to be almost certainly unhistorical.   In iv. 152, Epictetus seems to assert that Diogenes was not born of free parents.   He also quotes anecdotes that can be paralleled in Diogenes Laertius (cf. ii. xiii. 26, and D.L., vi. 29, iii. ii. 11, and D.L., vi. 34, iii. xii. iii., and D.L., vi. 23, iv. xxii. 88, and D.L., vi. 81, &c.) ; or from the *Epistles of the Cynics*.   Elsewhere, as Schenkl notes, he appears to have used letters ascribed to Diogenes that have not survived (Schenkl, on IV. i. 156).

[1] Ep., iv. i. 139.

[2] Nothing can safely be inferred from the fact that there is no mention of Demetrius in Musonius ; for the latter seldom refers to his contemporaries.

actual fact, it is to be doubted whether any came so near to it as did Epictetus himself.

If in Musonius and Epictetus we find a greater sympathy for Cynicism than in any later Stoic writing, it must not be assumed that the Stoicism of the second century was marked by a reaction from this attitude. It is through Marcus Aurelius that most of our knowledge of Stoicism at this period is derived, and the Stoic tutors of Marcus Aurelius had seen that phoenix, the Ideal Wise Man, in their own day, in the person of Epictetus. ' Marcus thoroughly Epictetizes ', says the Scholiast, and he is borne out by the Emperor's grateful recognition of the debt he owes to Rusticus for introducing him to the writings of Epictetus, and by the frequency of quotations from Epictetus in the *Meditations*. Marcus Aurelius shared the Stoic regard for Diogenes as one of the greatest of all philosophers ; he quotes Monimus and Crates ; and it is interesting to find him placing Dio Chrysostom in the company of Thrasea, Helvidius, Cassius, and Brutus. But his chief reverence was for Epictetus. What Demetrius had been to Seneca and Thrasea, such was Epictetus to the Stoics of the second century. Since the Stoicism of Epictetus was strongly flavoured with Cynicism, it is safe to assume a sympathy for Cynicism on the part of his enthusiastic admirers. And we have evidence that the connexion was maintained in the statement that the Cynic Demonax was one of the pupils of the Stoic Timocrates of Heraclia. Cynic influence is also to be found in that interesting and curious little book known as the *Pinax* of Cebes, which probably belongs to the second century.[1] Cebes' interest in Pythagoreanism is not surprising in a period when Stoicism was far less self-contained than formerly. The Pinax is another version of the old allegory of the Pythagorean Y—the Two Ways of Life, which is also the theme of Dio Chrysostom's story of the *Choice of Heracles*. Like Dio, by whom it was probably influenced, it makes great use of allegorical personification, a regular feature of Cynic diatribe, developed, though probably not invented, by Bion. The importance attached to $καρτερία$ and $ἐγκράτεια$

---

[1] The date of the *Pinax* is uncertain. The Teubner editor gives reason for thinking that it is later than Dio Chrysostom, and as we know it to be earlier than Lucian the first half of the second century seems the best conjecture.

in acquiring true ἀρετή recalls similar Cynic influence on Musonius.

Throughout this period, then, Cynicism was a kind of radical Stoicism : the relation between the two may be likened to that between the more ascetic monastic orders and the main body of the Catholic Church. Crates, and especially Diogenes, were major figures of Stoic hagiography ; the κυνικὸς τρόπος in garb and rationale differed in degree and not in kind from that of normal Stoic practice : the vehicle for Stoic popular propaganda was the diatribe, the chief genre of the κυνικὸς τρόπος in literature. Over the external aspects of Stoicism Cynicism thus exerted a powerful influence, as it had done in the days of Zeno and Chrysippus. In going back to the founders of the sect and neglecting the anti-Cynic developments of the Middle Stoa, the Stoics of the Empire were true to the retrospective and archaistic tendencies so general in the culture of their age. The Cynic leanings of Stoicism at this period, and especially the use of Cynic literary forms for popular preaching, are responsible for the traces of Cynicism that can be discovered at third-hand in eclectics who came under Stoic influence, such as Favorinus and Maximus of Tyre. The newly-discovered fragments of Favorinus περὶ φυγῆς are an excellent illustration of this point.[1]

(c) Favorinus must have been brought into contact with Cynic ideas through his association with Dio Chrysostom and with Epictetus ; he is said, though on more doubtful authority, to have been a warm admirer of Demetrius the Cynic. Exile was, of course, one of the most hackneyed themes of the Cynic diatribe, since voluntary or involuntary exile was so often the prelude to the vagrant Cynic life. The canons of the diatribe demanded stock figures, traditional metaphors and similes, which any one wishing to preach to one of the standard texts would find ready-made ; and in this fragment one can see how Favorinus has availed himself of them. Thus the familiar Cynic trio of Heracles, Odysseus, and Diogenes appear as examples of persons who became famous through exile. Odysseus also appears—again in the Cynic tradition—as Πολυτροπής in the good sense ; he is the wise man who willingly in his time plays many parts in the drama written by the Heavenly Playwright.

[1] *Studi et Testi*, No. 53 (il Papiro Vaticano).

Amid all the shifts of Fortune, I can imagine him each time saying
to God : ' Do you wish me to play the king ? I am willing. A
king will I be, but one unlike Echetus and Sardanapalus and
Arbaces. Do you wish me to be shipwrecked ? I am willing.
Shipwrecked will I be, and more piously than Ajax. Do you wish
me to suffer hunger ? I will do it, and more stoutly than my
comrades. Do you wish me to be a beggar ? I will be a beggar
more beggarly than Irus, and will endure though beaten and struck
most savagely by my foes. If you wish me again to be a king, I
will do it at your command. . . .'

The metaphor of the ' drama of life ', whose first elaboration
was probably due to Bion, was as much a favourite with
Favorinus as with his Stoic contemporaries ; besides the
example quoted, it is elaborated in 2, lines 20–3, line 15.
Another Cynic metaphor used is that of Life as an Olympic
contest, in which the athletes are the σοφοί whose training
(ἄσκησις) is to enable them to overcome their opponents, in
their case the numerous συμφοραί that beset human life. Our
contest is not ' on the stage, or at the Dionysia . . . but at
the feast of Heracles, in the stadium of virtue, a contest of
deeds, not of words '. Again, we find the metaphor of the
Voyage of Life, in which the σοφός will adapt himself to
conditions as sailors adapt the rigging to the winds. The
speech is also marked by appeals, in the favourite manner of
the Cynics, to the habits of animals as affording evidence for
the standards of the ' natural life '. Thus in 9, 15 ff., it is
asserted that

the earth is the common mother and nurse of all mankind. Now
God gave the finny creatures one fatherland, the sea, to dwell in,
and one to the winged race, the heavens, and to those animals that
dwell on land he allotted a safe refuge, the earth, roofing it over
with the heavens and walling it in with the ocean. Now the birds
and the fish preserve the distribution of God, and so do all other
animals, that dwell on land. But men alone through lust of greed
(πλεονεξία) portion out the earth, splitting up the gift of God and
dividing it up amongst themselves, &c.

Again, ' The cranes are wiser than we are. For they go from
Thrace to Egypt, and do not think Thrace their home nor
Egypt a land of exile, but to them this is but a change of place,
of dwellings for summer and winter.' The lesson that we

should be content with the qualities we possess κατὰ φύσιν and not seek δόξα and τιμή is enforced by appealing to

the horse, which never thinks of its repute or ill-repute amongst other beasts, but thinks that because of its speed it enjoys a kind of natural sovereignty amongst them. Nor does a lion much care what the other animals say and think about it, but thinks that it excels in strength, and they exert the most natural kind of sovereignty over those who are weaker.

Finally, there are reminiscences of well-known Cynic ἀποφθέγματα as Diogenes' remark that if the Sinopeans sentenced him to exile, he sentenced them to stay at home, or Antisthenes' definition of αὐτοχθονία as a property of slugs and worms. In fact, the thought of the fragment is essentially that of a Cynic diatribe. Were the piece anonymous, the only doubts as to its Cynic origin would be occasioned by the evidence of rhetorical ability by which it is marked.

(d) *Maximus.*—Similar traces of the influence of Cynicism are to be found in Maximus of Tyre. Diss. 36 is the most notable example, in which Maximus discusses the question as to whether the Cynic life is a προήγμενον, i.e. meet for the Stoic σοφός. In deciding in the affirmative he is following the view we have shown to be dominant in contemporary Stoicism. The familiar conception of the Cynic life as the life of man in the Golden Age is developed in the essay.

CHAPTER X

CYNICISM FROM THE THIRD TO THE
SIXTH CENTURIES A.D.

THE importance of Cynicism in the second century is strikingly reflected in the literature of the time. For its history during the last three centuries of the Ancient World there is but incomplete evidence. A few scattered references attest its existence during the turmoil of the third century : for the second half of the fourth century there is more detailed evidence to be had from the attacks of Julian on contemporary Cynics and from the reference in the Fathers to the career of the Cynic Maximus : a hundred years later something is known of the Cynic Sallustius. Of the Cynics known to us by name during the whole period only Maximus and Sallustius leave any impression as individuals ; but the general features of Cynicism are clearly the same as those noticed in the second century. Julian's description of the charlatans who masqueraded as Cynics recalls those of Epictetus and Lucian ; the connexion of Cynicism with Christianity is illustrated by Maximus ; while Sallustius reproduces the extreme austerity and the mysticism of a Peregrinus.

(a) The two orations (6 and 7) of Julian against the Cynics date from 361. Both by temperament and training Julian was sympathetic to the ideals of the austerer Cynicism. Though his tutor Mardonius had endeavoured to arouse him to disgust towards the unkempt appearance of his fellow-pupil, the Cynic Iphicles, Julian himself seems to have presented at Antioch a very model of Cynic squalor, and indeed his mode of life after he entered Constantinople as Augustus was of a Cynic simplicity. Moreover, among the Sophists most admired by Julian, such as Themistius and Libanius, it was fashionable to profess admiration for Diogenes and Crates. Yet Julian, while protesting his sympathy with the genuine Cynic, doubts whether there are any such left ; towards the

Cynics of his day he feels indignation and disgust. It is not hard to suggest reasons for this attitude. His adoption of the ' philosopher's garb ' after entering Constantinople as Augustus drew to his court swarms of Cynics who hoped to exploit an Imperial sympathizer. ' First arrived Asclepiades, then Serenianus, then Chytron, then a tall youth with yellow hair whose name I don't know—then you, and with you twice as many more . . . none of you ever visited a philosopher's school as diligently as you did my secretary.' But the cold baths, the simple fare, and the hard living of Julian were not to the taste of these Cynics ; they expressed their disgust by ridiculing as ' ostentatious ' the asceticism of a Diogenes, which Julian professed to follow, while Heraclios annoyed Julian by relating an ' impious myth ', in which Julian appeared as Pan, while he himself was Zeus. It was, therefore, to reprove the Cynics of his time and to recall them to their proper duties that Julian delivered the 6th and 7th orations— addressed ' to the uneducated Cynics ' and ' to the Cynic Heraclios '. He regards Cynicism as ' the most universal and natural philosophy ' ; its true founder was the Delphic god when he gave to mankind the precept, ' Know thyself '. Diogenes he refers to as a ' sacred personage ', and emphatically rejects as spurious the obscene tragedies attributed to him. Several anecdotes about Diogenes are quoted, and their meaning rather strained, to show that piety was one of his characteristics, a moral also deduced from Crates' *Hymn to Simplicity*, which was evidently a favourite reading of Julian's. There is much that recalls Epictetus in his bowdlerized and spiritualized account of the old Cynicism, and of the frame of mind in which that way of life must be entered. The Cynics of his own day disgust Julian by their effeminacy and shamelessness, which brought philosophy into general dis- repute, and, above all, by their impiety. ' A Cynic must not be, like Oenomaus, a scorner of all things human and divine.' For their shamelessness and impiety he likens them to the ' monks ' who had recently given him much trouble, and he expects the ' Egyptian Cynic ' of Oration 6 to recognize a quotation from ' the words of the Galilaeans '. The close association which then existed between Christianity and Cynicism is exemplified by the career of Maximus.

(*b*) The evidence for Maximus largely derives from hostile

sources, and the authority of such eminent Fathers as Gregory
Nazianzen and Jerome has caused Church historians to follow
them in depicting Maximus as an impudent impostor. But
the bitterness of ecclesiastical controversy did not make for
balanced judgements ; if the extravagant praise of Maximus in
Gregory's 23rd oration be discounted, similar allowance
should be made for his fierce attacks after the Cynic had tried
to oust him from the See of Constantinople.

Maximus was born at Alexandria, presumably earlier than
A.D. 350, of a family which had produced Christian martyrs.
Nothing is known of his training, but he seems to have adopted
Cynicism at an early age, and from the first may well have
combined the Cynic garb and the Christian faith. The Church
was then disturbed by the Arian dispute, and as an adherent
of Athanasius Maximus was involved in the turmoils of the
time. In the disorders of 374 he was whipped and later
banished to the desert, where, according to Gregory, his
constancy and his austerity were a notable example to others
of the faithful. After returning to Alexandria he won the
confidence of the Bishop, Peter II, who sent him to Constantinople in 379. The events that followed are explicable as the
product of cross-currents from two controversies—the Arian
conflict and the dispute over the See of Constantinople. The
Arians had then recently lost ground in Constantinople, though
as yet there was no Orthodox bishop ; Gregory Nazianzen
being ' diocesan ' in the Orthodox interest. He had been
appointed to this position by Peter II, whose action was in
accordance with the claim that the Bishop of Alexandria held
control over the appointment to the See of Constantinople.
But Gregory was highly popular with the Catholics of Constantinople, who wished for independence from Alexandria,
and Peter may perhaps have thought it better to have in
Maximus a nominee more under his control.

Gregory welcomed Maximus with enthusiasm, and took the
unusual step of pronouncing a public panegyric over him as
he stood by the altar of the famous church Anastasia. This
speech, known as ' Oration in praise of the philosopher Hero ',
is interesting as a Christian opinion of Cynicism. Alluding
to the καρτερία of the philosopher, Gregory remarks that
Maximus will demonstrate this quality by listening unmoved
to the recital of his own praises. Then he addresses him as

the best and most perfect of philosophers . . . one who follows our Faith in an alien garb, nay, perhaps not in an alien garb, if the wearing of bright and shining robes is the mark of angels, as it is so depicted. . . . This man is a Cynic not through shamelessness but through freedom of speech, not through gluttony but through the simplicity of his daily life . . . a Dog who greets virtue not with barking but with hearkening, who fawns on what is friendly because it is good, who snarls at what is alien because it is bad.

Elsewhere he praises the Cynic's neglect of speculative philosophy, his philanthropy, and his cosmopolitanism; and his superiority to 'the meat-eating of Diogenes, the quackery of Antisthenes, and the wedding of Crates'. However, adds Gregory, we must spare the ancient Cynics through our reverence for Maximus. He then proceeds to an account of Maximus' deeds and sufferings as a supporter of the Nicene faith, and concludes by exhorting him to continue to combat 'Gentile superstitions' and to uphold orthodoxy.

But Gregory was much deceived by Maximus. The Cynic intrigued against him in Constantinople and tried to form a party of his own supporters; finally he attempted a coup by getting himself ordained Bishop at a secret and midnight service in the church. But news of this attempt leaked out and the service was interrupted by the civil authorities and the populace, who drove Maximus and his adherents from the church; they fled to a 'flute-player's shop', where the ordination was completed. How long Maximus remained in the See on which he had thus imposed himself is uncertain, but it must have been long enough for him to carry out several acts and ordinations. But popular discontent forced him to appeal to Theodosius in Thessalonica, who charged the Bishop of Thessalonica to refer to Damasus, Bishop of Rome. Damasus replied with two letters, still extant, strongly condemning both Maximus and the manner of his ordination. Maximus then returned to Alexandria to claim the support of Peter II; the latter refused, perhaps because he thought it unwise to oppose the wishes of the Orthodox community in Constantinople, when they were so clearly expressed. Thereupon Maximus headed a 'disorderly mob' of supporters, and caused such a disturbance that he was expelled from Egypt by the Prefect. To this period belong the hostile references to Maximus in the *Carmina* and epistles of Gregory, whose admiration for ' the most perfect of philosophers ' had changed to bitter hatred of the man who had tried to supplant him on the Bishop's throne.

At the Oecumenical Council of 381 Maximus' ordination was pronounced uncanonical, and his acts invalidated. But this Council was held at Constantinople, where the interests of the Eastern Church may well have predominated. The issue was probably as much between Constantinople and Alexandria as between Gregory and Maximus, for the Second Canon of the Council restricted the authority of the Bishop of Alexandria to Egypt. Rebuffed in the East by both Emperor and Church, Maximus appealed to the West. He put his case to the Italian bishops at the Synod of Milan, and tried to strengthen his claims by presenting to the Emperor Gratian ' a notable polemic against the Arians ', which Sajdak [1] conjectures to be the ' writing ' included in the works of Athanasius as ' N. adversus Arianos '. The Latin bishops decided to support Maximus, and demanded that a new General Council should be held at which the whole question of the See of Constantinople might be settled. Theodosius, however, refused to re-open the question of Maximus' ordination, and at the Synod of Rome in 383 the Italian bishops withdrew their support. At this point Maximus disappears from history ; the only further reference is that of the Church Council of 861, which pronounced an anathema upon him.

Of the man himself it is hard to form a judgement when we hear little about him except unrelieved abuse or praise. The issues with which he was concerned were clearly of the highest importance to the Church, and the fact that he had the confidence to appeal to both the Eastern and Western Emperors, and that, at least temporarily, he gained the support of Peter II and Ambrose, suggests that he must have been a person of ability. It is true that on at least two occasions he was the cause of riots, but such disturbances were almost inseparable from the fierce ecclesiastical controversies of the time. In such ages as the fourth century A.D. there is a tendency for the judgements of History to be delivered on the formula *vae victis !* Maximus, as an unsuccessful claimant, may well have been a victim.

(*c*) There is little reason to doubt that for Cynicism in general

---

[1] *Quaest. Nazianzenicae*, Pt. i.

Gregory Nazianzen had a warm sympathy ; the enmity which developed between him and Maximus was a purely personal quarrel. The extensive influence of the Cynic diatribe and its ' commonplaces ' in his sermons has been fully shown by Geffcken.[1] And indeed it is not surprising that many in the Church should have welcomed the Cynics as allies in the fight for the ideals of poverty and asceticism. St. Basil expressed admiration for Diogenes, whose way of life he regarded as a heathen exemplar of that of the poor monk. But nowhere are these Cynic affinities better exemplified than in the works of Asterius, Bishop of Amasea. There Lazarus appears as the beggar-philosopher : the Cynic similes of the Doctor and the Scout are borrowed to describe the functions of the Apostles : and Christ preaching to the rich young man uses almost the accents of Crates in exhorting him to renounce worldly goods and cleave to Philosophy, the only mother of virtue. As Bretz [2] rightly says, Asterius and his like stand at the junction of the pagan and the Christian worlds.

(*d*) Sallustius, who is referred to in Damascius' *Life* of his friend Isidorus, is the last known to us by name of the long line of followers of Diogenes. He was probably born about A.D. 430, and since Damascius speaks of him as a contemporary, it is likely that he lived into the sixth century. The origins of Cynicism lay in the period of the end of Classical Greece and the beginnings of the Hellenistic Age ; Sallustius stands at the death of the Graeco-Roman civilization to which the Hellenistic world gave birth. In 529 the philosophical schools of Athens were closed.

The characteristic features of Cynicism were vigorously marked in its last-known adherent : the references to Sallustius would serve to describe a Cynic of the time of Lucian, or even, but for an element of mysticism, of the time of Crates. But in the sixth century Sallustius was an archaism : perhaps he was consciously so, for we hear that during his training in rhetoric he showed a preference for the ancient orators over the admired models of the day.

Born, like so many Cynics, in Syria, he had an education in rhetoric and sophistic that recalls that of Dio Chrysostom.

---

[1] *Kynika und Verwandtes* ; *vide* index, *sub.* Greg. Naz.
[2] ' Studien . . . zu Asterios von Amasea ', in *Harnack und Schmidt Texte und Untersuch*, 3te Reihe, 10.

He studied rhetoric at Emesa, for philosophy he went to Athens and later to Alexandria. But the dogmatic schools had no attraction for him. ' Philosophy ', he declared, ' is not only hard for mortal men, it is impossible.' He therefore set out as a vagrant Cynic to wander the world. He seems to have stayed for some time in Dalmatia with Marcellinus, in whom he may have found the Ideal Ruler sought by the Ideal Philosopher. After Marcellinus' death he went with Isidorus to Alexandria. Asmus [1] has shown how the Alexandrian neo-Platonists had an interest in Cynicism, and Sallustius would appear to have been adopted by the curious circle that worked for a revival of Hellenism. No doubt they saw in him the pattern of the σοφός, as Seneca did in Demetrius, and Marcus Aurelius in Epictetus. There are the same praises of his asceticism, his boldness before tyrants, his scorn for τῦφος. He was opposed to the Christians and to the Christianized Cynics ; though he himself was not devoid of mysticism. For he practised a curious kind of divination, ' by looking into people's eyes he could foretell the manner of their deaths ', as he is said to have done with Marcellinus. The neo-Platonists of Alexandria were dispersed in the Isaurian rising of 488, and nothing is known of Sallustius' life after that date.

Sallustius is chiefly interesting as a proof that in the last age of the Ancient World the ' Island of Pera ', the Cynic paradise, was still inhabited. How long it so continued is uncertain. It is likely that Cynics were known in the Byzantine Empire, but by then Pera must have been a veritable Easter Island. Long ago Onesicratus had praised the virtues of the ' noble savage ', by the sixth century A.D. the savage had come again and conquered the world. The State and its institutions, which Diogenes had found an intolerable burden on the individual, were shattered, and the ordinary individual worse off than ever before. Having little to hope for in this world, he turned to a religion that would promise him redress in the next. Cynicism had nothing further to offer mankind.

---

[1] ' Der Kyniker Sallustius bei Damascius ', *Neue Jahr*, xxv, 1910.

EPILOGUE

THE sixth century A.D. is the proper finishing-point for a History of Cynicism.

But the ' universal and most natural philosophy ' which Julian saw represented in Cynicism has continued to claim adherents ' in all ages and all places '. The Wise Men of the East teach the same lessons that they taught centuries before Diogenes, and the ' naked philosophers ' are as conspicuous in India to-day as when Onesicratus saw them on the banks of the Ganges. A similar continuity is lacking in the Western world ; but it is possible to point to outbreaks of kindred movements at various ages as manifestations of a tendency deeply rooted in human nature, and asserting itself whenever the rights of the individual need upholding against the political, moral, or economic constraints of society.

The link between the Ancient World and that of the Middle Ages is here to be found in the ascetic orders of Christianity, with whom the Cynics had had direct connexion. But the Cynics had confined themselves to Rome and to the Eastern half of the Roman Empire ; monasticism and anchoritism, originally hardly distinct, reached the West about A.D. 400. Later they spread to Britain and were adopted with enthusiasm by the Celtic Church, especially in Ireland.[1] The later revival of anchoritism in the eighth to tenth centuries under the Rule of Tallaght is particularly notable, for it gave rise to the finest expression of asceticism known to literature.

The ascetic fare, hard bed, and coarse clothing, were some of the means by which the hermits attained their chief objects, spiritual purity and communion with God unhampered by the defilements of the flesh ; continual prayer and penitence were to be their occupation, and peacefulness, free from disturbing emotions and alarms, was the way of life desired.[2]

---

[1] Cf. K. H. Jackson, *Early Celtic Nature Poetry* (Cambridge University Press).

[2] op. cit., p. 99.

The descriptions of the life of the Irish hermits contain remarkably close parallels to the austerities of Cynicism ; Coemgen is said to have lived at Glendaloch [1]

without food but the nuts of the wood and the plants of the ground and pure water to drink ; and he had no bed but a pillow of stone under his head and a flag under him and a flag on each side of him, and he had no dwelling above him, and the skins of wild beasts were clothing for him.

But the quiet humility of the Irish hermits was alien to the Cynic spirit ; and their love of wild nature and sympathy for the birds and animals which shared their life in the woods could scarcely be matched in the whole range of classical literature.

Centralizing tendencies were predominant in the Christian world between 1000 and 1200, marked by the great increase in the power of the papacy and the extension of the Roman pattern of Church organization throughout Christendom. The anchorite movements gave way before Benedictine monasticism, though they did not everywhere die out, as witness the Culdees in Scotland. But the great increase in the temporal power and material possessions of the Church soon aroused opposition,[2] which found its strongest expression in the sects known as Albigenses or Catharists, a movement which owed doctrinal allegiance to the anchorites of the Eastern Church. Violently anti-clerical, and insisting on asceticism, they offer a parallel to the reaction of the Cynics to official Stoicism, while the division of the sect into Credents and Perfecti recalls Epictetus' views of the relations between the ordinary ' good man ' and the Cynic philosopher. How widespread were dissatisfaction with monastic capitalism and a desire to return to simpler standards is unmistakably shown by the rapid growth of the Dominican and Franciscan orders at the beginning of the thirteenth century. St. Dominic realized that for the suppression of the Albigensian heresy it was necessary to have orthodox missionaries who could equal the poverty and asceticism of the Perfecti, and who could make similar use of the appeal to the Poverty of Christ. The parallel between the Cynics and the mendicant friars is of course widely familiar.

[1] op., cit., p. 98.
[2] Cf. G. G. Coulton, *Five Centuries of Religion*, Vol. ii, esp. c. 1 and 6–9.

When the Dominicans punned on their name and called themselves the 'Domini canes' it is most improbable that any reference to Diogenes was or could have been intended, but a modern observer may translate the phrase in a more special meaning as 'the Cynics of the Lord'. The Franciscans, wandering through the world, voluntarily living at subsistence level, getting money for their needs by toil in the fields or by begging, and everywhere preaching to the people, invite comparison with Epictetus' ideal of Cynicism as a special service in an emergency. Like Dio Chrysostom, St. Francis believed that poverty was in itself a good thing, and he, too, called on the poor not to endow themselves, but to despoil themselves.[1] But he did not believe that his followers should practise any greater degree of asceticism than was inseparable from their way of life, he discouraged mendicancy, and his spirituality and that of many of his followers are without parallel amongst the Cynics.

The more radical sects of the Reformation, with their insistence on the supreme importance of the individual and their appeal to the oppressed classes, also offer an interesting comparison with the Cynics. Particularly is this true of the Anabaptists, who opposed all constituted authority, and regarded the State as inherently evil. Their longing for a divine leader, expressed in such pamphlets as *The Reformation of the Emperor Frederick III*, are curiously like the Cynic Search for the True King. But they differed from the Cynics in that they had a programme of social amelioration; they were the 'religion of the proletariat' in a modern sense, we have seen that Cynicism was not its philosophy. That they represented a serious danger to the civil and religious authorities is shown by the energetic measures taken to suppress them. The sects which survived, such as the Quakers and Baptists, were less radical: their championship of individual rights was primarily concerned with securing freedom of worship and of personal religious experience.

In modern times the movement most akin to Cynicism is Anarchism. In the eighteenth century it appears, though not under that name, in the speculations of Rousseau and Diderot on the Golden Age, or later in Blake's vision of the Age of Innocence; all marked by nostalgia for an imaginary age when

[1] Cf. Coulton, op. cit., c. 8.

man as an individual had the widest scope for achieving happiness, untrammelled by the constraints of the social system. As a political factor Anarchism belongs to the nineteenth century, and dates from Proudhon, whose chief aim was to secure for the masses liberation from economic tyranny. Later Anarchists, such as Stirner, advocate the full liberation of the individual from all moral and social bands. Bakunin regarded the State as a ' historically necessary evil ', the necessity for which mankind will soon outgrow. It is especially interesting to find Kropotkin recognizing the ' best exposition from the Ancient World of the principles of Anarchism ' in the *Republic* of Zeno, which was of course composed when Zeno was under the influence of Cynicism. Anarchism was most important in the middle decades of the nineteenth century ; in 1871 the International Working Men's Association was formed. Its importance has since declined, partly due to its adoption, towards the end of the century, of a policy of violence, more particularly to the rival attractions of Communism, which also attacks the economic system and can point to some spectacular successes. But to the Anarchist, the State Capitalism envisaged by the Communists will merely mean replacing one tyranny by another. Though Anarchism has been of small importance of recent years it continues to exist, and recent events in Spain,[1] a country where it has taken root more deeply than in any other, have again brought it into general notice.

There remains another very different force to be considered among those working in favour of individualism in the modern world. Ever since the great explorations of the fifteenth and sixteenth centuries the Frontier has been a prominent feature in the life of the Western nations and has been both the refuge and the nursery of individualism. In the woods of America, on the African veldt, in the bush of Australia, men have won freedom from the constraints of society, and have developed the character of the Pioneer. This, in its insistence on the importance of the individual, in the self-sufficiency demanded by its environment, in its dislike for law and authority even where their effects are beneficial, and lastly, in its frequent contempt for learning and culture, has many features in common with Cynicism.

[1] Written in 1936.

Our own age is one in which centralizing tendencies are again dominant. In Germany, Italy, and Russia the State claims complete authority over the individual ; the material efficiency thus attained forces rival nations to similar measures. Modern industrial methods, which are being rapidly extended to cover all fields of labour, reduce the worker to the level of a cog in a machine. A standardized urban civilization is everywhere menacing local cultures. The Frontiers are closing down ; it may well be that within a generation the last frontier will have been reached. The precedents of history suggest that we may expect a reaction towards individualism. For this conflict between the claims of society and the claims of the individual is as fundamental as that of the Love and Strife of Empedocles :

ἄλλοτε μὲν Φιλότητι συνερχόμεν᾽ εἰς ἓν ἅπαντα
ἄλλοτε δὰυ διχ᾽ ἕκαστα φορεύμενα Νείκεος ἔχθει [1]

being rooted in the dual nature of Man, at once a gregarious animal, and a separate personality.

[1] *Emped.*, fr. 17. 11. 67–8.

APPENDIX I

The succession of the Ionian philosophy, according to Diogenes Laertius, i. 14.

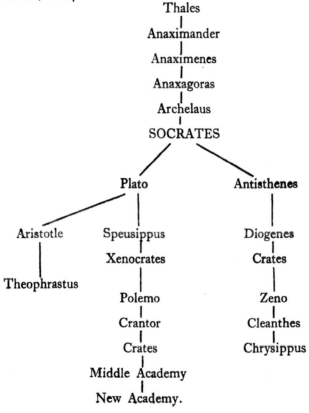

Thales
|
Anaximander
|
Anaximenes
|
Anaxagoras
|
Archelaus
|
SOCRATES

Plato · Antisthenes

Aristotle · Speusippus · Diogenes

Theophrastus · Xenocrates · Crates

Polemo · Zeno
|
Crantor · Cleanthes
|
Crates · Chrysippus
|
Middle Academy
|
New Academy.

APPENDIX II

THE whole passage is technical to a degree one does not associate with Diogenes ; and the expression ταύτην καθ' ἣν ἐν γυμνασίᾳ συνεχεῖ γινομέναι φαντασίαι εὐλυσίαν πρὸς τὰ τῆς ἀρετῆς ἔργα παρεχόνται is an obscure one. The wording at first sight seems Stoic, and von Fritz argues that the passage derives from one of the Stoic compilations which we have seen were foisted on to Diogenes ; he thinks it would be in place in the περὶ ἀρετῆς. But before refusing to accept the theory as that of Diogenes, it is necessary briefly to consider the use of the word φαντασία in the fourth century, particularly in Plato and Aristotle. (1) φαντασία is an abstract noun derived from the verb φαντάζεσθαι, and its primary meaning is simply that of ' appearance '. (When Aristotle says of φαντασία that it is ὄνομα ἀπὸ τοῦ φάος εἴληφεν one must admit that here is an ancient etymology that is substantially correct.) It is used in this simple and very general sense in Theaetetus 152C. Discussing Protagoras' proposition that οἷα ἕκαστα ἐμοὶ φαίνεται, τοιαῦτα μὲν ἔστιν ἐμοὶ Socrates points out that hence φαντασία καὶ αἴσθησις τ' αυτόν [ἐστὶν] ἐν τε θερμοῖς καὶ πᾶσι τοῖς τοιούτοις [i.e. ' seeming and perception are the same in cases of heat, &c.']. On this theory, he says, the whole science of dialectics is quite useless—τὸ γὰρ ἐπισκοπεῖν καὶ ἐπιχειρεῖν ἐλέγχειν τὰς ἀλλήλων φαντασίας καὶ δόξας, ὀρθὰς ἑκάστου οὔσας, οὐ μακρὰ μὲν καὶ διωλύγιος φλυαρία ; Aristotle also uses φαντασία in this sense in de Anima [402b, 23], where κατὰ τὴν φαντασίαν = κατὰ τοῦτο ὅ φαίνεται ἡμῖν.

(2) A more technical use is that of Sophist, 264A, B, where φαίνεται (= φαντασία) is defined as συμμείξις αἰσθήσεως καὶ δόξης ' a mixture of perception and judgement '. φαντασία in this passage is distinguished from δόξα as arising through sensation, while δόξα arises ' by thought in the soul ' (ἐν ψυχῇ κατὰ διανοίαν). φαντασία is, however, one of the most elastic words in Plato, and in Philebus 39A. Plato speaks of a δόξα ἐκ μνήμης καὶ αἰσθήσεως which is the same as the φαντασία of Sophist 264B.

(3) Philebus 39B describes ' imagination ' as a ' painter in the soul ' who produces φαντάσματα ἐζωγραφημένα, which are the εἰκόνες τῶν '. . . δοξασθέντων καὶ λεγομένων (i.e. ' imagination ' in a more ' fanciful ' sense than a recorder of sensations, the faculty for which is likened simply to a scribe).

(4) Aristotle's formal definition of φαντασία is to be found in
De Anima, c. iii. He uses it to denote the faculty of imagination,
but finds the Platonic definitions unsatisfactory. For the higher
animals have imagination in its ' reproductive sense ', since they
live ταῖς φαντασίαις καὶ ταῖς μνήμαις. Hence δόξα, which Plato had
introduced into his definition of φαντασία, must be divorced from
it. For δόξα is followed by πίστις, and one cannot talk of πίστις
amongst irrational creatures. Aristotle's own definition of φαντασία,
is κίνησις ὑπὸ τῆς αἰσθήσεως τῆς κατ᾽ ἐναργείαν γιγνομενη[1] (' a motion
generated by actual perception '—Hicks). In other words, while
for Plato φαντασία in the sense of imagination was a form of judgement, for Aristotle it was a form of perception—an ἀσθενὴς τις αἴσθησις,
a residuum of sense perception in the mind, made weaker by the
absence of real sensation. The *De Anima* and especially this
passage is of fundamental importance for Stoic epistemology : Zeno
really added nothing except the famous καταληπτικὴ φαντασία, which
is the basis for knowledge.[2]

The plural φαντασίαι was also used in a general and a technical
sense. Thus corresponding to (1) above is the phrase τὰς ἀλλήλων
φαντασίας καὶ δόξας of Theaetetus 162E, also Aristotle's remark
that ἀι φαντασίαι γιγνόνται ἀι πλείους ψευδεῖς. Corresponding to
the meaning of a residue of sense-perception are the ' writings in
the soul ' of *Philebus* (which Plato does not actually call φαντασίαι in
the passage), and Aristotle's reference to the φαντασίαι καὶ μνήμαι
which govern the life of the more highly developed animals, and
to the φαντασίαι which remain in us and are ὁμοίαι ταῖς αἰσθήσεσι.[3]
Hicks[4] rightly compares this use of φαντασίαι with the ' fancies '
which Hobbes defines as ' motions within us, reliques of those
made by the senses '. It is in this way that one must interpret
the educational theory under discussion. The ἄσκησις of gymnastics
gives rise to a set of φαντασίαι in the mind that make easy (παρεχόνται
πρὸς εὐλυσίαν) the performance of virtuous acts. Relevant in this
connexion is Aristotle's account of the part played by φαντασία in
the ' instincts ' of animals (οὐκ ὀρεκτικὸν τὸ ζῶον ἄνευ φαντασίας) ;
we are told that Diogenes[5] strongly insisted on the well-being
(εὐεξία of the body) ; such well-being existed when the natural
instincts had full play.

So much for an elucidation of the theory, which is seen to be
one that could have been propounded in the fourth century. But
can it be that of Diogenes ? Certainly he cannot have originated
it, for the theory of sensation which underlies it—that of the mind

---

[1] *De Anim.*, 429a. 1.   [2] Cf. von Arnim, *Stoic. vet. fr.*
[3] *De Anim.*, 429a. 13.   [4] Aristotle's *De Anima*, n. to 429a. 13.
                              [5] D.L., vi. 70.

as a wax tablet, the locus classicus for which is Theaetetus 191C—
was a familiar one in the fourth century. The importance of
gymnastics as a mental training is found in the Pythagoreans, with
their doctrine of ῥυθμός, which is expounded by Plato in the Timaeus
and Laws. Taylor says in his edition of the Timaeus [1]

> Two things are necessary if a man is to acquire virtue and wisdom.
> (a) He must get right nurture (ὀρθὴ τρόφη) from the first . . . his
> body must grow up in the right way. . . . For this reason Plato
> starts his great discussion in the Laws (vii, 788 seqq.) by demanding
> that even before the child is born its mother's diet and exercise shall
> be carefully regulated, and as soon as it is born the first care shall
> be to see that it grows ὀρθὸν ' straight-limbed '. . . . The Pytha-
> goreans were medical men as well as mathematicians—the later
> tradition was that the society attached the highest importance to diet
> and exercise, and made ἐπιμελεία σώματος a prominent part of the
> day's duty. . . . Later on, we see that Timaeus regards bad bodily
> condition, inherent or deprived from improper τρόφη, as a chief
> source of mental defects, (b) παίδευσις must come to the aid of ὀρθὴ
> τρόφη. In the section on the diseases of the soul we are expressly
> told that the two ways of avoiding badness are correct on the one
> hand, and moral and intellectual education on the other προθυμητέον
> . . . καὶ διὰ τρόφης καὶ δι' ἐπιτηδευμάτων μαθημάτων φεύγειν μὲν
> κακὸν, τοὐναντίον δὲ ἑλεῖν.

To return to the passage of Diogenes Laertius : von Fritz,[2] from
the fact that it contains an unusually large number of termini
technici, supposes it to be taken from one of the Stoic works foisted
on to Diogenes. Of these technical terms he enumerates ' die
bezeichendste ' as follows : (a) ἄσκησις, ἡδονή, πόνος, μελέτη,
(b) φαντασίαι, ἀτελής, τὰ προσήκοντα κατορθοῦσθαι, τὰ κατὰ φύσιν
αἱρεῖσθαι. Of these group (a) is ' aus Antisthenes und die κυνίσμος
auch sonst bekannt. Die ubrigen sind spezifische Schulausdrucke
der Stoa.' To (a) may be added εὐεξία, ἰσχύς, ἐλευθερία and a
reference to Heracles. As for (b)—φαντασία has been dealt with,
ἀτελής was in common use in fourth-century prose before it became
a Stoic technical term.[3] The phrase τὰ προσήκοντα κατορθοῦσθαι as
such I do not find in the passage ; τὰ προσήκοντα and κατορθοῦσθαι
occur separately, but the same remark applies to them as to ἀτελής.[4]
Nor does τὰ κατὰ φύσιν αἱρεῖσθαι occur expressis verbis ; the exact
phrase is δέον οὖν ἀντὶ τῶν ἀχρήστων πόνων τοὺς κατὰ φύσιν αἱρεῖσθαι ; the distinction between ' natural ' and ' unnatural ' πόνοι

---

[1] p. 273.   [2] op. cit., p. 58 seqq.
[3] cf. Plato, Phaedrus 248b ; Andoc, 30. 12.
[4] cf. Xen., Cyr., 3. 3. 1 ; Plato, Cratyl., 413a ; Xen., Mem., 3.
1. 3 ; Thuc. vi. 12.

probably was a contemporary Cynic doctrine, as we shall shortly see. Von Fritz' argument—that the passage ' best fits ' the treatise περὶ ἀρετῆς, that this work is only known in the catalogue of Sotion, which was compiled under Stoic influence, and that hence we have an additional reason for assigning the theory contained in the passage to the Stoics rather than to Diogenes—is decidedly arbitrary in the first link. The piece of Anaxagorean physics used by Diogenes to justify cannibalism and the ' sophism ' by which he showed the reasonableness of breakfasting in the market-place, suggest that he would borrow from science or dialectic when it suited his argument. And that this was true of contemporary Cynics is to be inferred from a reference of Menander to Diogenes' follower Monimus [1]; that he pronounced all suppositions to be illusions (τὸ γὰρ ὑποληφθὲν τῦφον εἶναι πᾶν ἔφη) ὑπόληψις as a technical term for ' supposition ' occurs not only in Aristotle,[2] but also in the epistemology of Epicurus.[3]

We do in fact possess evidence that the circle of Diogenes held the view ' abeunt studia (gymnastica) in mores '; I mean the curious and interesting fragments of Onesicratus of Astypalaea or Aegina, preserved in Strabo, xv. 1. 63. 64. Onesicratus was the Xenophon of the circle of Diogenes, ' for as Xenophon joined the expedition of Cyrus, so did Onesicratus that of Alexander ' (D.L., vi. 84). During Alexander's campaigns in India Onesicratus came into contact with a sect of ascetics, the Gymnosophists, whom, true to Greek habit, he portrays as so many Cynics. He tells us the names of two of them, Calanus and Mandanis ; and attributes to them doctrines which bear a close reference to those ascribed to Diogenes, particularly in our present passage. Calanus says : ' In the beginning the world was full of barley-meal and wheat . . . and the fountains flowed with honey and milk, with wine and olive oil. But by reason of luxury and gluttony man fell into ὕβρις ' (cf. the dictum of Diogenes that the gods had given to men the means of living easily, but by reason of the search after honeyed cakes and unguents and the like, this had been lost sight of).[4] Zeus, seeing this state of affairs, appointed for men a life of toil (πόνος). But when self-control and other virtues reappeared, then there was again an abundance of blessings (cf. in our passage . . . ' instead of useless toils men should choose those in accordance with nature, when they could live happily '). Still more relevant is the speech of Mandanis.

---

[1] D.L., vi. 83 : The passage is quoted from Menander's *Hippocomus*.

[2] *Magn. Mor.* 1. 35. 13 ; *Rhet.* 3. 15. 1.

[3] D.L., x. 34 ; Epic. Epist. iii, *apud* D.L., x. 123.

[4] D.L., vi. 44.

He said that the best form of discipline (λόγος), was that which removed from the mind ἡδονή and λύπη. Also that toil (πόνος) and pain (λύπη) differ—for pain is hostile (πολεμίον), but toil beneficial (φίλον). For they exercise their bodies in toil to strengthen their intelligence : by these means they put down discord and are present as advisers πᾶσιν ἀγαθῶν καὶ κοινῇ καὶ ἰδίᾳ.

(Cf. in our passage,

Diogenes would adduce indisputable evidence to show how easily from gymnastic training we arrive at virtue. For . . . take the case of athletes : what surpassing skill they acquire by their own incessant toil : if they had transferred their efforts to the training of the mind, how certainly their labours would not have been unprofitable or ineffective.)

After saying this Mandanis asked whether such doctrines were to be found among the Greeks. Onesicratus answered that such were taught by Pythagoras and Socrates and Diogenes ' and I was a pupil of his '.

We see, then, that the theory of sensation and the dependent theory of education contained in the passage were familiar in the fourth century ; that the interdependence of mental and gymnastic training was a doctrine current in the circle of Diogenes ; that Diogenes and the contemporary Cynics would borrow scientific terms when convenient. The inference is, that though the theories in the passage cannot have been the invention of Diogenes, they may well have been expounded in the ' germana Diogenis Scripta '.

APPENDIX III

TEXTS RELATING TO HIPPARCHIA

SEE Diels, *Frag. Poet. Phil. Crates ; Testimonia vitae*, fr. 1, 2, 3, and add.

1. *Menander*, Didumi (fr. 117K).

συμπεριπατήσεις γὰρ τρίβων' ἔχουσ' ἐμοὶ
ὥσπερ Κράτητι τῷ Κυνικῷ ποθ' ἡ γυνή,
καὶ θυγατέρ' ἐξέδωκ' ἐκεῖνος, ὡς ἔφη
αὐτός, ἐπὶ πείρᾳ δοὺς τριάκονθ' ἡμέρας.

2. *Antipater of Sidon*, Anth., vii. 413.

Ὀυχὶ βαθυστόλμων Ἱππάρχια ἔργα γυναικῶν
τῶν δὲ Κυνῶν ἑλόμαν ῥωμαλέον βίοτον.
οὐδὲ μοὶ ἀμπεχόναι περονήτιδες, οὐ βαθύπελμος
εὐμαρὶς, οὐ λιπόων εὖαδε κεκρύφαλος·
οὐλὰς δὲ σκίπωνι συνέμπορος, ἅ τε συνῳδός
δίπλαξ, καὶ κοίτας βλῆμα χαμαιλεχέος·
ἄμμι δὲ Μαιναλίας κάρρων † μνᾶμα † Ἀταλάντας
τόσσον, ὅσσον σοφία κρεῖσσον ὀριδρομίας.

3. *Epictetus iii.*, xxii. 76 especially.

ἀλλὰ Κράτης ἔγημεν—περίστασίν μοι λέγεις ἐξ ἔρωτος γενομενὴν καὶ γυναῖκα τίθεις ἄλλον Κράτητα. ἡμεῖς δὲ περὶ τῶν κοινῶν γάμων καὶ ἀπεριστάτων ζητοῦμεν, καὶ οὕτως ζητοῦντες οὐχ εὑρίσκομεν ἐν ταύτῃ τῇ καταστάσει προηγούμενον τῷ Κυνικῷ τὸ πρᾶγμα.

INDEX